Semantics and the
Philosophy of
Language

A COLLECTION OF READINGS

edited by Leonard Linsky

Semantics
and the
Philosophy of
Language

UNIVERSITY OF ILLINOIS PRESS
URBANA, CHICAGO, LONDON

The editor of this volume wishes to
dedicate it to the memory
of his teacher

PAUL MARHENKE

Preface

All of the essays in this volume have appeared previously in various philosophical publications, both American and foreign. They are reprinted here complete and unchanged. The one exception is the case of Nelson Goodman's "On Likeness of Meaning," which has been revised for this volume. A good number of these papers have already become classics and any student of semantics and linguistic philosophy will have met many references to them in the literature.

I have supplied a brief introduction and bibliography. The introduction aims to give the reader an acquaintance with the principal issues and problems dealt with in the book, and to show some respects in which the papers are related among themselves. The bibliography does not attempt to be complete, but only to offer some suggestions for further reading more or less closely related to the papers included here.

The papers are of various degrees of difficulty, although the attempt has been made to exclude material of a high technical level requiring background not usually to be met with in university students. It is my belief that the best way of proceeding in this field is through the study of important original papers. In selecting the essays I have attempted to include discussions of a large number of topics and to represent a variety of approaches to them. It should be obvious that success here can never be complete. A large number of excellent contributions have had to be omitted and there are points of view which are not represented.

I have sought the advice of many, though the full responsibility for the selections rests with me alone. With this understood, I should like to express my thanks to those whose suggestions have especially aided me in the preparation of this volume. They are Professor

Rudolf Carnap, Professor Nelson Goodman, Professor Benson Mates, Dr. Norman Martin, and Mr. Richard Wiebe.

Finally, I should like to express my gratitude to all of the authors for their willingness to have their papers reprinted, and to the original editors and publishers for granting the required permissions.

University of Illinois   Leonard Linsky
March, 1952

Contents

1

Introduction

By **LEONARD LINSKY**

Introduction

In this introduction I will comment on some of the central issues of the papers included in this volume and point out some of the relations between these papers. I should like to emphasize that I am not attempting an exhaustive analysis or summary of these papers and that many issues are raised in them which will not be mentioned here.

Tarski's paper, in its first expository portion, is a report of results achieved by him in his "Der Wahrheitsbegriff in den formalisierten Sprachen."[1] The task which Tarski sets for himself is that of finding a materially adequate and formally correct definition of truth. The requirement of material adequacy is simply the requirement that the definition, once achieved, shall correspond more or less closely with that concept of truth which all of us have in mind before we ever undertake the task of explication.

One of the most interesting aspects of Tarski's work, from the point of view of philosophers, is that he employs a means of expressing in precise terms the condition of material adequacy. Consider the following expression:

(T) X is true if, and only if, p

which will be called "the schema (T)." Any sentence resulting from the schema (T) by replacing the letter "p" by a sentence and the letter "X" by the name of that sentence is called "an equivalence of the form (T)." For example, if we replace "p" by "Snow is white" and "X" by ""Snow is white"" we get the following equivalence of the form (T):

"Snow is white" is true if, and only if, snow is white.

Now a definition of truth will be materially adequate, according to Tarski, if and only if, every equivalence of the form (T) is a logical consequence of that definition.

[1] *Studia Philosophica,* vol. I, 1935, pp. 261-405.

So that the above account may be fully intelligible it is necessary that the reader take account of the distinction between the *use* and *mention* of linguistic expressions. The principle governing this distinction is that in order to say something about (or *mention*) anything it is necessary to *use* a name or other means of designation for that thing. Consider, for example, the sentence:

(1) John is tall.

This sentence mentions the person John, but what appears in the sentence is not John but John's name. The sentence mentions John but does not use him; it uses John's name but does not mention it. Now we might attempt to use John himself in this sentence instead of using his name. We might attempt to do this by placing John himself on this page in approximately the same position now occupied by his name. The result would be a physical object consisting of John followed by the words "is tall." But nobody, I believe, would be inclined to call this a sentence of any language.

Nevertheless this fundamental confusion between a thing and its name is frequently made, particularly when the subject matter of our discourse happens to be language itself. If, for example, the same person who expressed the sentence (1) above were now to write:

(2) John consists of four letters

we should probably understand this to be a sentence about John's name and not about John himself. But our principle governing the distinction between use and mention has been violated in that case since there is no name for John's name in (2), but only a name for John.

A convenient device now extensively employed for distinguishing those cases in which linguistic expressions are mentioned rather than used is the device of quotation marks. According to the generally accepted convention regulating the use of this device, we may construct a name for a word or other linguistic expression by placing that expression between quotation marks. On the basis of this convention, for example, we could express our sentence (2) correctly as:

(3) "John" consists of four letters.

(3) mentions not John but his name. It is about "John" not about John. It does not use "John" but " "John"."

Now, if Tarski's criterion of material adequacy for the definition of truth is not to seem utterly confusing or trivial, the above principle must be kept in mind. In constructing an equivalence of the form (T) in accordance with Tarski's instructions, we must put a sentence in place of "p" and a name of that sentence in place of "X" in the schema (T). Normally this will mean putting in place of "X" the very sentence put in place of "p," but with the addition of a pair of quotation marks. Thus what appears on the left side of an equivalence of the form (T) is not a sentence but the name of a sentence and the whole equivalence is a sentence stating a necessary and sufficient condition for the truth of the sentence named.

Tarski insists that the problem of finding a satisfactory definition of truth has an exact meaning only for langauges of exactly specified structure. In his essay he says, "The problem of the definition of truth obtains a precise meaning and can be solved in a rigorous way only for those languages whose structure has been exactly specified." It is this conviction which has led Tarski and others to approach problems of definition and explication by way of the so-called "artificial languages." It seems obvious that the meaning of any term is relative to the language in which it occurs. Consequently the problem of specifying the meaning of any term will be a vague problem to the extent that the structure of the language in which it occurs is not precisely and completely known to us. Some philosophers have objected to this aspect of Tarski's method on the ground that it avoids philosophical issues. It seems to me, however, that the utility of artificial languages for the explication and clarification of concepts is sufficiently proven by Tarski's work itself, and by the work of modern logicians who have used such languages to achieve clarifications of the fundamental concepts of the deductive sciences and of their methodology.

The approach of Naess and his collaborators is unique. The investigations of Naess concern empirically given languages. Naess has attempted to develop a set of concepts which will enable him to formulate an adequate theory of such notions as synonymity, ambiguity, the relation of being more precise than, definiteness of intention. His method is empirical throughout, depending largely on questionnaire procedures. Much of contemporary philosophy in the United States and England has concerned itself with these same problems and others concerning "ordinary language," and the meanings of common sense. For example, the question has been much debated by philosophers as to whether or not the semantic conception of truth is the "ordinary" conception. Now Naess proposes to deal with such questions by the empirical questionnaire method rather than the method of philosophical debate, which some regard as "the method of revelation in semantics." Naess regards his empirical approach to the semantics of natural languages as a scientific development out of the analytical trends in contemporary philosophy.

The paper by Quine "On What There Is" and Carnap's "Empiricism, Semantics, and Ontology" deal with the ancient and perplexing questions of ontology. The approach here is, however, new in that the fundamental issues have received a linguistic formulation. The problem of ontology is put very simply by Quine, "What is there?" Historically the principal ontological dispute has concerned the admissibility of abstract entities such as classes, properties, and numbers. Quine expresses the belief that one strong stimulus to the acceptance of "bloated" ontologies has been the tangle which he calls "Plato's beard." If I deny that Pegasus exists, I seem to assume that the word "Pegasus" has meaning, else my denial contains a meaningless word and is therefore itself meaningless. In order to prevent my denial of Pegasus from thus falling into meaninglessness I seem forced to supply some entity for "Pegasus" to name. Now Pegasus itself cannot be the required object since I have just affirmed that there is no such thing. Consequently we seem led to unactualized possibles and perhaps also to unactualized impossibles as entities for "Pegasus" to name.

One of the aims of Russell's theory of definite descriptions is to provide a solution to the above puzzle. A definite description is a phrase such as "the present King of France," "the author of *Waverley*," "the man in the moon," or in general "the so-and-so," where the word "the" is used to indicate uniqueness. Russell treats these expressions as "incomplete symbols" meaningless outside of a sentence context but contributing to the meaning of sentences in which they occur. They would belong, according to Russell, among the syncategorematic expressions of traditional grammar. Thus Russell's theory provides us with meanings for whole sentences containing definite descriptions (by means of the so-called "contextual definition") but no meanings for such phrases in isolation from a sentence context. Words like "Pegasus" which purport to name but do not actually do so are regarded as truncated descriptions. "Pegasus," for example, might be regarded as an abbreviation for the descriptive phrase, "the winged horse captured by Bellerophon." Any sentence containing this phrase is then translated, in accordance with Russell's theory, into a sentence not containing it, but containing the English equivalent of the bound variables of logic, "everything," "nothing," "something." Since, according to Quine, all names are eliminable in favor of descriptions, the bound variable becomes the last remaining channel of extra-linguistic reference in language. The ontology then, to which we are committed by the language which we use, comprises just those entities encompassed by our use of "everything," "nothing," "something." It is this observation which prompts Quine to say that "to be is to be the value of a variable."

Rudolph Carnap, in his "Empiricism, Semantics, and Ontology," accepts Quine's view that it is the use of bound variables which refer to a certain class of entities which is the aspect of our linguistic usage involving us in ontological commitments. He insists, however, that in asking the ontological question, we must distinguish between what he calls the "internal question" and the "external question." If someone desires to speak in his language about a new kind of entity, he must introduce new ways of speaking and new rules governing these ways of speaking. In the first place this will involve the introduction of a new kind of variable. This procedure is called the construction of a "framework" for the new kind of entity. Now, we may ask questions of existence within the framework; these are the internal questions. Or we may ask questions of existence of the whole class of new entities independently of any reference to the framework. This is the external question. The importance of this distinction lies in the fact, according to Carnap, that the internal questions are meaningful ones (and moreover often trivial) because for each internal question there is a known method whereby a solution could be obtained. The external questions, however, have never been given a clear cognitive meaning, and Carnap argues that they are not theoretical questions at all. Consider, for example, a language framework for the system of numbers. Assume that we have within this framework the general term "number" for those objects which are taken as values of our variables; and assume finally that the sentence "2 is a number" is analytic relative to our language. Then the statement, "There are numbers" is likewise analytic within this framework since it follows logically from "2 is a number." But if when we ask "Are there numbers?" we do not mean this internal question, but a question prior to the acceptance of a linguistic framework, there does not seem to be any established method for uncovering an answer.

In their papers Carl Hempel and Paul Marhenke discuss the empiricist criterion of meaning, or the "verifiability" theory of meaning as it is commonly called. Hempel considers the fundamental tenet of modern empiricism to be that all non-analytic (factual) knowledge is based upon experience. Modern logical empiricists (or "logical positivists," as they are more usually called) have maintained further, as probably their principal doctrine, the verifiability criterion of meaning. In his paper Hempel states this theory as holding "that a sentence makes a cognitively meaningful assertion, and thus can be said to be either true or false, only if it is either (1) analytic or self-contradictory or (2) capable at least in principle, of experiential test."

The vagueness and lack of precision in this formulation are obvious. The attempts to make the criterion more exact and at the same time to retain its plausibility have led to very great difficulties. Hempel states many of these in his paper and attemps a restatement of the empiricist criterion of meaning.

Paul Marhenke, in his paper, seems to want to abandon the verifiability criterion altogether. In place of this he proposes to use the criterion of translatability into the "ordinary idiom" as a criterion of significance. The ordinary idiom is characterized, admittedly rather vaguely, as the idiom which we all use in communicating with each other. It is, I suppose, the "ordinary language" of the English philosophers. It is the language of everyday conversation, and of most non-philosophical books. It is the language which contains no technical terms. This, Marhenke claims, is what we all attempt to do when asked to tell the significance of one of our utterances. We try to translate it into a significant sentence of the ordinary idiom or of ordinary discourse.

Quine's "Notes on Existence and Necessity" deals with problems of identity, designation, meaning, ontology, and modality. The distinction between what Quine calls "purely designative" occurrences of names and indesignative occurrences is made with reference to the principle of substitutivity. This principle provides that "given a true statement of identity, one of its two terms may be substituted for the other in any true statement and the result will be true." Now in spite of the self-evidence of this principle it is easy to construct examples which seem to violate it. Consider one of the examples given by Quine. It involves the sentences:

(4) Tegucigalpa = the capital of Honduras

and

(5) Philip believes that Tegucigalpa is in Nicaragua.

Now both (4) and (5) are presumably true factual statements, but replacement of "Tegucigalpa" by "the capital of Honduras" in accordance with the principle of substitutivity will lead to the false sentence:

(6) Philip believes that the capital of Honduras is in Nicaragua.

The relation of a name to the object of which it is a name is the relation of designation. Thus "Cicero" designates Cicero. An occurrence of a name in a context in which the name refers simply to the object designated is what Quine calls a "purely designative" occurrence. The fact that the principle of substitutivity fails to apply for some occurrence of a name shows that the occurrence is indesignative, i.e., not purely designative. The principle of substitutivity is only plausible with respect to purely designative occurrences of names, and that is all that is revealed by the above puzzle. Quine constructs similar puzzles involving the modal concepts, necessity, possibility, contingency, etc., and regards the existence of these puzzles as giving ground for serious doubt concerning the possibility of a useful and significant employment of the modalities.

Quine was not the first to attempt to deal with antinomies of the above variety. In fact Russell's theory of descriptions was designed to solve it along with others, such as "Plato's beard." According to Russell, sentence (4) is not an identity sentence at all but is seen to be an existential generalization (a sentence governed by the word "something"), when the descriptive phrase occurring in it is removed in accordance with his theory. Consequently the principle of substitutivity does not apply here, and in fact has been misapplied to produce the antinomy.

Benson Mates in his "Synonymity" is led to a discussion of some of the same issues dealt with by Quine, Carnap, Russell, and Lewis, by way of an attempt to give a satisfactory account of the concept of synonymity or identity of meaning. Mates does not offer us a definition of "synonymity," but by a procedure remindful of Tarski's provides us with a criterion of adequacy for proposed definitions of this term. "Two expressions are synonymous in a language L if and only if they may be interchanged in each sentence in L without altering the truth value of that sentence." Since Mates's criterion requires that synonymous expressions obey Quine's rule of substitutivity, we would expect that puzzles of the kind involving Philip and Tegucigalpa would be relevant here. And in fact Mates regards these puzzles as confirming the correctness of his criterion. The failure of substitutivity in that example reveals merely that "Tegucigalpa" and "the capital of Honduras" are not synonymous. In the final portion of his paper Mates deals with matters concerning the interpretation of philosophical texts. In connection with this he discusses such matters as the "is" of predication and the "is" of identity, suggests the possibility of a third and more basic sense of that term, and critically comments on Quine's views concerning language and ontology.

Nelson Goodman, like Mates, is concerned in his first paper with identity of meaning. "Under what circumstances do two names or predicates in an ordinary language have the same meaning?" asks Goodman. He argues for the view that a satisfactory criterion is to be found in the identity of the extensions of the two terms. Two names or predicates have the same extension if and only if they apply to the same things. It is obvious that identity of extension is a necessary condition of synonymity, but against the view that it is also sufficient we have such examples as that of "centaur" and "unicorn." Both have the same (null) extension, but presumably they differ in meaning. It is clear that the criterion of extensional identity in this simple form is unacceptable. Nevertheless Goodman argues for a more complex version of this criterion as fully adequate. One of the most interesting consequences of Goodman's criterion is that, according to it, no two different words have the same meaning.

Lewis' theory of meaning centers about his analysis of the four-fold modes in which linguistic expressions have meaning. All terms have meaning in each of the four modes which Lewis calls "denotation," "comprehension," "connotation," and "signification." In terms of these categories Lewis distinguishes between abstract and concrete terms; singular and general terms. Since, according to Lewis' analysis, propositions and propositional functions are also terms, the fourfold analysis applies to them as well. One interesting application of Lewis' concepts is his construction of a definition stating conditions under which two expressions may be said to be synonymous.

Lewis' definition of "synonymity" (or "synonymy," as it is sometimes called) makes central the distinction between analytic and synthetic statements. Practically all contemporary philosophers would accept this division, but Morton White contends in his essay that it is an untenable dualism. White's problems concern the division between analytic and synthetic within natural languages. He deals with such sentences as "Every man is a rational animal," which is assumed to be analytic, and "Every man is a featherless biped," which is assumed to be synthetic. Making use of the observations made by Quine in his "Notes on Existence and Necessity," White reduces the problem of finding an adequate criterion for analyticity to the problem of finding an adequate criterion for synonymy. Supposing an adequate criterion for synonymy we could, following Quine, define a statement as analytic if and only if it was a result of putting synonyms for synonyms in a logical truth. Consider the logical truth:

(7) Every P is P.

From this, by substitution, White deduces:

(8) Every man is a man.

Now assuming "rational animal" to be synonymous with "man" and putting synonyms for synonyms, we get

(9) Every man is a rational animal

which, by the criterion being considered, is analytic. But the difficulty with the criterion is that the notion of synonymy which it employs is just as much in need of clarification as the concept of analyticity which it is supposed to clarify.

White observes that the criterion for analyticity is sometimes stated in terms of the counterfactual or subjunctive conditional. "If anything were not a rational animal, then we would refuse to call it a man." A counterfactual conditional is a sentence of the "If . . . then . . ." form which makes fundamental use of verbs in the subjunctive mood. Consider Goodman's sentence:

> If that piece of butter had been heated to 150° F., it
> would have melted.

Assuming the antecedent of this conditional to be false (as are, of course, the antecedents of all counterfactuals), it is obvious that the sentence cannot be interpreted simply as the conditional of truth-functional logic, since these are true whenever their antecedents are false. On such an interpretation, all counterfactuals would be true. The simple truth-functional analysis, then, is obviously not a satisfactory one. Goodman's second paper is devoted to a discussion of the importance, difficulty, and possible directions of an adequate treatment.

2

The Semantic
Conception
of Truth

by ALFRED TARSKI

Reprinted from *Philosophy and Phenomenological Research,* 4 (1944).

THE SEMANTIC CONCEPTION OF TRUTH

AND THE FOUNDATIONS OF SEMANTICS

This paper consists of two parts; the first has an expository character, and the second is rather polemical.

In the first part I want to summarize in an informal way the main results of my investigations concerning the definition of truth and the more general problem of the foundations of semantics. These results have been embodied in a work which appeared in print several years ago.[1] Although my investigations concern concepts dealt with in classical philosophy, they happen to be comparatively little known in philosophical circles, perhaps because of their strictly technical character. For this reason I hope I shall be excused for taking up the matter once again.[2]

Since my work was published, various objections, of unequal value, have been raised to my investigations; some of these appeared in print, and others were made in public and private discussions in which I took part.[3] In the second part of the paper I should like to express my views regarding these objections. I hope that the remarks which will be made in this context will not be considered as purely polemical in character, but will be found to contain some constructive contributions to the subject.

In the second part of the paper I have made extensive use of material graciously put at my disposal by Dr. Marja Kokoszyńska (University of Lwów). I am especially indebted and grateful to Professors Ernest Nagel (Columbia University) and David Rynin (University of California, Berkeley) for their help in preparing the final text and for various critical remarks.

I. EXPOSITION

1. THE MAIN PROBLEM—A SATISFACTORY DEFINITION OF TRUTH. Our discussion will be centered around the notion[4] of truth. The main problem is that of giving a *satisfactory definition of this notion*, i.e., a definition which is *materially adequate* and *formally correct*. But such a formulation of the problem, because of its generality, cannot be considered unequivocal, and requires some further comments.

In order to avoid any ambiguity, we must first specify the conditions under which the definition of truth will be considered adequate from the material point of view. The desired definition does not aim to specify the meaning of a familiar word used to denote a novel notion; on the contrary, it aims to catch hold of the actual meaning of an old notion. We must then characterize this notion precisely enough to enable anyone to determine whether the definition actually fulfills its task.

2) Secondly, we must determine on what the formal correctness of the definition depends. Thus, we must specify the words or concepts which we wish to use in defining the notion of truth; and we must also give the formal rules to which the definition should conform. Speaking more generally, we must describe the formal structure of the language in which the definition will be given.

The discussion of these points will occupy a considerable portion of the first part of the paper.

2. THE EXTENSION OF THE TERM "TRUE." We begin with some remarks regarding the extension of the concept of truth which we have in mind here.

The predicate "*true*" is sometimes used to refer to psychological phenomena such as judgments or beliefs, sometimes to certain physical objects, namely, linguistic expressions and specifically sentences, and sometimes to certain ideal entities called "propositions." By "sentence" we understand here what is usually meant in grammar by "declarative sentence"; as regards the term "proposition," its meaning is notoriously a subject of lengthy disputations by various philosophers and logicians, and it seems never to have been made quite clear and unambiguous. For several reasons it appears most convenient to *apply the term "true" to sentences,* and we shall follow this course.[5]

Consequently, we must always relate the notion of truth, like that of a sentence, to a specific language; for it is obvious that the same expression which is a true sentence in one language can be false or meaningless in another.

Of course, the fact that we are interested here primarily in the notion of truth for sentences does not exclude the possibility of a subsequent extension of this notion to other kinds of objects.

3. THE MEANING OF THE TERM "TRUE." Much more serious difficulties are connected with the problem of the meaning (or the intension) of the concept of truth.

The word "*true*," like other words from our everyday language, is certainly not unambiguous. And it does not seem to me that the philosophers who have discussed this concept have helped to diminish its ambiguity. In works and discussions of philosophers we meet many different conceptions of truth and falsity, and we must indicate which conception will be the basis of our discussion.

We should like our definition to do justice to the intuitions which adhere to the *classical Aristotelian conception of truth*—intuitions which find their expression in the well-known words of Aristotle's *Metaphysics*:

① *To say of <u>what is</u> that <u>it is not</u>, or of <u>what is not</u> that <u>it is</u>, is false, while to say of <u>what is</u> that <u>it is</u>, or of <u>what is not</u> that <u>it is not</u>, is <u>true</u>.*

If we wished to adapt ourselves to modern philosophical terminology, we could perhaps express this conception by means of the familiar formula:

①a *The <u>truth of a sentence consists in its agreement with (or correspondence to) reality</u>.*

(For a theory of truth which is to be based upon the latter formulation the term "correspondence theory" has been suggested.)

If, on the other hand, we should decide to extend the popular usage of the term *"designate"* by applying it not only to names, but also to sentences, and if we agreed to speak of the designata of sentences as "states of affairs," we could possibly use for the same purpose the following phrase:

② *A sentence is true if it designates an existing state of affairs.*[6]   Sachverhalt?

However, all these formulations can lead to various misunderstandings, for none of them is sufficiently precise and clear (though this applies much less to the original Aristotelian formulation than to either of the others); at any rate, <u>none of them can be considered a satisfactory definition of truth</u>. It is up to us to look for a more precise expression of our intuitions.

4. A CRITERION FOR THE MATERIAL ADEQUACY OF THE DEFINITION.[7] Let us start with a concrete example. Consider the sentence *"snow is white."* We ask the question under what conditions this sentence is true or false. It seems clear that if we base ourselves on the classical conception of truth, we shall say that the sentence is true if snow is white, and that it is false if snow is not white. Thus, if the definition of truth is to conform to our conception, it must imply the following equivalence:

The sentence "snow is white" is true if, and only if, snow is white.

Let me point out that the phrase *"snow is white"* occurs on the left side of this equivalence in quotation marks, and on the right without quotation marks. On the right side we have the sentence itself, and on the left the name of the sentence. Employing the medieval logical terminology we could also say that on the right side the words *"snow is white"* occur in *suppositio formalis*, and on the left in *suppositio materialis*. It is hardly necessary to explain why we must have the name of the sentence, and not the sentence itself, on the left side of the equivalence. For, in the first place, from the point of view of the grammar of our language, an expression of the form *"X is true"* will not become a meaningful sentence if we replace in it 'X' by a sentence or by anything other than a name—

since the subject of a sentence may be only a noun or an expression functioning like a noun. And, in the second place, the fundamental conventions regarding the use of any language require that in any utterance we make about an object it is the name of the object which must be employed, and not the object itself. In consequence, if we wish to say something about a sentence, for example, that it is true, we must use the name of this sentence, and not the sentence itself.[8]

It may be added that enclosing a sentence in quotation marks is by no means the only way of forming its name. For instance, by assuming the usual order of letters in our alphabet, we can use the following expression as the name (the description) of the sentence *"snow is white"*:

the sentence constituted by three words, the first of which consists of the 19th, 14th, 15th, and 23rd letters, the second of the 9th and 19th letters, and the third of the 23rd, 8th, 9th, 20th, and 5th letters of the English alphabet.

We shall now generalize the procedure which we have applied above. Let us consider an arbitrary sentence; we shall replace it by the letter *'p.'* We form the name of this sentence and we replace it by another letter, say *'X.'* We ask now what is the logical relation between the two sentences *"X is true"* and *'p.'* It is clear that from the point of view of our basic conception of truth these sentences are equivalent. In other words, the following equivalence holds:

(T)   *X is true if, and only if, p.*

We shall call any such equivalence (with *'p'* replaced by any sentence of the language to which the word *"true"* refers, and *'X'* replaced by a name of this sentence) an *"equivalence of the form* (T)."

Now at last we are able to put into a precise form the conditions under which we will consider the usage and the definition of the term *"true"* as adequate from the material point of view: we wish to use the term *"true"* in such a way that all equivalences of the form (T) can be asserted, and *we shall call a definition of truth "adequate" if all these equivalences follow from it.*

It should be emphasized that neither the expression (T) itself (which is not a sentence, but only a schema of a sentence) nor any particular instance of the form (T) can be regarded as a definition of truth. We can only say that every equivalence of the form (T) obtained by replacing *'p'* by a particular sentence, and *'X'* by a name of this sentence, may be considered a partial definition of truth, which explains wherein the truth of this one individual sentence consists. The general definition has to be, in a certain sense, a logical conjunction of all these partial definitions.

(The last remark calls for some comments. A language may admit the construction of infinitely many sentences; and thus the number of partial definitions of truth referring to sentences of such a language will also be infinite. Hence to give our remark a precise sense we should have to explain what is meant by a "logical conjunction of infinitely many sentences"; but this would lead us too far into technical problems of modern logic.)

5. TRUTH AS A SEMANTIC CONCEPT. I should like to propose the name *"the semantic conception of truth"* for the conception of truth which has just been discussed.

Semantics is a discipline which, speaking loosely, *deals with certain relations between expressions of a language and the objects* (or "states of affairs") *"referred to" by those expressions*. As typical examples of semantic concepts we may mention the concepts of *designation, satisfaction,* and *definition* as these occur in the following examples:

the expression *"the father of his country"* designates (denotes) George
Washington;

snow *satisfies the sentential function (the condition) "x is white";*

the equation *"2·x = 1"* defines (uniquely determines) the number 1/2.

While the words *"designates," "satisfies,"* and *"defines"* express relations (between certain expressions and the objects "referred to" by these expressions), the word *"true"* is of a different logical nature: it expresses a property (or denotes a class) of certain expressions, viz., of sentences. However, it is easily seen that all the formulations which were given earlier and which aimed to explain the meaning of this word (cf. Sections 3 and 4) referred not only to sentences themselves, but also to objects "talked about" by these sentences, or possibly to "states of affairs" described by them. And, moreover, it turns out that the simplest and the most natural way of obtaining an exact definition of truth is one which involves the use of other semantic notions, e.g., the notion of satisfaction. It is for these reasons that we count the concept of truth which is discussed here among the concepts of semantics, and the problem of defining truth proves to be closely related to the more general problem of setting up the foundations of theoretical semantics.

It is perhaps worth while saying that semantics as it is conceived in this paper (and in former papers of the author) is a sober and modest discipline which has no pretensions of being a universal patent-medicine for all the ills and diseases of mankind, whether imaginary or real. You will not find in semantics any remedy for decayed teeth or illusions of grandeur or class conflicts. Nor is semantics a device for establishing that everyone except the speaker and his friends is speaking nonsense.

From antiquity to the present day the concepts of semantics have played an important role in the discussions of philosophers, logicians, and philologists. Nevertheless, these concepts have been treated for a long time with a certain amount of suspicion. From a historical standpoint, this suspicion is to be regarded as completely justified. For although the meaning of semantic concepts as they are used in everyday language seems to be rather clear and understandable, still all attempts to characterize this meaning in a general and exact way miscarried. And what is worse, various arguments in which these concepts were involved, and which seemed otherwise quite correct and based upon apparently obvious premises, led frequently to paradoxes and antinomies. It is sufficient to mention here the *antinomy of the liar*, Richard's *antinomy of definability* (by means of a finite number of words), and Grelling-Nelson's *antinomy of heterological terms*.[9]

I believe that the method which is outlined in this paper helps to overcome these difficulties and assures the possibility of a consistent use of semantic concepts.

6. LANGUAGES WITH A SPECIFIED STRUCTURE. Because of the possible occurrence of antinomies, the problem of specifying the formal structure and the vocabulary of a language in which definitions of semantic concepts are to be given becomes especially acute; and we turn now to this problem.

There are certain general conditions under which the structure of a language is regarded as *exactly specified*. Thus, to specify the structure of a language, we must characterize unambiguously the class of those words and expressions which are to be considered *meaningful*. In particular, we must indicate all words which we decide to use without defining them, and which are called "*undefined* (or *primitive) terms*"; and we must give the so-called *rules of definition* for introducing new or *defined terms*. Furthermore, we must set up criteria for distinguishing within the class of expressions those which we call "*sentences*." Finally, we must formulate the conditions under which a sentence of the language can be *asserted*. In particular, we must indicate all *axioms* (or *primitive sentences*), i.e., those sentences which we decide to assert without proof; and we must give the so-called *rules of inference* (or *rules of proof*) by means of which we can deduce new asserted sentences from other sentences which have been previously asserted. Axioms, as well as sentences deduced from them by means of rules of inference, are referred to as "*theorems*" or "*provable sentences*."

If in specifying the structure of a language we refer exclusively to the form of the expressions involved, the language is said to be *formalized*. In such a language theorems are the only sentences which can be asserted.

At the present time the only languages with a specified structure are the formalized languages of various systems of deductive logic, possibly enriched by the introduction of certain non-logical terms. However, the field of application of these languages is rather comprehensive; we are able, theoretically, to develop in them various branches of science, for instance, mathematics and theoretical physics.

(On the other hand, we can imagine the construction of languages which have an exactly specified structure without being formalized. In such a language the assertability of sentences, for instance, may depend not always on their form, but sometimes on other, non-linguistic factors. It would be interesting and important actually to construct a language of this type, and specifically one which would prove to be sufficient for the development of a comprehensive branch of empirial science; for this would justify the hope that languages with specified structure could finally replace everyday language in scientific discourse.)

The problem of the definition of truth obtains a precise meaning and can be solved in a rigorous way only for those languages whose structre has been exactly specified. For other languages—thus, for all natural, "spoken" languages—the meaning of the problem is more or less vague, and its solution can have only an approximate character. Roughly speaking, the approximation consists in replacing a natural language (or a portion of it in which we are interested) by one whose structure is exactly specified, and which diverges from the given language "as little as possible."

7. THE ANTINOMY OF THE LIAR. In order to discover some of the more specific conditions which must be satisfied by languages in which (or for which) the definition of truth is to be given, it will be advisable to begin with a discussion of that antinomy which directly involves the notion of truth, namely, the antinomy of the liar.

To obtain this antinomy in a perspicuous form,[10] consider the following sentence:

The sentence printed in this paper on p. 347, l. 31, is not true.

For brevity we shall replace the sentence just stated by the letter '*s*.'

According to our convention concerning the adequate usage of the term "*true*," we assert the following equivalence of the form (T):

(1) '*s*' is true if, and only if, the sentence printed in this paper on p. 347, l. 31, is not true.

On the other hand, keeping in mind the meaning of the symbol '*s*,' we establish empirically the following fact:

(2) '*s*' is identical with the sentence printed in this paper on p. 347, l. 31.

Now, by a familiar law from the theory of identity (Leibniz's law), it follows from (2) that we may replace in (1) the expression *"the sentence printed in this paper on p. 347, l. 31"* by the symbol *" 's.' "* We thus obtain what follows:

(3) *'s' is true if, and only if, 's' is not true.*

In this way we have arrived at an obvious contradiction.

In my judgment, it would be quite wrong and dangerous from the standpoint of scientific progress to depreciate the importance of this and other antinomies, and to treat them as jokes or sophistries. It is a fact that we are here in the presence of an absurdity, that we have been compelled to assert a false sentence (since (3), as an equivalence between two contradictory sentences, is necessarily false). If we take our work seriously, we cannot be reconciled with this fact. We must discover its cause, that is to say, we must analyze premises upon which the antinomy is based; we must then reject at least one of these premises, and we must investigate the consequences which this has for the whole domain of our research.

It should be emphasized that antinomies have played a preeminent role in establishing the foundations of modern deductive sciences. And just as class-theoretical antinomies, and in particular Russell's antinomy (of the class of all classes that are not members of themselves), were the starting point for the successful attempts at a consistent formalization of logic and mathematics, so the antinomy of the liar and other semantic antinomies give rise to the construction of theoretical semantics.

8. THE INCONSISTENCY OF SEMANTICALLY CLOSED LANGUAGES.[7] If we now analyze the assumptions which lead to the antinomy of the liar, we notice the following:

(I) We have implicitly assumed that the language in which the antinomy is constructed contains, in addition to its expressions, also the names of these expressions, as well as semantic terms such as the term *"true"* referring to sentences of this language; we have also assumed that all sentences which determine the adequate usage of this term can be asserted in the language. A language with these properties will be called *"semantically closed."*

(II) We have assumed that in this language the ordinary laws of logic hold.

(III) We have assumed that we can formulate and assert in our language an empirical premise such as the statement (2) which has occurred in our argument.

It turns out that the assumption (III) is not essential, for it is possible to reconstruct the antinomy of the liar without its help.[11] But the assumptions (I) and (II) prove essential. Since every language which satisfies both of these assumptions is inconsistent, we must reject at least one of them.

It would be superfluous to stress here the consequences of rejecting the assumption (II), that is, of changing our logic (supposing this were possible) even in its more elementary and fundamental parts. We thus consider only the possibility of rejecting the assumption (I). Accordingly, we decide *not to use any language which is semantically closed* in the sense given.

This restriction would of course be unacceptable for those who, for reasons which are not clear to me, believe that there is only one "genuine" language (or, at least, that all "genuine" languages are mutually translatable). However, this restriction does not affect the needs or interests of science in any essential way. The languages (either the formalized languages or—what is more frequently the case—the portions of everyday language) which are used in scientific discourse do not have to be semantically closed. This is obvious in case linguistic phenomena and, in particular, semantic notions do not enter in any way into the subject-matter of a science; for in such a case the language of this science does not have to be provided with any semantic terms at all. However, we shall see in the next section how semantically closed languages can be dispensed with even in those scientific discussions in which semantic notions are essentially involved.

The problem arises as to the position of everyday language with regard to this point. At first blush it would seem that this language satisfies both assumptions (I) and (II), and that therefore it must be inconsistent. But actually the case is not so simple. Our everyday language is certainly not one with an exactly specified structure. We do not know precisely which expressions are sentences, and we know even to a smaller degree which sentences are to be taken as assertible. Thus the problem of consistency has no exact meaning with respect to this language. We may at best only risk the guess that a language whose structure has been exactly specified and which resembles our everyday language as closely as possible would be inconsistent.

9. OBJECT-LANGUAGE AND META-LANGUAGE. Since we have agreed not to employ semantically closed languages, we have to use two different languages in discussing the problem of the definition of truth and, more generally, any problems in the field of semantics. The first of these languages is the language which is "talked about" and which is the subject-matter of the whole discussion; the definition of truth which we are seeking

applies to the sentences of this language. The second is the language in which we "talk about" the first language, and in terms of which we wish, in particular, to construct the definition of truth for the first language. We shall refer to the first language as *"the object-language,"* and to the second as *"the meta-language."*

It should be noticed that these terms "object-language" and "meta-language" have only a relative sense. If, for instance, we become interested in the notion of truth applying to sentences, not of our original object-language, but of its meta-language, the latter becomes automatically the object-language of our discussion; and in order to define truth for this language, we have to go to a new meta-language—so to speak, to a meta-language of a higher level. In this way we arrive at a whole hierarchy of languages.

The vocabulary of the meta-language is to a large extent determined by previously stated conditions under which a definition of truth will be considered materially adequate. This definition, as we recall, has to imply all equivalences of the form (T):

(T) $\qquad\qquad\qquad\qquad$ *X is true if, and only if, p.*

The definition itself and all the equivalences implied by it are to be formulated in the meta-language. On the other hand, the symbol '*p*' in (T) stands for an arbitrary sentence of our object-language. Hence it follows that every sentence which occurs in the object-language must also occur in the meta-language; in other words, the meta-language must contain the object-language as a part. This is at any rate necessary for the proof of the adequacy of the definition—even though the definition itself can sometimes be formulated in a less comprehensive meta-language which does not satisfy this requirement.

(The requirement in question can be somewhat modified, for it suffices to assume that the object-language can be translated into the meta-language; this necessitates a certain change in the interpretation of the symbol '*p*' in (T). In all that follows we shall ignore the possibility of this modification.)

Furthermore, the symbol '*X*' in (T) represents the name of the sentence which '*p*' stands for. We see therefore that the meta-language must be rich enough to provide possibilities of constructing a name for every sentence of the object-language.

In addition, the meta-language must obviously contain terms of a general logical character, such as the expression "if, and only if."[12]

It is desirable for the meta-language not to contain any undefined terms except such as are involved explicitly or implicitly in the remarks above, i.e.: terms of the object-language; terms referring to the form of the expressions of the object-language, and used in building names for these expressions; and terms of logic. In particular, we desire *semantic terms* (referring to the object-language) *to be introduced into the meta-language only by definition.* For, if this postulate is satisfied, the definition of truth, or of any other semantic concept, will fulfill what we intuitively expect from every definition; that is, it will explain the meaning of the term being defined in terms whose meaning appears to be completely clear and unequivocal. And, moreover, we have then a kind of guarantee that the use of semantic concepts will not involve us in any contradictions.

We have no further requirements as to the formal structure of the object-language and the meta-language; we assume that it is similar to that of other formalized languages known at the present time. In particular, we assume that the usual formal rules of definition are observed in the meta-language.

10. CONDITIONS FOR A POSITIVE SOLUTION OF THE MAIN PROBLEM. Now, we have already a clear idea both of the conditions of material adequacy to which the definition of truth is subjected, and of the formal structure of the language in which this definition is to be constructed. Under these circumstances the problem of the definition of truth acquires the character of a definite problem of a purely deductive nature.

The solution of the problem, however, is by no means obvious, and I would not attempt to give it in detail without using the whole machinery of contemporary logic. Here I shall confine myself to a rough outline of the solution and to the discussion of certain points of a more general interest which are involved in it.

The solution turns out to be sometimes positive, sometimes negative. This depends upon some formal relations between the object-language and its meta-language; or, more specifically, upon the fact whether the meta-language in its logical part is *"essentially richer"* than the object-language or not. It is not easy to give a general and precise definition of this notion of "essential richness." If we restrict ourselves to languages based on the logical theory of types, the condition for the meta-language to be "essentially richer" than the object-language is that it contain variables of a higher logical type than those of the object-language.

If the condition of "essential richness" is not satisfied, it can usually be shown that an interpretation of the meta-language in the object-language is possible; that is to say, with any given term of the meta-language a well-determined term of the object-language can be correlated in such a way that the assertible sentences of the one language turn out to be correlated with assertible sentences of the other. As a result of this interpretation, the hypothesis that a satisfactory definition of truth has been formulated in the meta-language turns out to imply the possibility of reconstructing in that language the antinomy of the liar; and this in turn forces us to reject the hypothesis in question.

(The fact that the meta-language, in its non-logical part, is ordinarily more comprehensive than the object-language does not affect the possibility of interpreting the former in the latter. For example, the names of expressions of the object-language occur in the meta-language, though for the most part they do not occur in the object-language itself; but, nevertheless, it may be possible to interpret these names in terms of the object-language.)

Thus we see that the condition of "essential richness" is necessary for the possibility of a satisfactory definition of truth in the meta-language. If we want to develop the theory of truth in a meta-language which does not satisfy this condition, we must give up the idea of defining truth with the exclusive help of those terms which were indicated above (in Section 8). We have then to include the term *"true,"* or some other semantic term, in the list of undefined terms of the meta-language, and to express fundamental properties of the notion of truth in a series of axioms. There is nothing essentially wrong in such an axiomatic procedure, and it may prove useful for various purposes.[13]

It turns out, however, that this procedure can be avoided. For *the condition of the "essential richness" of the meta-language proves to be, not only necessary, but also sufficient for the construction of a satisfactory definition of truth;* i.e., if the meta-language satisfies this condition, the notion of truth can be defined in it. We shall now indicate in general terms how this construction can be carried through.

11. THE CONSTRUCTION (IN OUTLINE) OF THE DEFINITION.[14] A definition of truth can be obtained in a very simple way from that of another semantic notion, namely, of the notion of *satisfaction.*

Satisfaction is a relation between arbitrary objects and certain expressions called *"sentential functions."* These are expressions like *"x is white," "x is greater than y,"* etc. Their formal structure is analogous to that of sentences; however, they may contain the so-called free variables (like 'x' and 'y' in *"x is greater than y"*), which cannot occur in sentences.

In defining the notion of a sentential function in formalized languages, we usually apply what is called a "recursive procedure"; i.e., we first describe sentential functions of the simplest structure (which ordinarily presents no difficulty), and then we indicate the operations by means of which compound functions can be constructed from simpler ones. Such an operation may consist, for instance, in forming the logical disjunction or conjunction of two given functions, i.e., by combining them by the word *"or"* or *"and."*   A sentence can now be defined simply as a sentential function which contains no free variables.

As regards the notion of satisfaction, we might try to define it by saying that given objects satisfy a given function if the latter becomes a true sentence when we replace in it free variables by names of given objects.   In this sense, for example, snow satisfies the sentential function *"x is white"* since the sentence *"snow is white"* is true.   However, apart from other difficulties, this method is not available to us, for we want to use the notion of satisfaction in defining truth.

To obtain a definition of satisfaction we have rather to apply again a recursive procedure.   We indicate which objects satisfy the simplest sentential functions; and then we state the conditions under which given objects satisfy a compound function—assuming that we know which objects satisfy the simpler functions from which the compound one has been constructed.   Thus, for instance, we say that given numbers satisfy the logical disjunction *"x is greater than y or x is equal to y"* if they satisfy at least one of the functions *"x is greater than y"* or *"x is equal to y."*

Once the general definition of satisfaction is obtained, we notice that it applies automatically also to those special sentential functions which contain no free variables, i.e., to sentences.   It turns out that for a sentence only two cases are possible: a sentence is either satisfied by all objects, or by no objects.   Hence we arrive at a definition of truth and falsehood simply by saying that *a sentence is true if it is satisfied by all objects, and false otherwise.*[15]

(It may seem strange that we have chosen a roundabout way of defining the truth of a sentence, instead of trying to apply, for instance, a direct recursive procedure.   The reason is that compound sentences are constructed from simpler sentential functions, but not always from simpler sentences; hence no general recursive method is known which applies specifically to sentences.)

From this rough outline it is not clear where and how the assumption of the "essential richness" of the meta-language is involved in the discussion; this becomes clear only when the construction is carried through in a detailed and formal way.[16]

12. CONSEQUENCES OF THE DEFINITION.   The definition of truth which was outlined above has many interesting consequences.

In the first place, the definition proves to be not only formally correct, but also materially adequate (in the sense established in Section 4); in other words, it implies all equivalences of the form (T).   In this connection it is important to notice that the conditions for the material adequacy of the definition determine uniquely the extension of the term *"true."*

Therefore, every definition of truth which is materially adequate would necessarily be equivalent to that actually constructed. The semantic conception of truth gives us, so to speak, no possibility of choice between various non-equivalent definitions of this notion.

Moreover, we can deduce from our definition various laws of a general nature. In particular, we can prove with its help the *laws of contradiction and of excluded middle*, which are so characteristic of the Aristotelian conception of truth; i.e., we can show that one and only one of any two contradictory sentences is true. These semantic laws should not be identified with the related logical laws of contradiction and excluded middle; the latter belong to the sentential calculus, i.e., to the most elementary part of logic, and do not involve the term *"true"* at all.

Further important results can be obtained by applying the theory of truth to formalized languages of a certain very comprehensive class of mathematical disciplines; only disciplines of an elementary character and a very elementary logical structure are excluded from this class. It turns out that for a discipline of this class *the notion of truth never coincides with that of provability;* for all provable sentences are true, but there are true sentences which are not provable.[17] Hence it follows further that every such discipline is consistent, but incomplete; that is to say, of any two contradictory sentences at most one is provable, and—what is more—there exists a pair of contradictory sentences neither of which is provable.[18]

13. EXTENSION OF THE RESULTS TO OTHER SEMANTIC NOTIONS. Most of the results at which we arrived in the preceding sections in discussing the notion of truth can be extended with appropriate changes to other semantic notions, for instance, to the notion of satisfaction (involved in our previous discussion), and to those of *designation* and *definition.*

Each of these notions can be analyzed along the lines followed in the analysis of truth. Thus, criteria for an adequate usage of these notions can be established; it can be shown that each of these notions, when used in a semantically closed language according to those criteria, leads necessarily to a contradiction;[19] a distinction between the object-language and the meta-language becomes again indispensable; and the "essential richness" of the meta-language proves in each case to be a necessary and sufficient condition for a satisfactory definition of the notion involved. Hence the results obtained in discussing one particular semantic notion apply to the general problem of the foundations of theoretical semantics.

Within theoretical semantics we can define and study some further notions, whose intuitive content is more involved and whose semantic origin is less obvious; we have in mind, for instance, the important notions of *consequence*, *synonymity*, and *meaning.*[20]

We have concerned ourselves here with the theory of semantic notions related to an individual object-language (although no specific properties of this language have been involved in our arguments). However, we could also consider the problem of developing *general semantics* which applies to a comprehensive class of object-languages. A considerable part of our previous remarks can be extended to this general problem; however, certain new difficulties arise in this connection, which will not be discussed here. I shall merely observe that the axiomatic method (mentioned in Section 10) may prove the most appropriate for the treatment of the problem.[21]

II. POLEMICAL REMARKS

14. IS THE SEMANTIC CONCEPTION OF TRUTH THE "RIGHT" ONE? I should like to begin the polemical part of the paper with some general remarks.

I hope nothing which is said here will be interpreted as a claim that the semantic conception of truth is the "right" or indeed the "only possible" one. I do not have the slightest intention to contribute in any way to those endless, often violent discussions on the subject: "What is the right conception of truth?"[22] I must confess I do not understand what is at stake in such disputes; for the problem itself is so vague that no definite solution is possible. In fact, it seems to me that the sense in which the phrase "the right conception" is used has never been made clear. In most cases one gets the impression that the phrase is used in an almost mystical sense based upon the belief that every word has only one "real" meaning (a kind of Platonic or Aristotelian idea), and that all the competing conceptions really attempt to catch hold of this one meaning; since, however, they contradict each other, only one attempt can be successful, and hence only one conception is the "right" one.

Disputes of this type are by no means restricted to the notion of truth. They occur in all domains where—instead of an exact, scientific terminology—common language with its vagueness and ambiguity is used; and they are always meaningless, and therefore in vain.

It seems to me obvious that the only rational approach to such problems would be the following: We should reconcile ourselves with the fact that we are confronted, not with one concept, but with several different concepts which are denoted by one word; we should try to make these concepts as clear as possible (by means of definition, or of an axiomatic procedure, or in some other way); to avoid further confusions, we should agree to use different terms for different concepts; and then we may proceed to a quiet and systematic study of all concepts involved, which will exhibit their main properties and mutual relations.

Referring specifically to the notion of truth, it is undoubtedly the case that in philosophical discussions—and perhaps also in everyday usage—

some incipient conceptions of this notion can be found that differ essentially from the classical one (of which the semantic conception is but a modernized form). In fact, various conceptions of this sort have been discussed in the literature, for instance, the pragmatic conception, the coherence.theory, etc.[6]

It seems to me that none of these conceptions have been put so far in an intelligible and unequivocal form. This may change, however; a time may come when we find ourselves confronted with several incompatible, but equally clear and precise, conceptions of truth. It will then become necessary to abandon the ambiguous usage of the word *"true,"* and to introduce several terms instead, each to denote a different notion. Personally, I should not feel hurt if a future world congress of the "theoreticians of truth" should decide—by a majority of votes—to reserve the word *"true"* for one of the non-classical conceptions, and should suggest another word, say, *"frue,"* for the conception considered here. But I cannot imagine that anybody could present cogent arguments to the effect that the semantic conception is "wrong" and should be entirely abandoned.

15. FORMAL CORRECTNESS OF THE SUGGESTED DEFINITION OF TRUTH. The specific objections which have been raised to my investigations can be divided into several groups; each of these will be discussed separately.

I think that practically all these objections apply, not to the special definition I have given, but to the semantic conception of truth in general. Even those which were leveled against the definition actually constructed could be related to any other definition which conforms to this conception.

This holds, in particular, for those objections which concern the formal correctness of the definition. I have heard a few objections of this kind; however, I doubt very much whether anyone of them can be treated seriously.

As a typical example let me quote in substance such an objection.[23] In formulating the definition we use necessarily sentential connectives, i.e., expressions like *"if . . . , then," "or,"* etc. They occur in the definiens; and one of them, namely, the phrase *"if, and only if"* is usually employed to combine the definiendum with the definiens. However, it is well known that the meaning of sentential connectives is explained in logic with the help of the words *"true"* and *"false"*; for instance, we say that an equivalence, i.e., a sentence of the form *"p if, and only if, q,"* is true if either both of its members, i.e., the sentences represented by *'p'* and *'q,'* are true or both are false. Hence the definition of truth involves a vicious circle.

If this objection were valid, no formally correct definition of truth would be possible; for we are unable to formulate any compound sentence without using sentential connectives, or other logical terms defined with their help. Fortunately, the situation is not so bad.

It is undoubtedly the case that a strictly deductive development of logic is often preceded by certain statements explaining the conditions under which sentences of the form *"if p, then q,"* etc., are considered true or false. (Such explanations are often given schematically, by means of the so-called truth-tables.) However, these statements are outside of the system of logic, and should not be regarded as definitions of the terms involved. They are not formulated in the language of the system, but constitute rather special consequences of the definition of truth given in the meta-language. Moreover, these statements do not influence the deductive development of logic in any way. For in such a development we do not discuss the question whether a given sentence is true, we are only interested in the problem whether it is provable.[24]

On the other hand, the moment we find ourselves within the deductive system of logic—or of any discipline based upon logic, e.g., of semantics— we either treat sentential connectives as undefined terms, or else we define them by means of other sentential connectives, but never by means of semantic terms like *"true"* or *"false."* For instance, if we agree to regard the expressions *"not"* and *"if . . . , then"* (and possibly also *"if, and only if"*) as undefined terms, we can define the term *"or"* by stating that a sentence of the form *"p or q"* is equivalent to the corresponding sentence of the form *"if not p, then q."* The definition can be formulated, e.g., in the following way:

$$(p \ or \ q) \ if, \ and \ only \ if, \ (if \ not \ p, \ then \ q).$$

This definition obviously contains no semantic terms.

However, a vicious circle in definition arises only when the definiens contains either the term to be defined itself, or other terms defined with its help. Thus we clearly see that the use of sentential connectives in defining the semantic term *"true"* does not involve any circle.

I should like to mention a further objection which I have found in the literature and which seems also to concern the formal correctness, if not of the definition of truth itself, then at least of the arguments which lead to this definition.[25]

The author of this objection mistakenly regards scheme (T) (from Section 4) as a definition of truth. He charges this alleged definition with "inadmissible brevity, i.e., incompleteness," which "does not give us the means of deciding whether by 'equivalence' is meant a logical-formal, or a non-logical and also structurally non-describable relation." To remove this "defect" he suggests supplementing (T) in one of the two following ways:

(T′)   *X is true if, and only if, p is true,*

or

(T″)   *X is true if, and only if, p is the case (i.e., if what p states is the case).*

Then he discusses these two new "definitions," which are supposedly free from the old, formal "defect," but which turn out to be unsatisfactory for other, non-formal reasons.

This new objection seems to arise from a misunderstanding concerning the nature of sentential connectives (and thus to be somehow related to that previously discussed). The author of the objection does not seem to realize that the phrase "*if, and only if*" (in opposition to such phrases as "*are equivalent*" or "*is equivalent to*") expresses no relation between sentences at all since it does not combine names of sentences.

In general, the whole argument is based upon an obvious confusion between sentences and their names. It suffices to point out that —in contradistinction to (T)—schemata (T') and (T") do not give any meaningful expressions if we replace in them '*p*' by a sentence; for the phrases "*p is true*" and "*p is the case*" (i.e., "*what p states is the case*") become meaningless if '*p*' is replaced by a sentence, and not by the name of a sentence (cf. Section 4).[26]

While the author of the objection considers schema (T) "inadmissible brief," I am inclined, on my part, to regard schemata (T') and (T") as "inadmissibly long." And I think even that I can rigorously prove this statement on the basis of the following definition: An expression is said to be "inadmissibly long" if (i) it is meaningless, and (ii) it has been obtained from a meaningful expression by inserting superfluous words.

16. REDUNDANCY OF SEMANTIC TERMS—THEIR POSSIBLE ELIMINATION. The objection I am going to discuss now no longer concerns the formal correctness of the definition, but is still concerned with certain formal features of the semantic conception of truth.

We have seen that this conception essentially consists in regarding the sentence "*X is true*" as equivalent to the sentence denoted by '*X*' (where '*X*' stands for a name of a sentence of the object-language). Consequently, the term "*true*" when occurring in a simple sentence of the form "*X is true*" can easily be eliminated, and the sentence itself, which belongs to the meta-language, can be replaced by an equivalent sentence of the object-language; and the same applies to compound sentences provided the term "*true*" occurs in them exclusively as a part of the expressions of the form "*X is true*."

Some people have therefore urged that the term "*true*" in the semantic sense can always be eliminated, and that for this reason the semantic conception of truth is altogether sterile and useless. And since the same considerations apply to other semantic notions, the conclusion has been drawn that semantics as a whole is a purely verbal game and at best only a harmless hobby.

But the matter is not quite so simple.[27] The sort of elimination here discussed cannot always be made. It cannot be done in the case of universal statements which express the fact that all sentences of a certain type are true, or that all true sentences have a certain property. For instance, we can prove in the theory of truth the following statement:

All consequences of true sentences are true.

However, we cannot get rid here of the word *"true"* in the simple manner contemplated.

Again, even in the case of particular sentences having the form *"X is true"* such a simple elimination cannot always be made. In fact, the elimination is possible only in those cases in which the name of the sentence which is said to be true occurs in a form that enables us to reconstruct the sentence itself. For example, our present historical knowledge does not give us any possibility of eliminating the word *"true"* from the following sentence:

The first sentence written by Plato is true.

Of course, since we have a definition for truth and since every definition enables us to replace the definiendum by its definiens, an elimination of the term *"true"* in its semantic sense is always theoretically possible. But this would not be the kind of simple elimination discused above, and it would not result in the replacement of a sentence in the meta-language by a sentence in the object-language.

If, however, anyone continues to urge that—because of the theoretical possibility of eliminating the word *"true"* on the basis of its definition—the concept of truth is sterile, he must accept the further conclusion that all defined notions are sterile. But this outcome is so absurd and so unsound historically that any comment on it is unnecessary. In fact, I am rather inclined to agree with those who maintain that the moments of greatest creative advancement in science frequently coincide with the introduction of new notions by means of definition.

17. CONFORMITY OF THE SEMANTIC CONCEPTION OF TRUTH WITH PHILO-SOPHICAL AND COMMON-SENSE USAGE. The question has been raised whether the semantic conception of truth can indeed be regarded as a precise form of the old, classical conception of this notion.

Various formulations of the classical conception were quoted in the early part of this paper (Section 3). I must repeat that in my judgment none of them is quite precise and clear. Accordingly, the only sure way of settling the question would be to confront the authors of those statements with our new formulation, and to ask them whether it agrees with their intentions. Unfortunately, this method is impractical since they died quite some time ago.

As far as my own opinion is concerned, I do not have any doubts that our formulation does conform to the intuitive content of that of Aristotle. I am less certain regarding the later formulations of the classical conception, for they are very vague indeed.[28]

Furthermore, some doubts have been expressed whether the semantic conception does reflect the notion of truth in its common-sense and everyday usage. I clearly realize (as I already indicated) that the common meaning of the word *"true"*—as that of any other word of everyday language—is to some extent vague, and that its usage more or less fluctuates. Hence the problem of assigning to this word a fixed and exact meaning is relatively unspecified, and every solution of this problem implies necessarily a certain deviation from the practice of everyday language.

In spite of all this, I happen to believe that the semantic conception does conform to a very considerable extent with the common-sense usage—although I readily admit I may be mistaken. What is more to the point, however, I believe that the issue raised can be settled scientifically, though of course not by a deductive procedure, but with the help of the statistical questionnaire method. As a matter of fact, such research has been carried on, and some of the results have been reported at congresses and in part published.[29]

I should like to emphasize that in my opinion such investigations must be conducted with the utmost care. Thus, if we ask a highschool boy, or even an adult intelligent man having no special philosophical training, whether he regards a sentence to be true if it agrees with reality, or if it designates an existing state of affairs, it may simply turn out that he does not understand the question; in consequence his response, whatever it may be, will be of no value for us. But his answer to the question whether he would admit that the sentence *"it is snowing"* could be true although it is not snowing, or could be false although it is snowing, would naturally be very significant for our problem.

Therefore, I was by no means surprised to learn (in a discussion devoted to these problems) that in a group of people who were questioned only 15% agreed that *"true"* means for them *"agreeing with reality,"* while 90% agreed that a sentence such as *"it is snowing"* is true if, and only if, it is snowing. Thus, a great majority of these people seemed to reject the classical conception of truth in its "philosophical" formulation, while accepting the same conception when formulated in plain words (waiving the question whether the use of the phrase "the same conception" is here justified).

18. THE DEFINITION IN ITS RELATION TO "THE PHILOSOPHICAL PROBLEM OF TRUTH" AND TO VARIOUS EPISTEMOLOGICAL TRENDS. I have heard it remarked that the formal definition of truth has nothing to do with "the philosophical problem of truth."[30] However, nobody has ever pointed out to me in an intelligible way just what this problem is. I have been informed in this connection that my definition, though it states necessary and sufficient conditions for a sentence to be true, does not really grasp the "essence" of this concept. Since I have never been able to understand what the "essence" of a concept is, I must be excused from discussing this point any longer.

In general, I do not believe that there is such a thing as "the philosophical problem of truth." I do believe that there are various intelligible and interesting (but not necessarily philosophical) problems concerning the notion of truth, but I also believe that they can be exactly formulated and possibly solved only on the basis of a precise conception of this notion.

While on the one hand the definition of truth has been blamed for not being philosophical enough, on the other a series of objections have been raised charging this definition with serious philosophical implications, always of a very undesirable nature. I shall discuss now one special objection of this type; another group of such objections will be dealt with in the next section.

It has been claimed that—due to the fact that a sentence like "snow is white" is taken to be semantically true if snow is *in fact* white (italics by the critic)—logic finds itself involved in a most uncritical realism.[31]

If there were an opportunity to discuss the objection with its author, I should raise two points. First, I should ask him to drop the words *"in fact,"* which do not occur in the original formulation and which are misleading, even if they do not affect the content. For these words convey the impression that the semantic conception of truth is intended to establish the conditions under which we are warranted in asserting any given sentence, and in particular any empirical sentence. However, a moment's reflection shows that this impression is merely an illusion; and I think that the author of the objection falls victim to the illusion which he himself created.

In fact, the semantic definition of truth implies nothing regarding the conditions under which a sentence like (1):

(1)   *snow is white*

can be asserted. It implies only that, whenever we assert or reject this sentence, we must be ready to assert or reject the correlated sentence (2):

(2)   *the sentence "snow is white" is true.*

Thus, we may accept the semantic conception of truth without giving up any epistemological attitude we may have had; we may remain naive realists, critical realists or idealists, empiricists or metaphysicians—whatever we were before. The semantic conception is completely neutral toward all these issues.

In the second place, I should try to get some information regarding the conception of truth which (in the opinion of the author of the objection) does not involve logic in a most naive realism. I would gather that this conception must be incompatible with the semantic one. Thus, there must be sentences which are true in one of these conceptions without being true in the other. Assume, e.g., the sentence (1) to be of this kind. The truth of this sentence in the semantic conception is determined by an equivalence of the form (T):

The sentence "snow is white" is true if, and only if, snow is white.

Hence in the new conception we must reject this equivalence, and consequently we must assume its denial:

The sentence "snow is white" is true if, and only if, snow is not white (or perhaps: *snow, in fact, is not white*).

This sounds somewhat paradoxical. I do not regard such a consequence of the new conception as absurd; but I am a little fearful that someone in the future may charge this conception with involving logic in a "most sophisticated kind of irrealism." At any rate, it seems to me important to realize that every conception of truth which is incompatible with the semantic one carries with it consequences of this type.

I have dwelt a little on this whole question, not because the objection discussed seems to me very significant, but because certain points which have arisen in the discussion should be taken into account by all those who for various epistemological reasons are inclined to reject the semantic conception of truth.

19. ALLEGED METAPHYSICAL ELEMENTS IN SEMANTICS. The semantic conception of truth has been charged several times with involving certain metaphysical elements. Objections of this sort have been made to apply not only to the theory of truth, but to the whole domain of theoretical semantics.[32]

I do not intend to discuss the general problem whether the introduction of a metaphysical element into a science is at all objectionable. The only point which will interest me here is whether and in what sense metaphysics is involved in the subject of our present discussion.

The whole question obviously depends upon what one understands by "metaphysics." Unfortunately, this notion is extremely vague and equivocal. When listening to discussions in this subject, sometimes one gets the impression that the term "metaphysical" has lost any objective meaning, and is merely used as a kind of professional philosophical invective.

For some people metaphysics is a general theory of objects (ontology)—a discipline which is to be developed in a purely empirical way, and which differs from other empirical sciences only by its generality. I do not know whether such a discipline actually exists (some cynics claim that it is customary in philosophy to baptize unborn children); but I think that in any case metaphysics in this conception is not objectionable to anybody, and has hardly any connections with semantics.

For the most part, however, the term "metaphysical" is used as directly opposed—in one sense or another—to the term "empirical"; at any rate, it is used in this way by those people who are distressed by the thought that any metaphysical elements might have managed to creep into science. This general conception of metaphysics assumes several more specific forms.

Thus, some people take it to be symptomatic of a metaphysical element in a science when methods of inquiry are employed which are neither deductive nor empirical. However, no trace of this symptom can be found in the development of semantics (unless some metaphysical elements are involved in the object-language to which the semantic notions refer). In particular, the semantics of formalized languages is constructed in a purely deductive way.

Others maintain that the metaphysical character of ·a science depends mainly on its vocabulary and, more specifically, on its primitive terms. Thus, a term is said to be metaphysical if it is neither logical nor mathematical, and if it is not associated with an empirical procedure which enables us to decide whether a thing is denoted by this term or not. With respect to such a view of metaphysics it is sufficient to recall that a meta-language includes only three kinds of undefined terms: (i) terms taken from logic, (ii) terms of the corresponding object-language, and (iii) names of expressions in the object-language. It is thus obvious that no metaphysical undefined terms occur in the meta-language (again, unless such terms appear in the object-language itself).

There are, however, some who believe that, even if no metaphysical terms occur among the primitive terms of a language, they may be introduced by definitions; namely, by those definitions which fail to provide us with general criteria for deciding whether an object falls under the defined concept. It is argued that the term *"true"* is of this kind, since no universal criterion of truth follows immediately from the definition of this term, and since it is generally believed (and in a certain sense can even be proved) that such a criterion will never be found. This comment on the actual character of the notion of truth seems to be perfectly just. However, it should be noticed that the notion of truth does not differ in this respect from many notions in logic, mathematics, and theoretical parts of various empirical sciences, e.g., in theoretical physics.

In general, it must be said that if the term "metaphysical" is employed in so wide a sense as to embrace certain notions (or methods) of logic, mathematics, or empirical sciences, it will apply *a fortiori* to those of semantics. In fact, as we know from Part I of the paper, in developing the semantics of a language we use all the notions of this language, and we apply even a stronger logical apparatus than that which is used in the language itself. On the other hand, however, I can summarize the arguments given above by stating that in no interpretation of the term "metaphysical" which is familiar and more or less intelligible to me does semantics involve any metaphysical elements peculiar to itself.

I should like to make one final remark in connection with this group of objections. The history of science shows many instances of concepts which were judged metaphysical (in a loose, but in any case derogatory sense of this term) before their meaning was made precise; however, once they received a rigorous, formal definition, the distrust in them evaporated. As typical examples we may mention the concepts of negative and imaginary numbers in mathematics. I hope a similar fate awaits the concept of truth and other semantic concepts; and it seems to me, therefore, that those who have distrusted them because of their alleged metaphysical implications should welcome the fact that precise definitions of these concepts are now available. If in consequence semantic concepts lose philosophical interest, they will only share the fate of many other concepts of science, and this need give rise to no regret.

20. APPLICABILITY OF SEMANTICS TO SPECIAL EMPIRICAL SCIENCES. We come to the last and perhaps the most important group of objections. Some strong doubts have been expressed whether semantic notions find or can find applications in various domains of intellectual activity. For the most part such doubts have concerned the applicability of semantics to the field of empirical science—either to special sciences or to the general methodology of this field; although similar skepticism has been expressed regarding possible applications of semantics to mathematical sciences and their methodology.

I believe that it is possible to allay these doubts to a certain extent, and that some optimism with respect to the potential value of semantics for various domains of thought is not without ground.

To justify this optimism, it suffices I think to stress two rather obvious points. First, the development of a theory which formulates a precise definition of a notion and establishes its general properties provides *eo ipso* a firmer basis for all discussions in which this notion is involved; and, therefore, it cannot be irrelevant for anyone who uses this notion, and desires to do so in a conscious and consistent way. Secondly, semantic notions are actually involved in various branches of science, and in particular of empirical science.

The fact that in empirical research we are concerned only with natural languages and that theoretical semantics applies to these languages only with certain approximation, does not affect the problem essentially. However, it has undoubtedly this effect that progress in semantics will have but a delayed and somewhat limited influence in this field. The situation with which we are confronted here does not differ essentially from that which arises when we apply laws of logic to arguments in everyday life—or, generally, when we attempt to apply a theoretical science to empirical problems.

Semantic notions are undoubtedly involved, to a larger or smaller degree, in psychology, sociology, and in practically all the humanities. Thus, a psychologist defines the so-called intelligence quotient in terms of the numbers of *true* (right) and *false* (wrong) answers given by a person to certain questions; for a historian of culture the range of objects for which a human race in successive stages of its development possesses adequate *designations* may be a topic of great significance; a student of literature may be strongly interested in the problem whether a given author always uses two given words with the same *meaning*. Examples of this kind can be multiplied indefinitely.

The most natural and promising domain for the applications of theoretical semantics is clearly linguistics—the empirical study of natural languages. Certain parts of this science are even referred to as "semantics," sometimes with an additional qualification. Thus, this name is occasionally given to that portion of grammar which attempts to classify all words of a language into parts of speech, according to what the words mean or designate. The study of the evolution of meanings in the historical development of a language is sometimes called "historical semantics." In general, the totality of investigations on semantic relations which occur in a natural language is referred to as "descriptive semantics." The relation between theoretical and descriptive semantics is analogous to that between pure and applied mathematics, or perhaps to that between theoretical and empirical physics; the role of formalized languages in semantics can be roughly compared to that of isolated systems in physics.

It is perhaps unnecessary to say that semantics cannot find any direct applications in natural sciences such as physics, biology, etc.; for in none of these sciences are we concerned with linguistic phenomena, and even less with semantic relations between linguistic expressions and objects to which these expressions refer. We shall see, however, in the next section that semantics may have a kind of indirect influence even on those sciences in which semantic notions are not directly involved.

21. APPLICABILITY OF SEMANTICS TO THE METHODOLOGY OF EMPIRICAL SCIENCE. Besides linguistics, another important domain for possible applications of semantics is the methodology of science; this term is used here in a broad sense so as to embrace the theory of science in general. Independent of whether a science is conceived merely as a system of statements or as a totality of certain statements and human activities, the study of scientific language constitutes an essential part of the methodological discussion of a science. And it seems to me clear that any tendency to eliminate semantic notions (like those of truth and designation) from this discussion would make it fragmentary and inadequate.[33] Moreover, there is no reason for such a tendency today, once the main difficulties in using semantic terms have been overcome. The semantics of scientific language should be simply included as a part in the methodology of science.

I am by no means inclined to charge methodology and, in particular, semantics—whether theoretical or descriptive—with the task of clarifying the meanings of all scientific terms. This task is left to those sciences in which the terms are used, and is actually fulfilled by them (in the same way in which, e.g., the task of clarifying the meaning of the term *"true"* is left to, and fulfilled by, semantics). There may be, however, certain special problems of this sort in which a methodological approach is desirable or indeed necessary (perhaps, the problem of the notion of causality is a good example here); and in a methodological discussion of such problems semantic notions may play an essential role. Thus, semantics may have some bearing on any science whatsoever.

The question arises whether semantics can be helpful in solving general and, so to speak, classical problems of methodology. I should like to discuss here with some detail a special, though very important, aspect of this question.

One of the main problems of the methodology of empirical science consists in establishing conditions under which an empirical theory or hypothesis should be regarded as acceptable. This notion of acceptability must be relativized to a given stage of the development of a science (or to a given amount of presupposed knowledge). In other words, we may consider it as provided with a time coefficient; for a theory which is acceptable today may become untenable tomorrow as a result of new scientific discoveries.

It seems *a priori* very plausible that the acceptability of a theory some-how depends on the truth of its sentences, and that consequently a method-ologist in his (so far rather unsuccessful) attempts at making the notion of acceptability precise, can expect some help from the semantic theory of truth. Hence we ask the question: Are there any postulates which can be reasonably imposed on acceptable theories and which involve the notion of truth? And, in particular, we ask whether the following postulate is a reasonable one:

An acceptable theory cannot contain (or imply) any false sentences.

The answer to the last question is clearly negative. For, first of all, we are practically sure, on the basis of our historical experience, that every empirical theory which is accepted today will sooner or later be rejected and replaced by another theory. It is also very probable that the new theory will be incompatible with the old one; i.e., will imply a sentence which is contradictory to one of the sentences contained in the old theory. Hence, at least one of the two theories must include false sentences, in spite of the fact that each of them is accepted at a certain time. Secondly, the postulate in question could hardly ever be satisfied in practice; for we do not know, and are very unlikely to find, any criteria of truth which enable us to show that no sentence of an empirical theory is false.

The postulate in question could be at most regarded as the expression of an ideal limit for successively more adequate theories in a given field of research; but this hardly can be given any precise meaning.

Nevertheless, it seems to me that there is an important postulate which can be reasonably imposed on acceptable empirical theories and which involves the notion of truth. It is closely related to the one just discussed, but is essentially weaker. Remembering that the notion of acceptability is provided with a time coefficient, we can give this postulate the following form:

As soon as we succeed in showing that an empirical theory contains (or implies) false sentences, it cannot be any longer considered acceptable.

In support of this postulate, I should like to make the following remarks.

I believe everybody agrees that one of the reasons which may compel us to reject an empirical theory is the proof of its inconsistency: a theory becomes untenable if we succeed in deriving from it two contradictory sentences. Now we can ask what are the usual motives for rejecting a theory on such grounds. Persons who are acquainted with modern logic are inclined to answer this question in the following way: A well-known logical law shows that a theory which enables us to derive two contradictory sentences enables us also to derive every sentence; therefore, such a theory is trivial and deprived of any scientific interest.

I have some doubts whether this answer contains an adequate analysis of the situation. I think that people who do not know modern logic are as little inclined to accept an inconsistent theory as those who are thoroughly familiar with it; and probably this applies even to those who regard (as some still do) the logical law on which the argument is based as a highly controversial issue, and almost as a paradox. I do not think that our attitude toward an inconsistent theory would change even if we decided for some reasons to weaken our system of logic so as to deprive ourselves of the possibility of deriving every sentence from any two contradictory sentences.

It seems to me that the real reason of our attitude is a different one: We know (if only intuitively) that an inconsistent theory must contain false sentences; and we are not inclined to regard as acceptable any theory which has been shown to contain such sentences.

There are various methods of showing that a given theory includes false sentences. Some of them are based upon purely logical properties of the theory involved; the method just discussed (i.e., the proof of inconsistency) is not the sole method of this type, but is the simplest one, and the one which is most frequently applied in practice. With the help of certain assumptions regarding the truth of empirical sentences, we can obtain methods to the same effect which are no longer of a purely logical nature. If we decide to accept the general postulate suggested above, then a successful application of any such method will make the theory untenable.

22. APPLICATIONS OF SEMANTICS TO DEDUCTIVE SCIENCE. As regards the applicability of semantics to mathematical sciences and their methodology, i.e., to meta-mathematics, we are in a much more favorable position than in the case of empirical sciences. For, instead of advancing reasons which justify some hopes for the future (and thus making a kind of pro-semantics propaganda), we are able to point out concrete results already achieved.

Doubts continue to be expressed whether the notion of a true sentence— as distinct from that of a provable sentence—can have any significance for mathematical disciplines and play any part in a methodological discussion of mathematics. It seems to me, however, that just this notion of a true sentence constitutes a most valuable contribution to meta-mathematics by semantics. We already possess a series of interesting meta-mathematical results gained with the help of the theory of truth. These results concern the mutual relations between the notion of truth and that of provability; establish new properties of the latter notion (which, as well known, is one of the basic notions of meta-mathematics); and throw some light on the fundamental problems of consistency and completeness. The most significant among these results have been briefly discussed in Section 12.[34]

Furthermore, by applying the method of semantics we can adequately define several important meta-mathematical notions which have been used so far only in an intuitive way—such as, e.g., the notion of definability or that of a model of an axiom system; and thus we can undertake a systematic study of these notions. In particular, the investigations on definability have already brought some interesting results, and promise even more in the future.[35]

We have discussed the applications of semantics only to meta-mathematics, and not to mathematics proper. However, this distinction between mathematics and meta-mathematics is rather unimportant. For meta-mathematics is itself a deductive discipline and hence, from a certain point of view, a part of mathematics; and it is well known that—due to the formal character of deductive method—the results obtained in one deductive discipline can be automatically extended to any other discipline in which the given one finds an interpretation. Thus, for example, all meta-mathematical results can be interpreted as results of number theory. Also from a practical point of view there is no clear-cut line between meta-mathematics and mathematics proper; for instance, the investigations on definability could be included in either of these domains.

23. FINAL REMARKS. I should like to conclude this discussion with some general and rather loose remarks concerning the whole question of the evaluation of scientific achievements in terms of their applicability. I must confess I have various doubts in this connection.

Being a mathematician (as well as a logician, and perhaps a philosopher of a sort), I have had the opportunity to attend many discussions between specialists in mathematics, where the problem of applications is especially acute, and I have noticed on several occasions the following phenomenon: If a mathematician wishes to disparage the work of one of his colleagues, say, A, the most effective method he finds for doing this is to ask where the results can be applied. The hard pressed man, with his back against the wall, finally unearths the researches of another mathematician B as the locus of the application of his own results. If next B is plagued with a similar question, he will refer to another mathematician C. After a few steps of this kind we find ourselves referred back to the researches of A, and in this way the chain closes.

Speaking more seriously, I do not wish to deny that the value of a man's work may be increased by its implications for the research of others and for practice. But I believe, nevertheless, that it is inimical to the progress of science to measure the importance of any research exclusively or chiefly in terms of its usefulness and applicability. We know from the history of science that many important results and discoveries have had to wait centuries before they were applied in any field. And, in my opinion, there are

also other important factors which cannot be disregarded in determining·
the value of a scientific work.   It seems to me that there is a special domain
of very profound and strong human needs related to scientific research,
which are similar in many ways to aesthetic and perhaps religious needs.
And it also seems to me that the satisfaction of these needs should be
considered an important task of research.   Hence, I believe, the question
of the value of any research cannot be adequately answered without taking
into account the intellectual satisfaction which the results of that research
bring to those who understand it and care for it.   It may be unpopular and
out-of-date to say—but I do not think that a scientific result which gives
us a better understanding of the world and makes it more harmonious in
our eyes should be held in lower esteem than, say, an invention which reduces the cost of paving roads, or improves household plumbing.

It is clear that the remarks just made become pointless if the word
"application" is used in a very wide and liberal sense.   It is perhaps not
less obvious that nothing follows from these general remarks concerning
the specific topics which have been discussed in this paper; and I really do
not know whether research in semantics stands to gain or lose by introducing the standard of value I have suggested.

Notes

1 Compare Tarski [2] (see bibliography at the end of the paper).   This work may
be consulted for a more detailed and formal presentation of the subject of the paper,
especially of the material included in Sections 6 and 9–13.   It contains also references
to my earlier publications on the problems of semantics (a communication in Polish,
1930; the article Tarski [1] in French, 1931; a communication in German, 1932; and a
book in Polish, 1933).   The expository part of the present paper is related in its character to Tarski [3].   My investigations on the notion of truth and on theoretical
semantics have been reviewed or discussed in Hofstadter [1], Juhos [1], Kokoszyńska
[1] and [2], Kotarbiński [2], Scholz [1], Weinberg [1], *et al.*

2 It may be hoped that the interest in theoretical semantics will now increase, as a
result of the recent publication of the important work Carnap [2].

3 This applies, in particular, to public discussions during the I. International Congress for the Unity of Science (Paris, 1935) and the Conference of International
Congresses for the Unity of Science (Paris, 1937); cf., e.g., Neurath [1] and Gonseth [1].

4 The words "notion" and "concept" are used in this paper with all of the vagueness and ambiguity with which they occur in philosophical literature.   Thus, sometimes they refer simply to a term, sometimes to what is meant by a term, and in other
cases to what is denoted by a term.   Sometimes it is irrelevant which of these interpretations is meant; and in certain cases perhaps none of them applies adequately.
While on principle I share the tendency to avoid these words in any exact discussion,
I did not consider it necessary to do so in this informal presentation.

5 For our present purposes it is somewhat more convenient to understand by "expressions," "sentences," etc., not individual inscriptions, but classes of inscriptions
of similar form (thus, not individual physical things, but classes of such things).

[6] For the Aristotelian formulation see Aristotle [1], Γ, 7, 27. The other two formulations are very common in the literature, but I do not know with whom they originate. A critical discussion of various conceptions of truth can be found, e.g., in Kotarbiński [1] (so far available only in Polish), pp. 123 ff., and Russell [1], pp. 362 ff.

[7] For most of the remarks contained in Sections 4 and 8, I am indebted to the late S. Leśniewski who developed them in his unpublished lectures in the University of Warsaw (in 1919 and later). However, Leśniewski did not anticipate the possibility of a rigorous development of the theory of truth, and still less of a definition of this notion; hence, while indicating equivalences of the form (T) as premisses in the antinomy of the liar, he did not conceive them as any sufficient conditions for an adequate usage (or definition) of the notion of truth. Also the remarks in Section 8 regarding the occurrence of an empirical premiss in the antinomy of the liar, and the possibility of eliminating this premiss, do not originate with him.

[8] In connection with various logical and methodological problems involved in this paper the reader may consult Tarski [6].

[9] The antinomy of the liar (ascribed to Eubulides or Epimenides) is discussed here in Sections 7 and 8. For the antinomy of definability (due to J. Richard) see, e.g., Hilbert-Bernays [1], vol. 2, pp. 263 ff.; for the antinomy of heterological terms see Grelling-Nelson [1], p. 307.

[10] Due to Professor J. Lukasiewicz (University of Warsaw).

[11] This can roughly be done in the following way. Let S be any sentence beginning with the words *"Every sentence."* We correlate with S a new sentence S^* by subjecting S to the following two modifications: we replace in S the first word, *"Every,"* by *"The"*; and we insert after the second word, *"sentence,"* the whole sentence S enclosed in quotation marks. Let us agree to call the sentence S "(self-)applicable" or "non-(self-)applicable" dependent on whether the correlated sentence S^* is true or false. Now consider the following sentence:

Every sentence is non-applicable.

It can easily be shown that the sentence just stated must be both applicable and non-applicable; hence a contradiction. It may not be quite clear in what sense this formulation of the antinomy does not involve an empirical premiss; however, I shall not elaborate on this point.

[12] The terms "logic" and "logical" are used in this paper in a broad sense, which has become almost traditional in the last decades; logic is assumed here to comprehend the whole theory of classes and relations (i.e., the mathematical theory of sets). For many different reasons I am personally inclined to use the term "logic" in a much narrower sense, so as to apply it only to what is sometimes called "elementary logic," i.e., to the sentential calculus and the (restricted) predicate calculus.

[13] Cf. here, however, Tarski [3], pp. 5 f.

[14] The method of construction we are going to outline can be applied—with appropriate changes—to all formalized languages that are known at the present time; although it does not follow that a language could not be constructed to which this method would not apply.

[15] In carrying through this idea a certain technical difficulty arises. A sentential function may contain an arbitrary number of free variables; and the logical nature of the notion of satisfaction varies with this number. Thus, the notion in question when applied to functions with one variable is a binary relation between these functions and single objects; when applied to functions with two variables it becomes a ternary relation between functions and couples of objects; and so on. Hence, strictly

speaking, we are confronted, not with one notion of satisfaction, but with infinitely many notions; and it turns out that these notions cannot be defined independently of each other, but must all be introduced simultaneously.

To overcome this difficulty, we employ the mathematical notion of an infinite sequence (or, possibly, of a finite sequence with an arbitrary number of terms). We agree to regard satisfaction, not as a many-termed relation between sentential functions and an indefinite number of objects, but as a binary relation between functions and sequences of objects. Under this assumption the formulation of a general and precise definition of satisfaction no longer presents any difficulty; and a true sentence can now be defined as one which is satisfied by every sequence.

[16] To define recursively the notion of satisfaction, we have to apply a certain form of recursive definition which is not admitted in the object-language. Hence the "essential richness" of the meta-language may simply consist in admitting this type of definition. On the other hand, a general method is known which makes it possible to eliminate all recursive definitions and to replace them by normal, explicit ones. If we try to apply this method to the definition of satisfaction, we see that we have either to introduce into the meta-language variables of a higher logical type than those which occur in the object-language; or else to assume axiomatically in the meta-language the existence of classes that are more comprehensive than all those whose existence can be established in the object-language. See here Tarski [2], pp. 393 ff., and Tarski [5], p. 110.

[17] Due to the development of modern logic, the notion of mathematical proof has undergone a far-reaching simplification. A sentence of a given formalized discipline is provable if it can be obtained from the axioms of this discipline by applying certain simple and purely formal rules of inference, such as those of detachment and substitution. Hence to show that all provable sentences are true, it suffices to prove that all the sentences accepted as axioms are true, and that the rules of inference when applied to true sentences yield new true sentences; and this usually presents no difficulty.

On the other hand, in view of the elementary nature of the notion of provability, a precise definition of this notion requires only rather simple logical devices. In most cases, those logical devices which are available in the formalized discipline itself (to which the notion of provability is related) are more than sufficient for this purpose. We know, however, that as regards the definition of truth just the opposite holds. Hence, as a rule, the notions of truth and provability cannot coincide; and since every provable sentence is true, there must be true sentences which are not provable.

[18] Thus the theory of truth provides us with a general method for consistency proofs for formalized mathematical disciplines. It can be easily realized, however, that a consistency proof obtained by this method may possess some intuitive value—i.e., may convince us, or strengthen our belief, that the discipline under consideration is actually consistent—only in case we succeed in defining truth in terms of a meta-language which does not contain the object-language as a part (cf. here a remark in Section 9). For only in this case the deductive assumptions of the meta-language may be intuitively simpler and more obvious than those of the object-language—even though the condition of "essential richness" will be formally satisfied. Cf. here also Tarski [3], p. 7.

The incompleteness of a comprehensive class of formalized disciplines constitutes the essential content of a fundamental theorem of K. Gödel; cf. Gödel [1], pp. 187 ff. The explanation of the fact that the theory of truth leads so directly to Gödel's theorem is rather simple. In deriving Gödel's result from the theory of truth we make an essential use of the fact that the definition of truth cannot be given in a metalanguage which is only as "rich" as the object-language (cf. note 17); however, in establishing this fact, a method of reasoning has been applied which is very closely related to that used (for the first time) by Gödel. It may be added that Gödel was clearly guided in his proof by certain intuitive considerations regarding the notion of truth, although this notion does not occur in the proof explicitly; cf. Gödel [1], pp. 174 f.

[19] The notions of designation and definition lead respectively to the antinomies of Grelling-Nelson and Richard (cf. note 9). To obtain an antinomy for the notion of satisfaction, we construct the following expression:

The sentential function X does not satisfy X.

A contradiction arises when we consider the question whether this expression, which is clearly a sentential function, satisfies itself or not.

[20] All notions mentioned in this section can be defined in terms of satisfaction. We can say, e.g., that a given term designates a given object if this object satisfies the sentential function "x *is identical with* T" where 'T' stands for the given term. Similarly, a sentential function is said to define a given object if the latter is the only object which satisfies this function. For a definition of consequence see Tarski [4], and for that of synonymity—Carnap [2].

[21] General semantics is the subject of Carnap [2]. Cf. here also remarks in Tarski [2], pp. 388 f.

[22] Cf. various quotations in Ness [1], pp. 13 f.

[23] The names of persons who have raised objections will not be quoted here, unless their objections have appeared in print.

[24] It should be emphasized, however, that as regards the question of an alleged vicious circle the situation would not change even if we took a different point of view, represented, e.g., in Carnap [2]; i.e., if we regarded the specification of conditions under which sentences of a language are true as an essential part of the description of this language. On the other hand, it may be noticed that the point of view represented in the text does not exclude the possibility of using truth-tables in a deductive development of logic. However, these tables are to be regarded then merely as a formal instrument for checking the provability of certain sentences; and the symbols 'T' and 'F' which occur in them and which are usually considered abbreviations of "*true*" and "*false*" should not be interpreted in any intuitive way.

[25] Cf. Juhos [1]. I must admit that I do not clearly understand von Juhos' objections and do not know how to classify them; therefore, I confine myself here to certain points of a formal character. Von Juhos does not seem to know my definition of truth; he refers only to an informal presentation in Tarski [3] where the definition has not been given at all. If he knew the actual definition, he would have to change his argument. However, I have no doubt that he would discover in this definition some "defects" as well. For he believes he has proved that "on ground of principle it is impossible to give such a definition at all."

[26] The phrases "p *is true*" and "p *is the case*" (or better "*it is true that* p" and "*it is the case that* p") are sometimes used in informal discussions, mainly for stylistic reasons; but they are considered then as synonymous with the sentence represented by 'p'. On the other hand, as far as I understand the situation, the phrases in question cannot be used by von Juhos synonymously with 'p'; for otherwise the replacement of (T) by (T') or (T″) would not constitute any "improvement."

[27] Cf. the discussion of this problem in Kokoszyńska [1], pp. 161 ff.

[28] Most authors who have discussed my work on the notion of truth are of the opinion that my definition does conform with the classical conception of this notion; see, e.g., Kotarbiński [2] and Scholz [1].

[29] Cf. Ness [1]. Unfortunately, the results of that part of Ness' research which is especially relevant for our problem are not discussed in his book; compare p. 148, footnote 1.

[30] Though I have heard this opinion several times, I have seen it in print only once and, curiously enough, in a work which does not have a philosophical character—in fact, in Hilbert-Bernays [1], vol. II, p. 269 (where, by the way, it is not expressed as any kind of objection). On the other hand, I have not found any remark to this effect in discussions of my work by professional philosophers (cf. note 1).

[31] Cf. Gonseth [1], pp. 187 f.

[32] See Nagel [1], and Nagel [2], pp. 471 f. A remark which goes, perhaps, in the same direction is also to be found in Weinberg [1], p. 77; cf., however, his earlier remarks, pp. 75 f.

[33] Such a tendency was evident in earlier works of Carnap (see, e.g., Carnap [1], especially Part V) and in writings of other members of Vienna Circle. Cf. here Kokoszyńska [1] and Weinberg [1].

[34] For other results obtained with the help of the theory of truth see Gödel [2]; Tarski [2], pp. 401 ff.; and Tarski [5], pp. 111 f.

[35] An object—e.g., a number or a set of numbers—is said to be definable (in a given formalism) if there is a sentential function which defines it; cf. note 20. Thus, the term "definable," though of a meta-mathematical (semantic) origin, is purely mathematical as to its extension, for it expresses a property (denotes a class) of mathematical objects. In consequence, the notion of definability can be re-defined in purely mathematical terms, though not within the formalized discipline to which this notion refers; however, the fundamental idea of the definition remains unchanged. Cf. here—also for further bibliographic references—Tarski [1]; various other results concerning definability can also be found in the literature, e.g., in Hilbert-Bernays [1], vol. I, pp. 354 ff., 369 ff., 456 ff., etc., and in Lindenbaum-Tarski [1]. It may be noticed that the term "definable" is sometimes used in another, meta-mathematical (but not semantic), sense; this occurs, for instance, when we say that that a term is definable in other terms (on the basis of a given axiom system). For a definition of a model of an axiom system see Tarski [4].

BIBLIOGRAPHY

Only the books and articles actually referred to in the paper will be listed here.

Aristotle. [1]. *Metaphysica*. (*Works*, vol. VIII.) English translation by W. D. Ross. Oxford, 1908.

Carnap, R. [1]. *Logical Syntax of Language*. London and New York, 1937.

Carnap, R. [2]. *Introduction to Semantics*. Cambridge, 1942.

Gödel, K. [1]. "Über formal unentscheidbare Sätze der *Principia Mathematica* und verwandter Systeme, I." *Monatshefte für Mathematik und Physik*, vol. XXXVIII, 1931, pp. 173–198.

Gödel, K, [2]. "Über die Länge von Beweisen." *Ergebnisse eines mathematischen Kolloquiums*, vol. VII, 1936, pp. 23–24.

Gonseth, F. [1]. "Le Congrès Descartes. Questions de Philosophie scientifique." *Revue thomiste*, vol. XLIV, 1938, pp. 183–193.

Grelling, K., and Nelson, L. [1]. "Bemerkungen zu den Paradoxien von Russell und Burali-Forti." *Abhandlungen der Fries'schen Schule*, vol. II (new series), 1908, pp. 301–334.

Hofstadter, A. [1]. "On Semantic Problems." *The Journal of Philosophy*, vol. XXXV, 1938, pp. 225–232.

Hilbert, D., and Bernays, P. [1]. *Grundlagen der Mathematik*. 2 vols. Berlin, 1934–1939.

Juhos, B. von. [1]. "The Truth of Empirical Statements." *Analysis*, vol. IV, 1937, pp. 65–70.

Kokoszyńska, M. [1]. "Über den absoluten Wahrheitsbegriff und einige andere semantische Begriffe." *Erkenntnis*, vol. VI, 1936, pp. 143–165.

Kokoszyńska, M. [2]. "Syntax, Semantik und Wissenschaftslogik." *Actes du Congrès International de Philosophie Scientifique*, vol. III, Paris, 1936, pp. 9–14.

Kotarbiński, T. [1]. *Elementy teorji poznania, logiki formalnej i metodologji nauk*. (*Elements of Epistemology, Formal Logic, and the Methodology of Sciences*, in Polish.) Lwów, 1929.

Kotarbiński, T. [2]. "W sprawie pojęcia prawdy." (*"Concerning the Concept of Truth*," in Polish.) *Przegląd filozoficzny*, vol. XXXVII, pp. 85–91.

Lindenbaum, A., and Tarski, A. [1]. "Über die Beschränktheit der Ausdrucksmittel deduktiver Theorien." *Ergebnisse eines mathematischen Kolloquiums*, vol. VII, 1936, pp. 15–23.

Nagel, E. [1]. Review of Hofstadter [1]. *The Journal of Symbolic Logic*, vol. III, 1938, p. 90.

Nagel, E. [2]. Review of Carnap [2]. *The Journal of Philosophy*, vol. XXXIX, 1942, pp. 468–473.

Ness, A. [1]. " 'Truth' As Conceived by Those Who Are Not Professional Philosophers." *Skrifter utgitt av Det Norske Videnskaps-Akademi i Oslo, II. Hist.-Filos. Klasse*, vol. IV, Oslo, 1938.

Neurath, O. [1]. "Erster Internationaler Kongress für Einheit der Wissenschaft in Paris 1935." *Erkenntnis*, vol. V, 1935, pp. 377–406.

Russell, B. [1]. *An Inquiry Into Meaning and Truth*. New York, 1940.

Scholz, H. [1]. Review of *Studia philosophica*, vol. I. *Deutsche Literaturzeitung*, vol. LVIII, 1937, pp. 1914–1917.

Tarski, A. [1]. "Sur les ensembles définissables de nombres réels. I." *Fundamenta mathematicae*, vol. XVII, 1931, pp. 210–239.

Tarski, A. [2]. "Der Wahrheitsbegriff in den formalisierten Sprachen." (German translation of a book in Polish, 1933.) *Studia philosophica*, vol. I, 1935, pp. 261–405.

Tarski, A. [3]. "Grundlegung der wissenschaftlichen Semantik." *Actes du Congrès International de Philosophie Scientifique*, vol. III, Paris, 1936, pp. 1–8.

Tarski, A. [4]. "Über den Begriff der logischen Folgerung." *Actes du Congrès International de Philosophie Scientifique*, vol. VII, Paris, 1937, pp. 1–11.

Tarski, A. [5]. "On Undecidable Statements in Enlarged Systems of Logic and the Concept of Truth." *The Journal of Symbolic Logic*, vol. IV, 1939, pp. 105–112.

Tarski, A. [6]. *Introduction to Logic*. New York, 1941.

Weinberg, J. [1]. Review of *Studia philosophica*, vol. I. *The Philosophical Review*, vol. XLVII, pp. 70–77.

ALFRED TARSKI.

UNIVERSITY OF CALIFORNIA, BERKELEY.

3

The Modes of Meaning

by C. I. LEWIS

Reprinted from *Philosophy and Phenomenological Research,* 4 (1944).

A SYMPOSIUM ON MEANING AND TRUTH, PART I

THE MODES OF MEANING

The discussion will mainly be confined to meanings as conveyed by words; by series of ink-marks or of sounds. But it will be well to acknowledge at the outset that verbal meanings are not primitive: presumably the meanings to be expressed must come before the linguistic expression of them, however much language may operate retroactively to modify the meanings entertained. Also, other things than verbal expressions have meaning; in fact, one may well think that words are only surrogates for presentational items of other sorts which are the originals in exercise of the meaning-function. As Charles Peirce pointed out, the essentials of the meaning-situation are found wherever there is anything which, for some mind, stands as sign of something else. To identify meaning exclusively with the characters of verbal symbolization would be to put the cart before the horse, and run the risk of trivializing the subject. The generic significance of meaning is that in which A means B if A operates as representing or signifying B; if it stands for B, or calls it to mind. Still, it is doubtful that there are, or could be, any meanings which it is intrinsically impossible for words to express: it may well be that in discussing verbal meanings exclusively, we do not necessarily omit any kind of meanings, but merely limit our consideration to meanings as conveyed by a particular type of vehicle.

Even with this limitation to meaning as verbally expressed, it is impossible, within reasonable limits of space here, to present our topic otherwise than in outline only. Nor will it be possible to make desirable comparisons between the outline to be offered and other discussions of the same subject. But because such outline-presentation may easily have the air of dogmatism, I should like to express my conviction that if there be any one analysis of meaning in general which is correct, then any number of other analyses will be possible which are equally correct: for much the same reasons that if any set of primitive ideas and primitive propositions are sufficient for a mathematical system, then there will be any number of alternative sets of primitive ideas and propositions which likewise are sufficient. Amongst alternative analyses of meaning which should be so fortunate as to be correct in all details, choice would presumably be determined by such considerations as convenience, simplicity, and conformability to some purpose in hand.

In general, the connection between a linguistic sign and its meaning is determined by convention: linguistic signs are verbal symbols. A *verbal symbol* is a recognizable pattern of marks or of sounds used for purposes of expression. (What is recognized as the same pattern, in different instances, is partly a matter of physical similarity and partly a matter of conventional understanding.)   Two marks, or two sounds, having the same recognizable pattern, are two *instances* of the same symbol; not two different symbols.

A *linguistic expression* is constituted by the association of a verbal symbol and a fixed meaning; but the linguistic expression cannot be identified with the symbol alone nor with the meaning alone.   If in two cases, the meaning expressed is the same but the symbols are different, there are two expressions; not one.   If in two cases, the symbol is the same but the meanings are different, there are two expressions; not one.   But if in two cases—as in different places or at different times—the meaning is the same and the symbol is the same, then there are two *instances* of the expression but only one expression.

An instance of a symbol is often called a symbol, and an instance of an expression is often called an expression; but these modes of speech are unprecise.   An ink-spot or a noise is a concrete entity; but a symbol is an abstract entity; and an expression is a correlative abstraction.

A linguistic expression may be a term or a proposition or a propositional function.   As it will turn out, propositions and propositional functions are terms; but some terms only are propositions, and some only are propositional functions; and these two latter classifications are mutually exclusive.

A *term* is an expression which names or applies to a thing or things, of some kind, actual or thought of.

It is sometimes said that what is not actual cannot be named.   But such assertion is either an arbitrary and question-begging restriction upon use of the verb "to name"—since plainly whatever is thought of can be spoken of —or it is merely silly.   One does not easily imagine what those who make this assertion would say to persons who have named a hoped-for child or inventors who have named a never-completed machine.   However, there are difficulties connected with this point which are genuine; and it will be the intention so to write here as to minimize dependence upon it.   In line with that intention, the above definition of a term may be rephrased: A term is an expression *capable* of naming or applying to a thing or things, of some kind.

In common speech, a term is said to denote the existent or existents to which it is applied on any given occasion of its use.   For example, in the statement "Those three objects are books," "book" is said to denote the three objects indicated, or any one of them.   This usage has the awkward consequence that what a term is said to denote is not, in most instances, the denotation of it.   We shall, however, continue to use both "denote" and "denotation" with their commonplace significances.[1]

---

[1] Some avoid the awkward consequence mentioned by saying that a term *designates* a thing that it names.   This terminology is apt, but is not adopted here.

All terms have meaning in the sense or mode of denotation or extension; and all have meaning in the mode of connotation or intension.

The *denotation* of a term is the class of all actual or existent things to which that term correctly applies. The qualification "actual or existent" here is limiting and not merely explicative: things which are, or would be, namable by a term but which do not in fact exist are not included in its denotation.

A term which names nothing actual has *zero-denotation*. But it would be a mistake to say that such a term as "unicorn" or "Apollo" has no denotation; especially since this would suggest that it has no meaning in the correlative sense of meaning. A term has meaning in the mode of denotation if it is intended to function as a name; and any locution not so intended is not a term.

When it is desirable to refer to whatever a term would correctly name or apply to, whether existent or not, we shall speak of a *classification* instead of a class, and of the comprehension of the term. The *comprehension* of a term is, thus, the classification of all consistently thinkable things to which the term would correctly apply—where anything is consistently thinkable if the assertion of its existence would not, explicitly or implicitly, involve a contradiction. For example, the comprehension of "square" includes all imaginable as well as all actual squares, but does not include round squares.

Much confusion in analysis may be avoided by the clear distinction of denotation from comprehension.

The *connotation* or *intension* of a term is delimited by any correct definition of it. If nothing would be correctly namable by "T" unless it should also be namable by "A_1," by "A_2," and . . . and by "A_n," and if anything namable by the compound term, "A_1 and A_2 and . . . and A_n," would also be namable by "T" then this compound term, or any which is synonymous with it, specifies the connotation of "T" and may be said to have the same connotation as "T." This leaves "connotation" subject to one ambiguity, which will be discussed later. But for the present, the characterization given will be sufficiently clear.

Traditionally the term "essence" is used to indicate that characteristic of the object or objects named which is correlative with the connotation of the term. It is, of course, meaningless to speak of the essence of a thing except relative to its being named by some particular term. But for purposes of analysis, it is desirable or even necessary to have some manner of marking this distinction between characters of an object which are essential to its being named by a term in question, and other characters of the object which are not thus essential. We shall say that a term *signifies* the comprehensive character such that everything having this character is correctly namable by the term, and whatever lacks this character, or anything included in it, is not so namable. And we shall call this comprehensive essential character the *signification* of the term.[2]

Abstract terms are those which name what they signify. Thus for abstract terms, signification and denotation coincide. Things which incorporate the signification of an abstract term, *"A,"* but possess other characters not included in what *"A"* names, are *instances* of A but are not named by *"A."*

Non-abstract terms, whose denotation is distinct from their signification, are *concrete*.

By the idiom of language, there are certain words and phrases—e.g., predicate-adjectives like "red"—which when they occur as grammatical subject are abstract terms, but which may occur as concrete terms in the predicate. Such words and phrases are sometimes called *attributive*. But this classification is primarily linguistic; the words and phrases in question are not strictly terms but only ambiguous symbolizations having now one, now another meaning. The classification "attributive" is worth remarking only in order that certain confusions about abstract and concrete terms may be avoided.

A *singular* term is one whose connotation precludes application of it to more than one actual thing. A non-singular term is *general*. (The dichotomy, singular or general, is not significant in the case of abstract terms; if it be applied to them, all abstract terms must be classed as singular.)

It should be observed that singularity or generality is a question of connotation, not of denotation. "The red object on my desk" is a singular term, and "red object on my desk" is a general term, regardless of the facts about red objects on my desk. If there is no red object on my desk, or if there is more than one, then "the red object on my desk" has zero-denotation, but its being a singular term is not affected.

The question what should be regarded as comprehended by a singular term, involves the consideration that, although singularity is connoted, still the connotation of a singular term is never sufficient—without recourse to other and logically adventitious facts—to determine *what* individual is named; i.e., to select this individual from amongst all thinkable things satisfying the connotation of the term. Thus the denotation of a singular

---

[2] Some may be minded to insist that it is the *sign* which *signifies*, and not the term or linguistic expression, constituted by association of the sign with a meaning. Our usage here of the words "signify" and "signification" is, of course, arbitrary: other and possibly more appropriate words might have been chosen instead. But what we use these words to refer to is a function of the term or expression, and is *not* a property which (like its shape) can be attributed to the sign regardless of the meaning associated with it.

term is a class which is either a class of one or is empty. But its comprehension is the classification of *all* the things consistently thinkable as being the one and only member of that class.

It will be noted that, for any term, its connotation determines its comprehension; and conversely, any determination of its comprehension would determine its connotation; by determining what characters alone are common to all the things comprehended. In point of fact, however, there is no way in which the comprehension can be precisely specified except by reference to the connotation, since exhaustive enumeration of all the thinkable things comprehended is never possible.

The connotation of a term and its denotation do not, however, mutually determine one another. The connotation being given, the denotation is thereby limited but not fixed. Things which lack any essential attribute, specified or implied in the connotation, are *excluded from* the denotation; but what is *included in* the denotation, and what not, depends also on what happens to exist; since the class of things denoted—as distinguished from what the term comprehends—is confined to existents.

Also, the denotation of a term being determined, the connotation is thereby limited but not fixed. The connotation cannot include any attribute absent from one or more of the things named; but it may or may not include an attribute which is common to all existents named by the term; since such an attribute may or may not be essential to their being so named. "Featherless biped," for example, does not connote rationality, even if the class denoted contains only rational beings.

We should also remark that a term may have zero-comprehension. For example, "round square" has zero-comprehension; the classification of consistently-thinkable things so named is empty. But many terms—e.g., "unicorn" and "non-rational animal that laughs"—have zero-denotation without having zero-comprehension; things which would be correctly so named are consistently thinkable.

The classic dictum that denotation varies inversely as connotation, is false; e.g., "rational featherless biped" has the same denotation as "featherless biped." But this relation does hold between connotation and comprehension. Any qualification added to a connotation (and not already implied) further restricts the comprehension; and with any omission of a qualification from a connotation, the classification comprehended is enlarged to include thinkable things which retention of that qualification would exclude.

This relation of connotation and comprehension is worth remarking for the sake of one consequence of it: a term of zero-comprehension has *universal* connotation. This may at first strike the reader as a paradox. But the correctness of it may be observed from two considerations. Only terms naming nothing which is consistently thinkable have zero-comprehension. And "A is both round and square," for example, entails "A is y," for any value of y. That is, the attribution of "both round and square" entails *every* attribute; and the connotation of "round square," since it includes every mentionable attribute, is universal.[3]

This fact clarifies one matter which might otherwise be puzzling. Plainly, it is incorrect to say that terms like "round square" have no connotation, or that they are meaningless. This term is distinguished from a nonsense-locution like "zuke" by definitely implying the properties of roundness and squareness. And it is only by reason of this meaning—this connotation—which it has, that one determines its inapplicability to anything consistently thinkable.

Thus what is (presumably) intended by the inaccurate statement that such terms are meaningless, can be stated precisely by saying that they have zero-comprehension, or that their connotation is universal.

The diametrically opposite kind of term—those having universal comprehension and zero-connotation—are also often said to be meaningless. "Being" and "entity"—supposing everything one could mention is a being or entity—are such terms. And again, the accurate manner of indicating the lack of significance which characterizes these terms, is to observe that attribution of them implies no attribute that could be absent from anything; that their connotation is zero and their comprehension unlimited. But if they genuinely lacked any meaning—any connotation—this character of them could not be determined.

The modes of meaning mentioned above for terms—denotation or extension, connotation or intension, comprehension, and signification—are likewise the modes of meaning of propositions and of propositional functions. This is the case because propositions are a kind of terms; and propositional functions are another kind of terms.

A proposition is a term capable of signifying a state of affairs. To define a proposition as an expression which is either true or false, is correct enough but inauspicious; because it may lead to confusion of a proposition with the

---

[3] "A is both x and not-x" entails "A is x."

And "A is x" entails "Either A is both x and y or A is x but not y."

Hence "A is both x and not-x" entails "Either A is both x and y or A is x but not y."

But also "A is both x and not-x" entails "A is not x."

And "A is not x" entails "It is false that A is x but not y."

Hence "A is both x and not-x" entails "It is false that A is x but not y."

But "Either A is both x and y or A is x but not y" and "It is false that A is x but not y" together entail "A is both x and y."

And "A is both x and y" entails "A is y."

Hence "A is both x and not-x" entails "A is y."

statement or *assertion* of it, whereas the element of assertion in a statement is extraneous to the proposition asserted. The proposition is the assertable content; and this same content, signifying the same state of affairs, can also be questioned, denied, or merely supposed, and can be entertained in other moods as well.[4]

"Fred is buying groceries" asserts the state of affairs participially signifiable by "Fred buying groceries (now)." "Is Fred buying groceries?" questions it; "Let Fred buy groceries" presents it in the hortatory mood; "Oh that Fred may be buying groceries" in the optative mood; and "Suppose Fred is buying groceries" puts it forward as an hypothesis. Omitting, then, this adventitious element of assertion—or any other mode of entertainment—we find the assertable content, here identified with the proposition itself, as some participial term, signifying a state of affairs, actual or thinkable.

It will be noted that the state of affairs is the *signification* of the proposition; not its denotation. When any term denotes a thing, it names that thing as a whole, not merely the character or attribute signified. And what a term denotes or applies to is, by the law of the Excluded Middle, also denoted by one or the other of every pair of mutually negative terms which could meaningfully be applied to it. Thus there would be a failure of analogy, on a most important point, between propostional terms and the more familiar kind of terms, if we should regard propositions as denoting the state of affairs they refer to. And the denotation or extension of propositions would not be subject to the law of the Excluded Middle. The denotation or extension of a proposition, as application of that law leads us to see, is something which is likewise denoted by one or other of every pair of mutually negative propositional terms; i.e., one or other of every pair of mutually contradictory propositions. And this thing denoted is not that limited state of affairs which the proposition refers to, but the kind of *total* state of affairs we call a world. The limited state of affairs signified is merely the *essential attribute* which any world must possess in order that the proposition in question should denote or apply to it. A statement asserting a proposition *attributes* the state of affairs signified to the actual world. And the denotation or extension of a proposition—since denotation is in all cases confined to what exists—is either the actual world or it is empty. Thus all *true* propositions have the same extension, namely, this actual world; and all *false* propositions have the same extension, namely, zero-extension. The distinctive extensional property of a proposition is, thus, its truth or falsity.

---

[4] I am indebted to conversations with Professor C. W. Morris for this way of putting the matter—though he may not approve the conception that a proposition is a term.

A proposition *comprehends* any consistently thinkable world which would incorporate the state of affairs it signifies; a classification of Leibnitzian possible worlds. This conception of possible world is not jejune: the actual world, so far as anyone knows it, is merely one of many such which are possible. For example, I do not know at the moment how much money I have in my pocket, but let us say it is thirty cents. The world which is just like this one except that I should have thirty-five cents in my pocket now, is a consistently thinkable world—consistent even with all the facts I know. When I reflect upon the number of facts of which I am uncertain, the plethora of possible worlds which, for all I know, might be this one, becomes a little appalling.

The *intension* of a proposition includes whatever the proposition entails; it comprises whatever must be true of any possible world in order that the proposition should apply to or be true of it—a sense of the meaning of propositions which is familiar and fundamental.

An *analytic* proposition is one which would apply to or be true of every possible world; one, therefore, whose comprehension is universal, and cor-relatively, one which has zero-intension. At this point, the distinction previously remarked between terms of zero-intension and locutions which have no meaning, becomes important. An analytic proposition does not fail to have implications—though all entailments of it are likewise analytic or necessary propositions which would hold true of any world which is con-sistently thinkable. That an analytic proposition has zero-intension is correlative with the fact that in being true of reality it imposes no restriction or limitation on the actual which could conceivably be absent.

A *self-contradictory* or self-inconsistent proposition has zero-compre-hension, and could apply to or be true of no world which is consistently thinkable. Correlatively, such a proposition has universal intension: it entails all propositions, both true and false.

All *synthetic* propositions, excepting the self-contradictory, have an intension which is neither zero nor universal, and a comprehension which is neither universal nor zero. They entail some things and not other things. Consonantly, their truth is compatible with some consistently thinkable states of affairs and incompatible with other consistently thinkable states of affairs.

The discussion of propositional functions must be even more compressed —suggested rather than outlined.

A propositional function is essentially a kind of predicate or predication; a characterization meaningfully applicable to the kind of entities names of which are values of the variables. For a propositional function of the gen-eral form "x is A" (where "A" is some non-variable expression), it is "being A" which is this predicate or characterization; for one of the general form

"$x R y$" (where "R" is some constant), it is "(the first mentioned) being in the relation R (to the second mentioned)," or "(the ordered couple mentioned) being in the relation R."

Speaking most judiciously, there is only one variable in any propositional function. In what are called functions of two variables, x and y, this one variable is the ordered couple (x, y); in what are called functions of three variables, it is the ordered triad (x, y, z), etc. In the verbal form of the propositional function, so construed, the characterization which essentially is the function itself, is predicated of this one variable. What are called variables are, in fact, merely syntatic devices for preserving the essential structure of the predication itself. Otherwise put: variables are constituents of discourse which have no meaning except one conferred by their context, including the syntax of that context.

Propositional functions are participial terms, as propositions are. But whereas the propositional characterization (if we may so call it for the moment) "John being now angry" could only characterize reality or some thinkable world; the propositional-function characterization "being angry" or any of the form "being A" or of the form "being in the relation R," could not be a characterization of a world, but only of a thing, or a pair of things, etc. And a function-characterization which is predicable of one thing would be meaningfully predicable of many.[5]

The denotation or *extension* of a propositional function is the class of existent things (individuals or ordered couples or triads, etc.) for which this predication holds true. It may be a class of many or a class of one or an empty class.

The *comprehension* of a function is the classification of things consistently thinkable as being characterized by this predication. This comprehension may be universal or zero or may include some consistently thinkable things and exclude others.

The *connotation* or intension of a function comprises all that the attribution of this predicate to anything entails as also attributable to that thing. This intension may be universal or zero or neither.

Propositional functions of the sort sometimes called *assertable*—the kind that logicians write down in expounding their subject (when they do not make mistakes)—are functions having universal comprehension; falsely predicable of nothing which is consistently thinkable. And they have zero-intension, imposing no limitation on anything thinkable in being held

---

[5] This does not mean that the kind of term which is a function, is necessarily a general term. "Being now the President" is meaningfully predicable of many things; but by its intension it must be *falsely* predicable of any existent but one: hence it is a singular term.

true of it. It is by this fact alone that their status as assertable functions can be certified.

At almost every point of this outline, questions requiring to be met have been omitted. But even with this condensation, insufficient space remains for indicating applications of it to moot questions of theory. We shall mention briefly two such only; application to the question of meaningfulness in general; and the ambiguity of "intension" which was mentioned earlier.

If one should wish to speak of *the* meaning of a term or proposition or propositional function, it will be evident that meaning in the mode of intension would be the best candidate for this preferred status. Expressions having the same connotation or intension must also have the same denotation or extension, the same signification, and the same comprehension. One might suppose, in consequence, that two expressions having the same intension would have the same meaning in every called-for sense of the word "meaning." Nevertheless that would be an error.

That two locutions expressing the same intensional meaning may still be *distinct expressions*—and not two instances of one expression—is a point which has already been covered; they may be distinct by the fact that the *symbols* are different, though the meaning is the same. However, not every pair of expressions having the same intension would be called synonymous; and there is good reason for this fact.

Two expressions are commonly said to be synonymous (or in the case of propositions, equipollent) if they have the same intension, and *that intension is neither zero nor universal.*[6] But to say that two expressions with the same intension have the same meaning, without qualification, would have the anomalous consequence that any two analytic propositions would then be equipollent, and any two self-contradictory propositions would be equipollent. Also, any two terms like "round square" and "honorable poltroon" would then be synonymous.

The desirable restriction requires us to add a further specification to intensional meaning in the case of complex expressions.

An expression in question is *elementary* in case it has no symbolized constituent, the intension of which is a constituent of the intension of the expression in question itself. Otherwise the expression in question is *complex*.

The intension of any complex expression has, in addition to the intensions of its symbolized elementary constituents, an element of syntax. But we can avoid discussion of syntax here if we recognize that the syntax of a complex expression, so far as it is not already implicit in the intension of

---

6 "Equipollent" is doubtfully appropriate here; there is no term which unambiguously names that relation of propositions which is parallel to the relation of synonymity between terms.

constituents taken separately (e.g., by their being substantives or verbs, etc.), is conveyed by the *order* of these constituents.

When we think of the ways in which complex expressions can be analyzed into constituents and a syntactic order of them, we may refer to *analytic meaning*. This expression will not be defined: instead, we shall characterize the relation "equivalent in analytic meaning." Two expressions are *equivalent in analytic meaning*, (1) if at least one is elementary and they have the same intension, or (2) if, both being complex, they can be so analyzed into constituents that (a) for every constituent distinguished in either, there is a corresponding constituent in the other which has the same intension, (b) no constituent distinguished in either has zero-intension or universal intension, and (c) the order of corresponding constituents is the same in both, or can be made the same without alteration of the intension of either whole expression.

Thus "round excision" and "circular hole" are equivalent in analytic meaning. Likewise "square" and "rectangle with equal sides," since these terms have the same intension and one is elementary. But "equilateral triangle" and "equiangular triangle," though they have the same intension, when taken as whole expressions, are not equivalent in analytic meaning, since there is no constituent of the former which has the intension of "equiangular" and no constituent of the latter which has the same intension as "equilateral."

We shall be in conformity with good usage if we say that two expressions are synonymous or equipollent, (1) if they have the same intension and that intension is neither zero nor universal, or (2) if, their intension being either zero or universal, they are equivalent in analytic meaning. And we shall be in conformity with good usage if we take the statement that two expressions have the *same meaning*, when the intended mode of meaning is unspecified, as indicating that these expressions are synonymous or equipollent.

We turn now to the ambiguity of "intension" which has been referred to.

Intension or connotation may be thought of in either of two ways, which we shall call respectively linguistic meaning and sense meaning.

Linguistic meaning is intension as constituted by the pattern of definitive and other analytic relationships of the expression in question to other *expressions*.[7] One who, for example, tried to learn the meaning of a French word with only a French dictionary at hand, might—if he be poorly acquainted with French—be obliged to look up also words used in defining the

---

[7] Some would say "syntactic" here, instead of "analytic." A relationship is analytic if the statement of it is an analytic statement.

one whose meaning he sought; and the words defining them; and so on. He might thus eventually determine a quite extended pattern of linguistic relations of the word in question to other words in French. If the process of this example could, by some miracle, be carried to its logical limit, a person might thus come to grasp completely and with complete accuracy the linguistic pattern relating a large body of foreign words but—in an obvious sense—without learning what any one of them meant. What he would grasp would be their linguistic meaning. And what he would still fail to grasp would be their sense meaning.

Sense meaning is intension in the mode of a criterion in mind by which one is able to apply or refuse to apply the expression in question in the case of presented things or situations. One who should be able thus to apply or refuse to apply an expression correctly under all imaginable circumstances, would grasp its sense meaning perfectly. But if, through faulty language sense or poor analytic powers, he could still not offer any correct definition, then he would fail to grasp (at least to grasp explicitly) its linguistic meaning.

Because many logicians have of late been somewhat preoccupied with language, intension as linguistic (or "syntactic") meaning has been over-emphasized, and sense meaning has been relatively neglected. These two modes of intensional meaning are supplementary, not alternative. But for many purposes of theory of knowledge it is sense meaning the investigation of which is more important. For example, those who would demand theoretical verifiability or confirmability for significance in a statement, have in mind sense meaning as the prime requisite for meaningfulness in general. Likewise those who would set up the criterion of making some (practical) difference. And those who would emphasize the operational significance of concepts are emphasizing sense meaning.

For sense meaning, imagery is obviously requisite. Only through the capacity called imagination could one have in mind, in advance of presentation, a workable criterion for applying or refusing to apply an expression to what should be presented. But for reasons made familiar by the long controversy between nominalists, conceptualists, and realists, sense meaning cannot be vested directly and simply in imagery. The nominalist denies the possibility of sense meaning on such grounds as the impossibility of imagining dog in general or triangle in general, or of having in mind an image of a chiliagon which is sufficiently specific to distinguish between a polygon of 1000 sides and one having 999. It is the persistence of such nominalism which, in large measure, is responsible for the current tendency to identify meaning with linguistic meaning exclusively.

The answer was given by Kant. A sense meaning, when precise, is a schema; a rule or prescribed routine and an imagined result of it which will determine applicability of the expression in question. We cannot imagine a chiliagon, but we easily imagine counting the sides of a polygon and getting 1000 as the result. We cannot imagine triangle in general, but we easily imagine following the periphery of a figure with the eye or a finger and discovering it to be a closed figure with three angles. (Many protagonists of operational significance forget to mention the imaged result, and would—according to what they *say*—identify the concept or meaning exclusively with the routine. Presumably this is merely an oversight: no procedure of laying meter sticks on things would determine length without some anticipatory imagery of a perceivable result which would, e.g., corroborate statement that the thing is three meters long.)

Many epistemological problems may be clarified by reference to sense meaning. For example, question as to the meaningfulness of asserting that there are mountains on the other side of the moon. Practical difficulties of confirmation have no relevance: the routine and result which would corroborate the statement are in mind with a clarity sufficient for determination—perhaps with a clarity equal to that with which we grasp what it would mean to verify that there are elephants in Africa. The two assertions equally have sense meaning.

If it be said that analytic statements have no sense meaning, then it is in point that all analytic statements have zero-intension, and impose no limitation upon any consistently thinkable total state of affairs or world in being true of it. Analytic statements are, so to say, verifiable by the fact that no total state of affairs in which they should fail of truth can be imagined. But if *constituents* in analytic statements did not have sense meaning, in the more limited fashion of having criteria of their application which are sometimes satisfied and sometimes not, then this universal applicability of the analytic statement could not be certified by reference to imagination and without recourse to particular perceptions; and hence would not be knowable *a priori*.

Likewise, if it be said that the self-contradictory has no sense meaning, it is in point that the self-contradictory expression has universal intension and zero-comprehension. The situation in which it should apply is precluded in ways which imagination alone is sufficient to discover. But again, this fact would not be certifiable *a priori* if constituents in the self-contradictory expression did not have sense meanings which are self-consistent. We can certify the impossibility of what is expressed, by the experiment of trying to relate these sense meanings of constituents in the manner which the expression as a whole prescribes.

By their ultimate reference to concrete sense meaning, even the analytic and the self-contradictory have a kind of empirical reference. And without that, they would be genuinely non-significant for any experience in the world of fact. They are independent of any *particular* state of affairs or of what the world that exists is like in its details, because their applicability or inapplicability in general, or their truth or falsity in general, is certifiable from experiments in imagination.

C. I. LEWIS.

HARVARD UNIVERSITY.

4

On Likeness of Meaning

by NELSON GOODMAN

Revision of a paper which originally appeared in *Analysis,* 10 (1949).

ON LIKENESS OF MEANING[1]

by NELSON GOODMAN

Under what circumstances do two names or predicates in an ordinary language have the same meaning? Many and widely varied answers have been given to this question, but they have one feature in common: they are all unsatisfactory.

One of the earliest answers is to the effect that two predicates have the same meaning if they stand for the same real Essence or Platonic Idea; but this does not seem to help very much unless we know, as I am afraid we do not, how to find out whether two terms stand for the same Platonic Idea.

A more practical proposal is that two terms have the same meaning if they stand for the same mental idea or image; or in other words, that two predicates differ in meaning only if we have a mental picture of something that satisfies one but not the other of the two. Thus even though in fact all and only pelicans have gallon-sized bills, we can easily imagine a sparrow or a kangaroo with a gallon-sized bill; and thus the predicates "is a pelican" and "has a gallon-sized bill," even though satisfied by exactly the same actual individuals, do not have the same meaning. There are two familiar difficulties with this theory. In the first place, it is not very clear just what we can and what we cannot imagine. Can we imagine a man ten miles high or not? Can we imagine a tone we have never heard? To decide these cases is only to be confronted by new and harder ones. But the second and more serious difficulty is that of predicates that pretty clearly have no corresponding image, such as "clever" or "supersonic." Of course there is imagery associated with these terms; but that is hardly to the point. There is imagery associated with nonsense syllables.

The image theory thus sometimes gives way to the concept theory — the theory that two predicates differ in meaning if and only if we can conceive of something that satisfies one but not the other. This enables us to transcend the narrow boundaries of imagination, but unfortunately it hardly seems to provide us with any criterion at all. Presumably we can conceive a five-dimensional body since we can define it although we cannot imagine it. But similarly we can define a square-circle very easily (as a rectangle with four equal sides and such that every point of it is equidistant from a center) or a five-sided

[1] Read before the Fullerton Club, at Bryn Mawr College, Pennsylvania, on May 14, 1949. I am deeply indebted to Drs. Morton G. White and W. V. Quine, with whom I have frequently and profitably discussed the problem dealt with in this paper.

triangle. If it be objected that because such definitions are not self-consistent they do not represent genuine concepts, I must point out that the claim of inconsistency here can be supported only by appeal to just such meaning-relationships as we are trying to explain. We cannot use them in trying to define them. If the objection is put rather in the form that although we can define a square-circle there is no possible thing that can satisfy the definition, then it is clear that we are not judging possibility by conceivability but rather judging conceivability by possibility. Our criterion of sameness of meaning has thus changed: we are saying that two predicates have the same meaning if and only if there is nothing possible that satisfies one but not the other.

The possibility theory is somewhat ambiguous. Does it say that two terms differ in meaning only if it is possible that there is something that satisfies one but not the other? If that is all, then any two terms we know to have the same extension have the same meaning. If I know that Mr. Jones is in New York, I no longer regard it as possible that he is not in New York; and similarly if I know that two predicates are satisfied by exactly the same individuals, the possibility is excluded that they are not satisfied by the same individuals. But this formulation seldom satisfies proponents of the possibility theory, who will cite cases of terms that, even though they are known to have the same extension, have different meanings. The thesis, they say, is rather that two predicates differ in meaning if there "might have been" something that satisfied one but not the other; or in other words, if there is a possible but non-actual entity that does satisfy one but not the other predicate. The notion of possible entities that are not and cannot be actual is a hard one for many of us to understand or accept. And even if we do accept it, how are we to decide when there is and when there is not such a possible that satisfies one but not the other of two terms? We have already seen that we get nowhere by appealing to conceivability as a test of possibility. Can we, then, determine whether two predicates "P" and "Q" apply to the same possibles by asking whether the predicate "is a P or a Q but not both" is self-consistent? This is hardly helpful; for so long as "P" and "Q" are different predicates the compound predicate is logically self-consistent, and we have no ready means for determining whether it is otherwise self-consistent. Indeed the latter question amounts to the very question whether "P" and "Q" have the same meaning. And since we began by asking how to determine when two predicates have the same meaning, we are back where we started.

All these difficulties suggest that we might try the very different and radical theory that two predicates have the same meaning if and only if they apply to exactly the same things — or in other words, have the same extension. This thesis has been attacked more often than it has been advanced; but some of the familiar arguments against it seem to me worthless. An example is the absurd argument that the extension of a term is different at different times and that therefore by this thesis two terms may be synonymous at one time and not at another. The extension of a predicate consists, of course, of everything past, present, and future, to which the term applies; neither the making nor the eating of cakes changes the extension of the term "cake."

Certain other similar arguments apply not against the thesis that two terms have the same meaning if they have the same extension, but against the different thesis — that does not concern us here — that the extension of a term is its meaning. For example, against the latter thesis, one may argue as follows: before we can investigate whether a given predicate "P" applies to a given thing a we must know what "P" means, and if the meaning of "P" is its extension we must know the extension of "P" — and therefore must know whether it applies to a — before we can set about finding out whether "P" applies to a. But this argument does not apply against the weaker thesis that two predicates have the same meaning if they have the same extension; for obviously we may decide by induction, conjecture, or other means that two predicates have the same extension without knowing exactly all the things they apply to.

And yet, while many of the apparent objections seem to me unsound, I think we cannot maintain the unqualified thesis that two predicates have the same meaning if they have the same extension. There are certain clear cases where two words that have the same extension do not have the same meaning. "Centaur" and "unicorn," for example, since neither applies to anything, have the same (null) extension; yet surely they differ in meaning. I do not mean to suggest that identity of extension with difference of meaning occurs only where the extension is null, but such cases are enough and are the most striking.

Now the precise way in which the proposed thesis failed must be particularly noted. Obviously if two terms have the same meaning they have the same extension; the trouble is that two terms may have the same extension and yet not have the same meaning. Extensional identity is a necessary but not a sufficient condition for sameness of meaning. In other words, difference of extension does not draw distinctions as fine as those drawn by difference of meaning.

Does this mean, then, that we must return to the dismal search through never-never land for some ghostly entities called "meanings" that are distinct from and lie between words and their extensions? I don't think so. Despite the obvious inadequacy of the thesis we have been considering, I think that difference of meaning between any two terms can be fully accounted for without introducing anything beyond terms and their extensions. For while it is clear that difference in meaning of two terms "P" and "Q" is not always accompanied by difference in extension, I think it is always accompanied by difference in the extension of certain terms other than "P" and "Q." Let me explain:

Since there are no centaurs or unicorns, all unicorns are centaurs and all centaurs are unicorns. Furthermore, all uncles of centaurs are uncles of unicorns; and all feet of unicorns are feet of centaurs. How far can we generalize on this? Leaving aside absurd or ungrammatical variations, we must exclude the analogues in terms of "thoughts," or "concepts" or even "meaning" itself; for there is no guarantee that thoughts of centaurs are thoughts of unicorns. This is usually attributed to the mental reference or the vagueness of such terms. We have in logic the theorem that if all α's are β's, then all the things that bear the relation P to an α are things that bear the relation P to a β (see *Principia Mathematica*, 37.2); and it might naturally be supposed that this guarantees the truth of sentences like those we have been considering about centaurs and unicorns, provided the phrases involved apply only to physical objects if to anything. But actually this is not the case; for *pictures* — i.e., paintings, drawings, prints, statues — are physical objects, yet not all pictures of centaurs are pictures of unicorns, nor are all pictures of unicorns pictures of centaurs. At first sight this seems to violate the cited theorem of logic. Actually, what it shows is that "picture of" is not always a relation-term like "foot of" or "uncle of." If x is a foot of a centaur, then x bears the relation "foot of" to some y that is a centaur. Thus if there is any foot of a centaur or any uncle of a centaur then there is a centaur. But in contrast, if there is — as indeed there is — something that is a picture of a centaur, we cannot infer that there is some centaur — as there certainly is not. A phrase like "picture of a centaur" is a single predicate, and the fact that it applies to one or many things plainly does not enable us to conclude that there are objects that these things are pictures of. To avoid the temptation to make such unjustified inferences, perhaps we had better speak during the rest of our discussion not of "pictures of" centaurs or unicorns but rather of "centaur-pictures" and "unicorn-pictures," etc.

A centaur-picture differs from a unicorn-picture not by virtue of its resemblance to a centaur and lack of resemblance to a unicorn; for there are neither unicorns nor centaurs. "Centaur-picture" and "unicorn-picture" merely apply to different objects just as "chair" and "desk" apply to different objects, and we need no more ask why in the one case than in the other. The simple fact is that although "centaur" and "unicorn" apply to nothing and so have the same extension, the term "centaur-picture" applies to many things and the term "unicorn-picture" applies to many others.

Now the important point here is this: Although two words have the same extension, certain predicates composed by making identical additions to these two words may have different extensions. It is then perhaps the case that for every two words that differ in meaning either their extensions or the extensions of some corresponding compounds of them are different. If so, difference of meaning among extensionally identical predicates can be explained as difference in the extensions of certain other predicates. Or, if we call the extension of a predicate by itself its *primary* extension, and the extension of any of its compounds a *secondary* extension, the thesis is formulated as follows: two terms have the same meaning if and only if they have the same primary and secondary extensions. Let us, in order to avoid entanglement with such terms as "thought of . . . ," "concept of . . . ," "attribute of . . . ," and "meaning of . . . ," exclude from consideration all predicates that apply to anything but physical things, classes of these, classes of classes of these, etc. If the thesis is tenable, we have answered our question by stating, without reference to anything other than terms and the things to which they apply, the circumstances under which two terms have the same meaning.

This explanation takes care of well-known cases discussed in the literature. For instance, Frege has used the terms "(is the) Morningstar" and "(is the) Eveningstar" as examples of two predicates that have the same extension — since they apply to the same one thing — but obviously differ in meaning. This difference of meaning is readily explained according to our present thesis, since the two terms differ in their secondary extensions. There are, for example, "Morningstar-pictures" that are not "Eveningstar-pictures" — and also, indeed, "Eveningstar-pictures" that are not "Morningstar-pictures."

But is our thesis satisfactory in general? Perhaps the first question that arises is whether it takes care of cases where we have two terms "P" and "Q" such that there are no P-pictures or Q-pictures — say where "P" and "Q" are predicates applying to odors or electric charges. These present no difficulty; for the secondary extensions of a predicate "Q" consist not merely of the extension of "Q-picture" but also of the extensions of "Q-diagram," "Q-symbol," and any number of other such compound terms. Indeed *actual word-inscriptions* are as genuine physical objects as anything else; and so if there is such an actual physical inscription that is a P-description and is not a Q-description, or vice versa, then "P" and "Q" differ in their secondary extensions and thus in meaning.

This makes it look more and more as if every difference in meaning will be reflected by a difference in primary or secondary extension. Indeed, I think we can now show this to be true. For, given any two predicates whatsoever, say "P" and "Q," do we not have in an inscription of the phrase "a P that is not a Q" something that is a P-description and not a Q-description? Clearly the predicate "centaur-description" applies while the predicate "unicorn-description" does not apply to an inscription of "a centaur that is not a unicorn." Likewise, the predicate "acrid-odor-description" applies while the predicate "pungent-odor-description" does not apply to an inscription of "a pungent odor that is not an acrid odor"; and thus the two predicates "pungent-odor" and "acrid-odor" — whatever may be the relationship of their primary extensions — differ in secondary extension and thus in meaning. Again "triangle" and "trilateral" differ in meaning because "triangle that is not trilateral" is a triangle-description but not a trilateral-description. We do not, however, get the absurd result that "triangle" differs in meaning from "triangle"; for of course it is not the case that "triangle that is not a triangle" is and is not a triangle-description.[2]

But now see how far we have come. If difference of meaning is

---

[2] One basic principle is: *any phrase such as "—— that is . . ." is a —— -description and a . . . -description.* Thus "—— that is not a . . ." is both a —— -description and a not-a- . . . -description. Being a not-a- . . . -description is not a sufficient condition for not being a . . . -description. By a second principle, however, a not-a- . . . -description is not a . . . -description unless the first principle (or some other) makes it also a . . . -description. Formulation of complete and exact principles deciding whether any phrase is or is not a . . . -description would be difficult and is neither possible nor necessary here.

explained in the way I have proposed, then *no two different words have the same meaning.* We have assuredly answered the complaint that in terms of extensions alone we cannot draw fine enough distinctions. Here we get distinctions that are as fine as anyone could ask. But now we risk the opposite complaint: for can we accept the conclusion that a word has the same meaning as no other word than itself?

Before we decide that we cannot tolerate this conclusion, let me note that in the course of developing our criterion we have incidentally shown that there are no two predicates such that each can be replaced by the other in every sentence without changing the truth-value, *even if we exclude all the so-called intensional contexts in which such words as* "necessary," "possible," "attribute of," or "thought of" occur. Thus if we maintain that two different words have the same meaning, their lack of interreplaceability in some non-intensional context can immediately be offered as evidence that the words do not have the same meaning. It seems apparent, therefore, that the demands we commonly make upon a criterion of sameness of meaning can be satisfied only if we recognize that no two different predicates ever have the same meaning.

Theoretically, then, we shall do better never to say that two predicates have the same meaning but rather that they have a greater or lesser degree, or one or another kind, of *likeness* of meaning. In ordinary speech when we say that two terms have the same meaning, we usually indicate only that their kind and degree of likeness of meaning is sufficient for the purposes of the immediate discourse. This is quite harmless. But we must remember that the requirements vary greatly from discourse to discourse; often it is enough if two terms have the same primary extension; in other cases, identity in certain secondary extensions or others is also required. If we overlook this variation and seek a fixed criterion of sameness of meaning that will at once conform to these differing usages and satisfy our theoretical demands, we are doomed to perpetual confusion.

To repeat, it is commonly supposed that a satisfactory definition of synonymy must meet two requirements: that some predicates be synonymous with others, and that either of a pair of synonyms be replaceable by the other in all non-intensional contexts without change of truth-value. But we have seen that these two requirements are incompatible. The sound course seems to be to construe degree of synonymy as, so to speak, degree of interreplaceability — along lines above suggested — and to recognize that the relation of exact synonymy between diverse predicates is null.

Just a few further words to suggest a bearing this paper has on another question. It is sometimes said that a sentence like "All A's are B's" is *analytic* if the meaning of B is contained in that of A. Our investigation has shown not only that two different predicates like "A" and "B" never have quite the same meaning; but further that, so to speak, neither is meaning-included in the other; for there is an A-description that is not a B-description, *and* a B-description that is not an A-description. Thus, at least according to the suggested interpretation of "analytic," no non-repetitive statement will be analytic. The most we can say is that it is more, or less, nearly analytic. This will be enough to convince many of us that likewise a non-repetitive statement is never absolutely necessary, but only more or less nearly so.

5

Notes on Existence
and Necessity

By WILLARD V. QUINE

Reprinted from *The Journal of Philosophy*, 40 (1943).

NOTES ON EXISTENCE AND NECESSITY

THIS paper [1] concerns two points of philosophical controversy. One is the question of admission or exclusion of the modalities—necessity, possibility, and the rest—as operators attaching to statements. The other is the ontological question, "What *is* there?" It is my purpose here to set forth certain considerations, grounded in elementary logic and semantics, which—while not answering either question—must seriously condition any tenable answers.

The logical notions that prove crucial to these considerations are the notions of identity and quantification; and the semantical ones are the notions of designation and meaning, which are insufficiently distinguished in some of the current literature. A new semantical notion that makes its appearance here and plays a conspicuous part is that of the "purely designative occurrence" of a name.

1. DESIGNATION AND IDENTITY

One of the fundamental principles governing identity is that of *substitutivity*—or, as it might well be called, that of *indiscernibility of identicals*. It provides that, *given a true statement of identity, one of its two terms may be substituted for the other in any true statement and the result will be true.* It is easy to find cases contrary to this principle. For example, the statements:

(1)   Giorgione = Barbarelli,

(2)   Giorgione was so-called because of his size

are true; however, replacement of the name 'Giorgione' by the name 'Barbarelli' turns (2) into the falsehood:

Barbarelli was so-called because of his size.

Furthermore, the statements:

(3)   Cicero = Tully,

(4)   'Cicero' contains six letters

are true, but replacement of the first name by the second turns (4)

---

[1] Mainly a translation, from the Portuguese, of portions of my forthcoming book *O sentido da nova lógica* (São Paulo, Brazil).

false. Yet the basis of the principle of substitutivity appears quite solid; whatever can be said about the person Cicero (or Giorgione) should be equally true of the person Tully (or Barbarelli), this being the same person.

In the case of (4), this paradox resolves itself immediately. The fact is that (4) is not a statement about the person Cicero, but simply about the word 'Cicero.' The principle of substitutivity should not be extended to contexts in which the name to be supplanted occurs without referring simply to the object.

The relation of name to the object whose name it is, is called *designation;* the name 'Cicero' designates the man Cicero. An occurrence of the name in which the name refers simply to the object designated, I shall call *purely designative*. Failure of substitutivity reveals merely that the occurrence to be supplanted is not purely designative, and that the statement depends not only upon the object but on the form of the name. For it is clear that whatever can be affirmed about the *object* remains true when we refer to the object by any other name.

An expression which consists of another expression between single quotes constitutes a name of that other expression; and it is clear in general that the occurrence of that other expression or any part of it, within the context of quotes, is not designative. In particular the occurrence of the personal name within the context of quotes in (4) is not designative, nor subject to the substitutivity principle. The personal name occurs there merely as a fragment of a longer name which contains, beside this fragment, the two quotation marks. To make a substitution upon a personal name, within such a context, would be no more justifiable than to make a substitution upon the term 'cat' within the context 'cattle'.

The example (2) is a little more subtle, for it is a statement about a man and not merely about his name. It was the man, not his name, that was called so and so because of his size. Nevertheless, the failure of substitutivity shows that the occurrence of the personal name in (2) is not *purely* designative. It is easy in fact to translate (2) into another statement which contains two occurrences of the name, one purely designative and the other not:

(5)   Giorgione was called 'Giorgione' because of his size.

The first occurrence is purely designative. Substitution on the basis of (1) converts (5) into another statement equally true:

Barbarelli was called 'Giorgione' because of his size.

The second occurrence of the personal name is no more designative than any other occurrence within a context of quotes.

To get an example of another common type of statement in which names do not occur designatively, consider any person who is called Philip and satisfies the condition:

(6)   Philip is unaware that Tully denounced Catiline,

or perhaps the condition:

(7)   Philip believes that Tegucigalpa is in Nicaragua.

Substitution on the basis of (3) transforms (6) into the statement:

(8)   Philip is unaware that Cicero denounced Catiline,

no doubt false.   Substitution on the basis of the true identity:

Tegucigalpa = Capital of Honduras

transforms the truth (7) likewise into the falsehood:

(9)   Philip believes that the capital of
                Honduras is in Nicaragua.

We see, therefore, that the occurrences of the names 'Tully' and 'Tegucigalpa' in (6)–(7) are not purely designative.

In this there is a fundamental contrast between (6), or (7), and:

Crassus heard Tully denounce Catiline.

This statement affirms a relation between three persons, and the persons remain so related independently of the names applied to them.   But (6) can not be considered simply as affirming a relation between three persons, nor (7) a relation between person, city, and country—at least, not so long as we interpret our words in such a way as to admit (6) and (7) as true and (8) and (9) as false.

Some readers may wish to construe unawareness and belief as relations between persons and statements, thus writing (6) and (7) in the manner:

Philip is unaware of 'Tully denounced Catiline',

Philip believes 'Tegucigalpa is in Nicaragua',

the purpose being to put within a context of single quotes every not purely designative occurrence of a name.   It is not necessary, however, to force an analogy thus between cases of the type (6)–(7) and those of the type (4)–(5).   It is unnecessary to insist that every indesignative occurrence of a name form part of the name of an expression.   What is important is to insist that the contexts 'is unaware that . . .' and 'believes that . . .' are, like the context of single quotes, contexts in which names do not occur purely designatively.   The same is true of the contexts 'knows that . . .', 'says that . . .', 'doubts that . . .', 'is surprised that . . .', etc.

2. Designation and Quantification

We have observed a basic connection between designation and identity. We have next to examine a connection, equally basic, between designation and existence—existence as expressed in the prefix '$\exists x$' of existential quantification in logic.

It must be noted carefully, to begin with, that this prefix has the very broad sense 'there is something x such that', and does not connote existence in any peculiarly spatial or temporal sense. The statement:

$$\exists x(x \text{ is a fish} \cdot x \text{ flies})$$

does affirm the existence of something in space and time, but only because fishes and things that fly are always in space and time, and not because of any spatial sense of '$\exists x$'. The prefix is no less suited to the context:

$$\exists x(x \text{ is a prime number} \cdot x \text{ is between 5 and 11}).[2]$$

The intimate connection between designation and existential quantification is implicit in the operation of *existential generalization* —the operation whereby, from 'Socrates is mortal', we infer '$\exists x(x$ is mortal)', i.e., 'Something is mortal'. The idea behind such inference is that whatever is true of the object designated by a given substantive is true of something; and clearly the inference loses its justification when the substantive in question does not happen to designate. From:

There is no such thing as Pegasus,

for example, we do not infer:

$$\exists x(\text{there is no such thing as } x),$$

i.e., 'There is something which there is no such thing as', or 'There is something which there is not'.

Inference by existential generalization is of course equally unwarranted in the case of an indesignative occurrence of any substantive, whether of 'Pegasus' (which never occurs designatively) or of 'Giorgione', 'Cicero', 'Tegucigalpa', etc. (which often do occur designatively). Let us see what in fact happens in some of

---

[2] The special emphasis put by philosophers on the distinction between existence as applied to spatio-temporal objects and existence (or subsistence or being) as applied to abstract objects, or universals, is partly prompted by an idea that the methods of knowing existence in the two cases are basically different. But this idea, according to which the observation of nature is relevant only to determining the existence of spatio-temporal particulars and never the being of universals, is readily refuted by counter-instances such as that of "hyperendemic fever" in my paper "Designation and Existence," this Journal, Vol. XXXVI (1939), p. 703.

these further cases. From (2), existential generalization would lead to:

$\exists x(x$ was so-called because of its size),

i.e., 'Something was so-called because of its size'. This is clearly meaningless, there being no longer any suitable antecedent for 'so-called'. Note, in contrast, that existential generalization with respect to the purely designative occurrence in (5) yields the sound conclusion:

$\exists x(x$ was called 'Giorgione' because of its size),

i.e., 'Something was called 'Giorgione' because of its size'.

Applied to the occurrence of the personal name in (4), existential generalization would lead us to:

(10) $\exists x('x'$ contains six letters),

i.e.:

(11)   There is something such that 'it' contains six letters,

or perhaps:

(12)   'Something' contains six letters.

Any expression formed by single quotes is a name of the expression within the quotes. In particular, thus, the expression:

        'x' contains six letters

means simply:

    The 24th letter of the alphabet contains six letters.

In (10) the occurrence of the letter within the context of quotes is as irrelevant to the quantifier that precedes it as is the occurrence of the same letter in the context 'six'. (10) consists merely of a falsehood preceded by an irrelevant quantifier. (11) is similar; its part:

        'it' contains six letters

is false, and the prefix 'there is something such that' is irrelevant. (12), again, is false—if by 'contains six' we mean 'contains exactly six'.

It is less obvious, and correspondingly more important to recognize, that existential generalization is unwarranted likewise in the case of (6) and (7). Applied to (6), it leads to:

      $\exists x(Philip$ is unaware that x denounced Catiline),

i.e.:

(13)   Something is such that Philip is unaware
          that it denounced Catiline.

What is this object, that denounced Catiline without Philip yet having become aware of the fact? Tully, i.e., Cicero? But to suppose this would conflict with the fact that (8) is false.

Note that (13) is not to be confused with:

Philip is unaware that $\exists x(x$ denounced Catiline),

which, though it happens to be false, is quite straightforward and in no danger of being inferred by existential generalization from (6).

The logical operation of *application* is that whereby we infer from 'Everything is itself', for example, or in symbols '$(x)(x = x)$', the conclusion that Socrates = Socrates. This and existential generalization are in fact two aspects of a single principle; for instead of saying that '$(x)(x = x)$' implies 'Socrates = Socrates', we could as well say that the denial 'Socrates $\neq$ Socrates' implies '$\exists x(x \neq x)$'. The principle embodied in these two operations is the link between quantifications and the singular statements that are related to them as instances. Yet it is a "principle" only by courtesy. It holds only in the case where a substantive designates, and, furthermore, occurs designatively. It is simply the logical content of the idea that a given occurrence is designative.[3]

The ontology which one accepts, or which a given context presupposes, is not revealed by an examination of mere vocabulary; for we know that substantives can be used indesignatively without depriving them of meaning. Use of the word 'Pegasus' does not imply acceptance of Pegasus, nor does the mere use of the signs '9' or '9^{99}' imply that there are abstract objects, numbers, such as 9 and 9^{99}. It is not the mere use of a substantive, but its designative use, that commits us to the acceptance of an object designated by the substantive.

In order to determine whether a substantive is used designatively in a given context we have to look beyond the substantive and observe the behavior of the pronouns. Ways of using the substantive that do commit one to recognition of the object are embodied in the operations of existential generalization and application. The ontology to which one's use of language commits him comprises simply the objects that he treats as falling with the subject-matter of his quantifiers—within the range of values of his variables.

[3] The principle is, for this reason, anomalous as an adjunct to the purely logical theory of quantification. Hence the theoretical importance of the fact that all substantives, except the variables that serve as pronouns in connection with quantifiers, are dispensable and eliminable by paraphrase. See my *Mathematical Logic*, §27. Such elimination of names does not, of course, eliminate any objects; but the contact between language and object comes to be concentrated in the variable, or pronoun.

3. MEANING AND NECESSITY

To say that two names designate the same object is not to say that they are *synonymous*, that is, that they have the same meaning. To determine the synonymity of two names or other expressions it should be sufficient to understand the expressions; but to determine that two names designate the same object, it is commonly necessary to investigate the world. The names 'Evening Star' and 'Morning Star', for example, are not synonymous, having been applied each to a certain ball of matter according to a different criterion. But it appears from astronomical investigations that it is the same ball, the same planet, in both cases; that is, the names designate the same thing. The identity:

(14)   Evening Star = Morning Star

is a truth of astronomy, not following merely from the meanings of the words.

It results equally from astronomical researches, and not merely from the meanings of the words, that the object (the number, or degree of multiplicity) designated by the numeral '9' is the same as that designated by the complex name 'the number of planets'. The identity:

(15)   The number of planets = 9

is a truth (so far as we know at the moment) of astronomy. The names the 'number of planets' and '9' are not synonymous; they do not have the same meaning. This fact is emphasized by the possibility, ever present, that (15) be refuted by the discovery of another planet.

Another contrast between designation and meaning is that only certain very definite expressions designate (viz., the names of the objects designated), whereas perhaps all words and other more complex unities capable of figuring in statements have meaning. In particular, substantives such as 'Pegasus' that fail to designate are not without meaning; in fact, it is only with an eye to the meaning of 'Pegasus' that we are able to conclude from a study of zoology that the word does not designate.

It is confusion of meaning and designation that gives rise to the quandary: "If there is no such thing as Pegasus, then there is nothing for 'Pegasus' to mean; but then this word and its contexts, even the context 'Pegasus does not exist', are meaningless." This quandary and its like no doubt have constituted a main motive for admitting, in addition to abstract objects and in addition to the concrete objects in space and time, certain further concrete objects which are more or less like the ones in space and time but are merely possible, not actual. Pegasus is admitted as an object, in this widened domain of concrete objects, but one which lacks merely the special property of actuality. It should be apparent, though, that this extravagant multiplication of entities is a very temporary palliative, for in place of 'Pegasus' we can pick an example not accommodated even by the realm of possible objects—say 'the spinster wife of Pegasus'.

Just what the *meaning* of an expression is—what kind of object— is not yet clear; but it is clear that, given a notion of meaning, we can explain the notion of *synonymity* easily as the relation between expressions that have the same meaning. Conversely also, given the relation of synonymity, it would be easy to derive the notion of meaning in the following way: the meaning of an expression is the class of all the expressions synonymous with it. No doubt this second direction of construction is the more promising one. The relation of synonymity, in turn, calls for a definition or a criterion in psychological and linguistic terms. Such a definition, which up to the present has perhaps never even been sketched, would be a fundamental contribution at once to philology and philosophy.

The relation of synonymity is presupposed, as we have seen, in the notion of meaning, which is used so abundantly in every-day discourse. The notion of synonymity figures implicitly also when-ever we use the method of indirect quotations. In indirect quota-tion we do not insist on a literal repetition of the words of the person quoted, but we insist on a *synonymous* sentence; we require reproduc-tion of the *meaning*. Such synonymity differs even from logical equivalence; and exactly what it is remains unspecified.

The relation of synonymity is presupposed also in the notion, so current in philosophical circles since Kant, of *analytic* statements. It is usual to describe an analytic statement as a statement that is true by virtue of the *meanings* of the words; or as a statement that follows logically from the meanings of the words. Given the notion of synonymity, given also the general notion of truth, and given finally the notion of logical form (perhaps by an enumeration of the logical vocabulary), we can define an analytic statement as any statement which, by putting synonyms for synonyms, is convertible into an instance of a logical form all of whose instances are true. For example, Professor Stevenson's favorite analytic statement, 'No spinster is married', is converted into an instance of the form 'No A not B is B' by putting 'woman not married' for its synonym 'spinster'; and this form 'No A not B is B', which is logical in the sense of preserving only words of the logical vocabulary ('no', 'not', 'is'), is a form all of whose instances are true.

Among the various possible senses of the vague adverb 'necessarily', we can single out one—the sense of *analytic* necessity—according to the following criterion: the result of applying 'necessarily' to a statement is true if, and only if, the original statement is analytic.

(16)   Necessarily no spinster is married,

for example, is equivalent to:

(17)   'No spinster is married' is analytic,

and is therefore true. The statement:

(18)   9 is necessarily greater than 7

is equivalent to

(19)   '9 > 7' is analytic

and is therefore true (if we recognize the reducibility of arithmetic to logic). The statement:

(20)   Necessarily, if there is life on the Evening Star then
                there is life on the Evening Star

is equivalent to:

(21)   'If there is life on the Evening Star, then there is life
                on the Evening Star' is analytic

(or, as we could also formulate it:

(22)   'There is life on the Evening Star'
                implies itself analytically,

if we explain a statement as implying another analytically when the conditional formed from the respective statement is analytic). (20) is then true, since the conditional in question is logically true and therefore analytic.

On the other hand the statements:

(23)   The number of planets is necessarily greater than 7,

(24)   Necessarily, if there is life on the Evening Star
                then there is life on the Morning Star

are false, since the statements:

            The number of planets is greater than 7,

            If there is life on the Evening Star, then
                there is life on the Morning Star

are true only because of circumstances outside logic.

The prefixes 'possibly' and 'it is impossible that' are definable immediately on the basis of 'necessarily' in the fashion 'not necessarily not' and 'necessarily not'. Thus, for example, (16) can be paraphrased in the manner:

(25)   It is impossible that some spinsters be married.

4. NON-TRUTH-FUNCTIONAL COMPOSITION OF STATEMENTS

The statements (17), (19), (21), and (22) are explicitly statements about statements. They attribute the property of analyticity or the relation of analytic implication to statements, referring to statements by use of their names (constructed with single quotes). On the other hand, (16), (18), (20), and (25) do not refer to other statements by use of their names; they are rather compounds of the statements themselves. The prefixes 'necessarily' and 'it is impossible that' are applied, like the sign of denial, to statements to form others.

The contrast between 'necessarily' and 'is analytic' is exactly analogous to the contrast between ' $\sim$ ' and 'is false'. To write the denial sign before the statement itself in the manner:

$$\sim 9 < 7$$

means the same as to write the words 'is false' after the name of the statement, in the manner:

'9 < 7' is false.

In the example (20) we can recognize a complex connective, 'necessarily, if-then'. This connective, like 'if-then' or the dot of conjunction, joins statements to form others.

There is nevertheless a striking difference between the compounds reducible to conjunction and denial on the one hand and the compounds (16), (18), (20), and (25) on the other. These latter are _intensional_ compounds, in the sense that the truth-value of the compound is not determined merely by the truth-value of the components.

The statements (17), (19), (21), and (22), besides containing names of statements, are also literally _compounds_ of these same statements, the quotation marks being part of an expression applied to the component statement to form the compound. Just as the statements ' $\sim 9 > 7$ ' and (18) are formed from the component statement '9 > 7' by the application of ' $\sim$ ' and 'necessarily', we may consider that (19) is formed from the same component by application of two quotation marks and the words 'is analytic'. Similarly for (17), (21), and (22).[4]

---

[4] Cf. E. V. Huntington, "Note on a recent set of postulates," _Journal of Symbolic Logic_, Vol. 4 (1939), pp. 10–14.

The way in which such statements occur in the "compounds" (17), (19), (21), and (22) is, indeed, rather irregular and accidental. In general, we know that all matter within a context of single quotes is isolated, in an important sense, from the broader context. We know that a name within a context of single quotes does not occur designatively, and that a pronoun within such a context does not succeed in referring to a quantifier anterior to the quotes.

It is in the supposed freedom from these defects that the intensional composition of statements by means of 'necessarily', 'possibly', and 'necessarily if-then', like extensional composition by means of '$\sim$' and '·', is thought to constitute composition of statements in a more genuine sense than that which puts the component within quotes. The prefixes 'necessarily' and 'possibly' aspire to such uses as:

If an object necessarily has one or other of two attributes,
   then it is not possible that it lack both attributes,

that is:

$$(x)(y)(z) \sim (y \text{ and } z \text{ are attributes } \cdot \text{ necessarily}$$
$$x \text{ has } y \text{ or } z \cdot \text{ possibly } x \text{ lacks } y \text{ and } z),$$

in which a pronoun within the context 'necessarily . . .' or 'possibly . . .' refers beyond that context.

However, the cited modes of intensional composition of statements are, in fact, subject to the same defects as the context of quotes. For, in view of the fact that a substitution on the basis of the true identity (14) transforms the truth (20) into the falsehood (24), we have to conclude that the terminal occurrence of the name 'Evening Star' in (20) is not purely designative. Equally, in view of the fact that a substitution on the basis of the true identity (15) transforms the truth (18) into the falsehood (23) we conclude that the occurrence of the name '9' in (18) is not purely designative.

It follows that the context 'necessarily . . .', at least in the analytic sense which we are considering, is similar to the context of single quotes and to the contexts 'is unaware that . . .', 'believes that . . .', etc. It does not admit pronouns which refer to quantifiers anterior to the context.[5]

The expression:

$$\text{Necessarily} \sim (x) \sim x > 7,$$

that is, 'Necessarily something is greater than 7', still makes sense, being in fact a true statement; but the expression:

$$\sim (x) \sim x \text{ is necessarily greater than 7,}$$

---

[5] These circumstances must be carefully considered in any appraisal of a calculus of necessity such, for example, as that of C. I. Lewis.

that is, 'There is something which is necessarily greater than 7', is meaningless. For, would 9, that is, the number of planets, be one of the numbers necessarily greater than 7? But such an affirmation would be at once true in the form (18) and false in the form (23). Similar observations apply to the use of pronouns in connection with the example (20). This resistance to quantification, observed in relation to the context 'necessarily . . .', is encountered equally in connection with the derivative contexts 'possibly . . .' etc.

We see, therefore, that the apparent compounds (16), (18), (20), and (25) are compounds of the contained statements only in the irregular or accidental sense noted in the case of contexts which use quotes. It would be clearer, perhaps, to adhere explicitly to the forms (17), (19), (21), and (22), instead of the alternative forms (16), (18), (20), and (25). These observations apply, naturally, to the prefix 'necessarily' only in the explained sense of analytic necessity; and correspondingly for possibility, impossibility, and the necessary conditional. As for other notions of necessity, possibility, etc., for example, notions of physical necessity or possibility, the first problem would be to formulate the notions clearly and exactly. Afterwards we could investigate whether such notions involve non-designative occurrences of names and hence resist the introduction of pronouns and exterior quantifiers. This question concerns intimately the practical use of language. It concerns, for example, the use of the contrary-to-fact conditional within a quantification; for it is reasonable to suppose that the contrary-to-fact conditional reduces to the form 'necessarily, if p and q' in some sense of necessity. Upon the contrary-to-fact conditional depends in turn, for example, this definition of solubility in water: To say that an object is soluble in water is to say that it would dissolve if it were in water. In discussions of physics, naturally, we need quantifications containing the clause 'x is soluble in water', or the equivalent in words; but, according to the definition suggested, we should then have to admit within quantifications the expression 'if x were in water then x would dissolve', that is, 'necessarily if x is in water then x dissolves'. Yet we do not know whether there is a suitable sense of "necessity" that admits pronouns referring thus to exterior quantifiers.[6]

The effect of these considerations is rather to raise questions than to answer them. The one important result is the recognition that any intensional mode of statement composition, whether based on some notion of "necessity" or, for example, on a notion of

[6] For a theory of "disposition terms," like 'soluble,' see Rudolf Carnap, "Testability and Meaning," *Philosophy of Science*, Vol. 3 (1936), pp. 419–471; Vol. 4 (1937), pp. 1–40.

"probability" (as in Reichenbach's system), must be carefully examined in relation to its susceptibility to quantification. Perhaps the only useful modes of statement composition susceptible to quantification are the extensional ones, reducible to '$\sim$' and '$\cdot$'. Up to now there is no clear example to the contrary. It is known, in particular, that no intensional mode of statement composition is needed in mathematics.

5. ATTRIBUTES AND CLASSES

The use of general terms, like 'man' or 'blue', or of abstract terms, like 'justice' or '9', does not commit us to recognizing the existence of abstract objects. As is already clear, the question of our ontological presuppositions rests rather on our designative use of such terms, and depends finally on our manner of using pronouns and quantifiers. In fact, the question of ontological presuppositions reduces completely to the question of the domain of objects covered by the quantifier.

It turns out, nevertheless, that mathematics depends on the recognition of abstract objects—such as numbers, functions, relations, classes, attributes. The abstract objects upon whose recognition mathematics depends are, in fact, reducible to a part which includes only classes or attributes.[7] But abstract objects, these or others, have to be admitted in the domain of the quantifier.

The nominalist, admitting only concrete objects, must either regard classical mathematics as discredited, or, at best, consider it a machine which is useful despite the fact that it uses ideograms of the form of statements which involve a fictitious ontology. However, anyone who cares to explore the foundations of mathematics must, whatever his private ontological dogma, begin with a provisional tolerance of classes or attributes. But what is the difference between classes and attributes? It is common to speak of a class as a "mere aggregate", and to imagine it as having its members inside it, according to a spatial analogy; whereas an attribute tends to be imagined rather on the analogy of a power that inheres in the object that has the attribute, or as a feature that the object exhibits. This appeal to opposing analogies is pointless. Classes are as abstract and non-spatial as attributes, as I have emphasized elsewhere,[8] and there is no difference between classes and attributes beyond perhaps this: classes are the same when their members are the same, whereas attributes may be regarded as distinct even though possessed by the same objects.

The opinion is sometimes held that the idea of attribute (or property) is more intuitive than that of class, and that the idea of

[7] Cf. by *Mathematical Logic*, Chapters III–VI.
[8] *Op. cit.*, p. 120.

class should be derived from that of attribute. The derivation presents little difficulty,[9] but the idea that such a derivation is desirable is very curious. It rests perhaps on a confusion between attribute and *matrix*, this latter being an expression which has the form of a statement but contains a free variable. Certainly, in order to specify a class we usually have to present a matrix that is satisfied by the members of the class and by them only; but in this respect classes and attributes are alike, for the determination of an attribute also depends, usually, on presenting a matrix satisfied by the objects, and only those that have the attribute. The matrix is not the attribute.

Classes, being abstract objects, are less clear and familiar than we might wish, but attributes are even more obscure; for the only difference between classes and attributes resides, as we have seen, in the condition of identity, and in this respect classes are much clearer than attributes. Two matrices determine the same class when satisfied by the same objects; but under what condition do the matrices determine the same attribute?

Usually no criterion is offered. The only one I know is the following: matrices determine the same attributes if, and only if, they are logically equivalent. But this criterion leads to awkward results. Consider the attributes determined by the respective matrices:

(26) $x >$ number of planets,

(27) $x > 9$;

that is, the attribute of exceeding the number of planets and the attribute of exceeding 9. Since (26) and (27) are not logically equivalent, it follows that the attributes will not be identical. The statement:

(28) The attribute of exceeding the number of planets = the attribute of exceeding 9

is false. Still, substitution in the true statement:

The attribute of exceeding 9 = the attribute of exceeding 9

on the basis of (15) leads to (28). We have to conclude that the occurrence of '9' in the context 'the attribute of exceeding 9' is not purely designative. Likewise, more generally, we must conclude that the occurrences of names within names of attributes are not designative. Expressions of the type that specify attributes are not contexts accessible to pronouns referring to anterior quantifiers.

9 Cf. Whitehead and Russell, *Principia Mathematica*, vol. 1, *20; also my essay "Whitehead and the rise of modern logic," in *The Philosophy of A. N. Whitehead* (Library of Living Philosophers, 1941), pp. 147 f.

Clearly this constitutes a fundamental restriction on the use of attributes. It is, in particular, a restriction which makes attributes inadequate to the ends of mathematics and inadequate even as a basis for the subsequent introduction of classes. The only recourse would be to adopt another standard for identity of attributes not based on logical equivalence. But what might such an alternative standard be? And would attributes so construed still be as intuitive as classes?

There may still be a reason to maintain that certain attributes are more intuitive than classes—namely, the attributes, properties, or qualities of sense experience, for example, those of color and sound. It is possible to maintain that these attributes are sometimes distinct even though possessed by the same objects, and still to maintain that the difficulty noted in the case of the matrices (26) and (27) does not arise, since (26) and (27) are not among the matrices to which the simple attributes of sense experience correspond. However, such a domain of special attributes, not corresponding to matrices in general, would not suffice for the purposes of mathematics, nor for the derivation of a general theory of classes.

The main conclusions reached in the five sections of this paper are as follows. A substantive word or phrase which designates an object may occur purely designatively in some contexts and not purely designatively in others. This second type of context, though no less "correct" than the first, is not subject to the law of substitutivity of identity nor to the laws of application and existential generalization. Moreover, no pronoun (or variable of quantification) within a context of this second type can refer back to an antecedent (or quantifier) prior to that context. This circumstance imposes serious restrictions, commonly unheeded, upon the significant use of modal operators, as well as challenging that philosophy of mathematics which assumes as basic a theory of attributes in a sense distinct from classes.

WILLARD V. QUINE.

HARVARD UNIVERSITY.

6

Descriptions

by BERTRAND RUSSELL

Reprinted from Chap. XVI, *Introduction to Mathematical Philosophy,* 2nd ed. London: Allen and Unwin, 1920.

CHAPTER XVI

DESCRIPTIONS

WE dealt in the preceding chapter with the words *all* and *some*; in this chapter we shall consider the word *the* in the singular, and in the next chapter we shall consider the word *the* in the plural. It may be thought excessive to devote two chapters to one word, but to the philosophical mathematician it is a word of very great importance: like Browning's Grammarian with the enclitic $\delta\epsilon$, I would give the doctrine of this word if I were " dead from the waist down " and not merely in a prison.

We have already had occasion to mention " descriptive functions," *i.e.* such expressions as " the father of *x* " or " the sine of *x*." These are to be defined by first defining " descriptions."

A " description " may be of two sorts, definite and indefinite (or ambiguous). An indefinite description is a phrase of the form " a so-and-so," and a definite description is a phrase of the form " the so-and-so " (in the singular). Let us begin with the former.

" Who did you meet ? " " I met a man." " That is a very indefinite description." We are therefore not departing from usage in our terminology. Our question is : What do I really assert when I assert " I met a man " ? Let us assume, for the moment, that my assertion is true, and that in fact I met Jones. It is clear that what I assert is *not* " I met Jones." I may say " I met a man, but it was not Jones "; in that case, though I lie, I do not contradict myself, as I should do if when I say I met a man I really mean that I met Jones. It is clear also that the person to whom I am speaking can understand what I say, even if he is a foreigner and has never heard of Jones.

But we may go further: not only Jones, but no actual man, enters into my statement. This becomes obvious when the statement is false, since then there is no more reason why Jones should be supposed to enter into the proposition than why anyone else should. Indeed the statement would remain significant, though it could not possibly be true, even if there were no man at all. "I met a unicorn" or "I met a sea-serpent" is a perfectly significant assertion, if we know what it would be to be a unicorn or a sea-serpent, *i.e.* what is the definition of these fabulous monsters. Thus it is only what we may call the *concept* that enters into the proposition. In the case of "unicorn," for example, there is only the concept: there is not also, somewhere among the shades, something unreal which may be called "a unicorn." Therefore, since it is significant (though false) to say "I met a unicorn," it is clear that this proposition, rightly analysed, does not contain a constituent "a unicorn," though it does contain the concept "unicorn."

The question of "unreality," which confronts us at this point, is a very important one. Misled by grammar, the great majority of those logicians who have dealt with this question have dealt with it on mistaken lines. They have regarded grammatical form as a surer guide in analysis than, in fact, it is. And they have not known what differences in grammatical form are important. "I met Jones" and "I met a man" would count traditionally as propositions of the same form, but in actual fact they are of quite different forms: the first names an actual person, Jones; while the second involves a propositional function, and becomes, when made explicit: "The function 'I met x and x is human' is sometimes true." (It will be remembered that we adopted the convention of using "sometimes" as not implying more than once.) This proposition is obviously not of the form "I met x," which accounts

$= (\exists x) Mx \cdot Hx$?

what semantic fn. of 'x' here? refer to an object?
hold place in lieu of proper name?

ie, for substi of all names for x, some substi yields
a true singular sent. (BR's old-fashioned langu. for
e.t. of gen. sent. & quantif.)

for the existence of the proposition " I met a unicorn " in spite of the fact that there is no such thing as " a unicorn."

For want of the apparatus of propositional functions, many logicians have been driven to the conclusion that there are unreal objects. It is argued, *e.g.* by Meinong,[1] that we can speak about " the golden mountain," " the round square," and so on ; we can make true propositions of which these are the subjects ; hence they must have some kind of logical being, since otherwise the propositions in which they occur would be meaningless. In such theories, it seems to me, there is a failure of that feeling for reality which ought to be preserved even in the most abstract studies. Logic, I should maintain, must no more admit a unicorn than zoology can ; for logic is concerned with the real world just as truly as zoology, though with its more abstract and general features. To say that unicorns have an existence in heraldry, or in literature, or in imagination, is a most pitiful and paltry evasion. What exists in heraldry is not an animal, made of flesh and blood, moving and breathing of its own initiative. What exists is a picture, or a description in words. Similarly, to maintain that Hamlet, for example, exists in his own world, namely, in the world of Shakespeare's imagination, just as truly as (say) Napoleon existed in the ordinary world, is to say something deliberately confusing, or else confused to a degree which is scarcely credible. There is only one world, the " real " world : Shakespeare's imagination is part of it, and the thoughts that he had in writing Hamlet are real. So are the thoughts that we have in reading the play. But it is of the very essence of fiction that only the thoughts, feelings, etc., in Shakespeare and his readers are real, and that there is not, in addition to them, an objective Hamlet. When you have taken account of all the feelings roused by Napoleon in writers and readers of history, you have not touched the actual man ; but in the case of Hamlet you have come to the end of him. If no one thought about Hamlet, there would be nothing

[1] *Untersuchungen zur Gegenstandstheorie und Psychologie,* 1904.

left of him ; if no one had thought about Napoleon, he would have soon seen to it that some one did. The sense of reality is vital in logic, and whoever juggles with it by pretending that Hamlet has another kind of reality is doing a disservice to thought. A robust sense of reality is very necessary in framing a correct analysis of propositions about unicorns, golden mountains, round squares, and other such pseudo-objects.

In obedience to the feeling of reality, we shall insist that, in the analysis of propositions, nothing " unreal " is to be admitted. But, after all, if there *is* nothing unreal, how, it may be asked, *could* we admit anything unreal ? The reply is that, in dealing with propositions, we are dealing in the first instance with symbols, and if we attribute significance to groups of symbols which have no significance, we shall fall into the error of admitting unrealities, in the only sense in which this is possible, namely, as objects described. In the proposition " I met a unicorn," the whole four words together make a significant proposition, and the word " unicorn " by itself is significant, in just the same sense as the word " man." But the *two* words " a unicorn " do not form a subordinate group having a meaning of its own. Thus if we falsely attribute meaning to these two words, we find ourselves saddled with " a unicorn," and with the problem how there can be such a thing in a world where there are no unicorns. " A unicorn " is an indefinite description which describes nothing. It is not an indefinite description which describes something unreal. Such a proposition as " *x* is unreal " only has meaning when " *x* " is a description, definite or indefinite ; in that case the proposition will be true if " *x* " is a description which describes nothing. But whether the description " *x* " describes something or describes nothing, it is in any case not a constituent of the proposition in which it occurs ; like " a unicorn " just now, it is not a subordinate group having a meaning of its own. All this results from the fact that, when " *x* " is a description, " *x* is unreal " or " *x* does not exist " is not nonsense, but is always significant and sometimes true.

We may now proceed to define generally the meaning of propositions which contain ambiguous descriptions. Suppose we wish to make some statement about "a so-and-so," where "so-and-so's" are those objects that have a certain property ϕ, i.e. those objects x for which the propositional function ϕx is true. (E.g. if we take "a man" as our instance of "a so-and-so," ϕx will be "x is human.") Let us now wish to assert the property ψ of "a so-and-so," i.e. we wish to assert that "a so-and-so" has that property which x has when ψx is true. (E.g. in the case of "I met a man," ψx will be "I met x.") Now the proposition that "a so-and-so" has the property ψ is *not* a proposition of the form "ψx." If it were, "a so-and-so" would have to be identical with x for a suitable x; and although (in a sense) this may be true in some cases, it is certainly not true in such a case as "a unicorn." It is just this fact, that the statement that a so-and-so has the property ψ is not of the form ψx, which makes it possible for "a so-and-so" to be, in a certain clearly definable sense, "unreal." The definition is as follows :—

The statement that "an object having the property ϕ has the property ψ"

means :

"The joint assertion of ϕx and ψx is not always false."

So far as logic goes, this is the same proposition as might be expressed by "some ϕ's are ψ's"; but rhetorically there is a difference, because in the one case there is a suggestion of singularity, and in the other case of plurality. This, however, is not the important point. The important point is that, when rightly analysed, propositions verbally about "a so-and-so" are found to contain no constituent represented by this phrase. And that is why such propositions can be significant even when there is no such thing as a so-and-so.

The definition of *existence*, as applied to ambiguous descriptions, results from what was said at the end of the preceding chapter. We say that "men exist" or "a man exists" if the propositional function " x is human " is sometimes true; and generally " a so-and-so exists " if " x is so-and-so " is sometimes true. We may put this in other language. The proposition " Socrates is a man " is no doubt *equivalent* to " Socrates is human," but it is not the very same proposition. The *is* of " Socrates is human " expresses the relation of subject and predicate; the *is* of " Socrates is a man " expresses identity. It is a disgrace to the human race that it has chosen to employ the same word " is " for these two entirely different ideas—a disgrace which a symbolic logical language of course remedies. The identity in " Socrates is a man " is identity between an object named (accepting " Socrates " as a name, subject to qualifications explained later) and an object ambiguously described. An object ambiguously described will " exist " when at least one such proposition is true, *i.e.* when there is at least one true proposition of the form " x is a so-and-so," where " x " is a name. It is characteristic of ambiguous (as opposed to definite) descriptions that there may be any number of true propositions of the above form—Socrates is a man, Plato is a man, etc. Thus " a man exists " follows from Socrates, or Plato, or anyone else. With definite descriptions, on the other hand, the corresponding form of proposition, namely, " x is the so-and-so " (where " x " is a name), can only be true for one value of x at most. This brings us to the subject of definite descriptions, which are to be defined in a way analogous to that employed for ambiguous descriptions, but rather more complicated.

We come now to the main subject of the present chapter, namely, the definition of the word *the* (in the singular). One very important point about the definition of " a so-and-so " applies equally to " the so-and-so "; the definition to be sought is a definition of propositions in which this phrase occurs, not a definition of the phrase itself in isolation. In the case of " a so-and-so," this is fairly obvious: no one could suppose that " a man " was a definite object, which could be defined by itself.

Socrates is a man, Plato is a man, Aristotle is a man, but we cannot infer that " a man " means the same as " Socrates " means and also the same as " Plato " means and also the same as " Aristotle " means, since these three names have different meanings. Nevertheless, when we have enumerated all the men in the world, there is nothing left of which we can say, " This is a man, and not only so, but it is *the* ' a man,' the quintessential entity that is just an indefinite man without being anybody in particular." It is of course quite clear that whatever there is in the world is definite : if it is a man it is one definite man and not any other. Thus there cannot be such an entity as " a man " to be found in the world, as opposed to specific men. And accordingly it is natural that we do not define " a man " itself, but only the propositions in which it occurs.

In the case of " the so-and-so " this is equally true, though at first sight less obvious. We may demonstrate that this must be the case, by a consideration of the difference between a *name* and a *definite description*. Take the proposition, " Scott is the author of *Waverley*." We have here a name, " Scott," and a description, " the author of *Waverley*," which are asserted to apply to the same person. The distinction between a name and all other symbols may be explained as follows :—

A name is a simple symbol whose meaning is something that can only occur as subject, *i.e.* something of the kind that, in Chapter XIII., we defined as an " individual " or a " particular." And a " simple " symbol is one which has no parts that are symbols. Thus " Scott " is a simple symbol, because, though it has parts (namely, separate letters), these parts are not symbols. On the other hand, " the author of *Waverley* " is not a simple symbol, because the separate words that compose the phrase are parts which are symbols. If, as may be the case, whatever *seems* to be an " individual " is really capable of further analysis, we shall have to content ourselves with what may be called " relative individuals," which will be terms that, throughout the context in question, are never analysed and never occur otherwise than as subjects. And in that case we shall have correspondingly to content ourselves with "relative names." From the standpoint of our present problem, namely, the definition of descriptions, this problem, whether these are absolute names or only relative names, may be ignored, since it concerns different stages in the hierarchy of "types," whereas we have to compare such couples as "Scott" and "the author of *Waverley*," which both apply to the same object, and do not raise the problem of types. We may, therefore, for the moment, treat names as capable of being absolute; nothing that we shall have to say will depend upon this assumption, but the wording may be a little shortened by it.

We have, then, two things to compare: (1) a *name*, which is a simple symbol, directly designating an individual which is its meaning, and having this meaning in its own right, independently of the meanings of all other words; (2) a *description*, which consists of several words, whose meanings are already fixed, and from which results whatever is to be taken as the "meaning" of the description. *ie, is a function of components*

A proposition containing a description is not identical with what that proposition becomes when a name is substituted, even if the name names the same object as the description describes. "Scott is the author of *Waverley*" is obviously a different proposition from "Scott is Scott": the first is a fact in literary history, the second a trivial truism. And if we put anyone other than Scott in place of "the author of *Waverley*," our proposition would become false, and would therefore certainly no longer be the same proposition. But, it may be said, our proposition is essentially of the same form as (say) "Scott is Sir Walter," in which two names are said to apply to the same person. The reply is that, if "Scott is Sir Walter" really means "the person named 'Scott' is the person named 'Sir Walter,'" then the names are being used as descriptions: *i.e.* the individual, instead of being named, is being described as the person having that name. This is a way in which names are frequently used in practice, and there will, as a rule, be nothing in the phraseology to show whether they are being used in this way or *as* names. When a name is used directly, merely to indicate what we are speaking about, it is no part of the *fact* asserted, or of the falsehood if our assertion happens to be false: it is merely part of the symbolism by which we express our thought. What we want to express is something which might (for example) be translated into a foreign language; it is something for which the actual words are a vehicle, but of which they are no part. On the other hand, when we make a proposition about " the person called ' Scott,' " the actual name " Scott " enters into what we are asserting, and not merely into the language used in making the assertion. Our proposition will now be a different one if we substitute " the person called ' Sir Walter.' " But so long as we are using names *as* names, whether we say " Scott " or whether we say " Sir Walter " is as irrelevant to what we are asserting as whether we speak English or French. Thus so long as names are used *as* names, " Scott is Sir Walter " is the same trivial proposition as " Scott is Scott." This completes the proof that " Scott is the author of *Waverley* " is not the same proposition as results from substituting a name for " the author of *Waverley*," no matter what name may be substituted.

 When we use a variable, and speak of a propositional function, ϕx say, the process of applying general statements about x to particular cases will consist in substituting a name for the letter " x," assuming that ϕ is a function which has individuals for its arguments. Suppose, for example, that ϕx is " always true "; let it be, say, the " law of identity," $x=x$. Then we may substitute for " x " any name we choose, and we shall obtain a true proposition. Assuming for the moment that " Socrates," " Plato," and " Aristotle " are names (a very rash assumption), we can infer from the law of identity that Socrates is Socrates, Plato is Plato, and Aristotle is Aristotle. But we shall commit a fallacy if we attempt to infer, without further premisses, that the author of *Waverley* is the author of *Waverley*. This results

from what we have just proved, that, if we substitute a name for
"the author of *Waverley*" in a proposition, the proposition
we obtain is a different one. That is to say, applying the result
to our present case : If "*x*" is a name, "*x=x*" is not the same
proposition as "the author of *Waverley* is the author of *Waverley*,"
no matter what name "*x*" may be. Thus from the fact that
all propositions of the form "*x=x*" are true we cannot infer,
without more ado, that the author of *Waverley* is the author of
Waverley. In fact, propositions of the form "the so-and-so
is the so-and-so" are not always true : it is necessary that the
so-and-so should *exist* (a term which will be explained shortly).
It is false that the present King of France is the present King of
France, or that the round square is the round square. When we
substitute a description for a name, propositional functions
which are "always true" may become false, if the description
describes nothing. There is no mystery in this as soon as we
realise (what was proved in the preceding paragraph) that when
we substitute a description the result is not a value of the
propositional function in question.

We are now in a position to define propositions in which a
definite description occurs. The only thing that distinguishes
"the so-and-so" from "a so-and-so" is the implication of
uniqueness. We cannot speak of "*the* inhabitant of London,"
because inhabiting London is an attribute which is not unique.
We cannot speak about "the present King of France," because
there is none; but we can speak about "the present King of
England." Thus propositions about "the so-and-so" always
imply the corresponding propositions about "a so-and-so,"
with the addendum that there is not more than one so-and-so.
Such a proposition as "Scott is the author of Waverley" could
not be true if *Waverley* had never been written, or if several
people had written it; and no more could any other proposition
resulting from a propositional function *x* by the substitution
of "the author of *Waverley*" for "*x*." We may say that "the
author of *Waverley*" means "the value of *x* for which '*x* wrote

*Zeus is
Zeus?
cf. p. 97-8*

(1920)

*direct analog of propositional
function in math.
or solution-set?*

Waverley' is true." Thus the proposition "the author of *Waverley* was Scotch," for example, involves :

(1) " *x* wrote *Waverley* " is not always false ; *— subj. term must describe s.th.*

(2) "if *x* and *y* wrote *Waverley*, *x* and *y* are identical " is always true ; *uniqueness of "the"*

(3) "if *x* wrote *Waverley*, *x* was Scotch " is always true.

(∃x) *(x)* *(x)* [handwritten margin symbols]

These three propositions, translated into ordinary language, state :

(1) at least one person wrote *Waverley* ;

(2) at most one person wrote *Waverley* ;

(3) whoever wrote *Waverley* was Scotch.

All these three are implied by " the author of *Waverley* was Scotch." Conversely, the three together (but no two of them) imply that the author of *Waverley* was Scotch. Hence the three together may be taken as <u>defining</u> what is meant by the proposition " the author of *Waverley* was Scotch." *∴ an "analysis"* [handwritten margin note]

We may somewhat simplify these three propositions. The first and second together are equivalent to : " There is a term *c* such that ' *x* wrote *Waverley* ' is true when *x* is *c* and is false when *x* is not *c*." In other words, " There is a term *c* such that ' *x* wrote *Waverley* ' is always equivalent to ' *x* is *c*.' " (Two propositions are " equivalent " when both are true or both are false.) We have here, to begin with, two <u>functions</u> of *x*, " *x* wrote *Waverley* " and " *x* is *c*," and we form a function of *c* by considering the equivalence of these two functions of *x* for all values of *x* ; we then proceed to assert that the resulting function of *c* is " sometimes true," *i.e.* that it is true for at least one value of *c*. (It obviously cannot be true for more than one value of *c*.) *uniqueness* [handwritten margin note] These two conditions together are defined as giving the meaning of " the author of *Waverley* exists."

We may now define " <u>the term satisfying the function ϕx exists</u>." This is the general form of which the above is a particular case. " The author of *Waverley* " is " the term satisfying the function ' *x* wrote *Waverley*.' " And " the so-and-so " will *Existence* [handwritten margin note] always involve reference to some propositional function, namely, that which defines the property that makes a thing a so-and-so. Our definition is as follows :—

"The term satisfying the function ϕx exists" means :

"There is a term c such that ϕx is always equivalent to 'x is c.'"

In order to define "the author of *Waverley* was Scotch," we have still to take account of the third of our three propositions, namely, "Whoever wrote *Waverley* was Scotch." This will be satisfied by merely adding that the c in question is to be Scotch. Thus "the author of *Waverley* was Scotch" is :

"There is a term c such that (1) 'x wrote *Waverley*' is always equivalent to 'x is c,' (2) c is Scotch."

And generally : "the term satisfying ϕx satisfies ψx" is defined as meaning : *or, "The so & so is such & such" :*

"There is a term c such that (1) ϕx is always equivalent to 'x is c,' (2) ψc is true." *how unpack?*

This is the definition of propositions in which descriptions occur.

It is possible to have much knowledge concerning a term described, *i.e.* to know many propositions concerning "the so-and-so," without actually knowing what the so-and-so is, *i.e.* without knowing any proposition of the form "x is the so-and-so," where "x" is a name. In a detective story propositions about "the man who did the deed" are accumulated, in the hope that ultimately they will suffice to demonstrate that it was A who did the deed. We may even go so far as to say that, in all such knowledge as can be expressed in words—with the exception of "this" and "that" and a few other words of which the meaning varies on different occasions—no names, in the strict sense, occur, but what seem like names are really descriptions. We may inquire significantly whether Homer existed, which we could not do if "Homer" were a name. The proposition "the so-and-so exists" is significant, whether true or false ; but if a is the so-and-so (where "a" is a name), the words "a exists" are meaningless. It is only of descriptions

—definite or indefinite—that existence can be significantly asserted; for, if "*a*" is a name, it *must* name something: what does not name anything is not a name, and therefore, if intended to be a name, is a symbol devoid of meaning, whereas a description, like "the present King of France," does not become incapable of occurring significantly merely on the ground that it describes nothing, the reason being that it is a *complex* symbol, of which the meaning is derived from that of its constituent symbols. And so, when we ask whether Homer existed, we are using the word "Homer" as an abbreviated description: we may replace it by (say) "the author of the *Iliad* and the *Odyssey*." The same considerations apply to almost all uses of what look like proper names.

When descriptions occur in propositions, it is necessary to distinguish what may be called "primary" and "secondary" occurrences. The abstract distinction is as follows. A description has a "primary" occurrence when the proposition in which it occurs results from substituting the description for "*x*" in some propositional function ϕx; a description has a "secondary" occurrence when the result of substituting the description for *x* in ϕx gives only *part* of the proposition concerned. An instance will make this clearer. Consider "the present King of France is bald." Here "the present King of France" has a primary occurrence, and the proposition is false. Every proposition in which a description which describes nothing has a primary occurrence is false. But now consider "the present King of France is not bald." This is ambiguous. If we are first to take "*x* is bald," then substitute "the present King of France" for "*x*," and then deny the result, the occurrence of "the present King of France" is secondary and our proposition is true; but if we are to take "*x* is not bald" and substitute "the present King of France" for "*x*," then "the present King of France" has a primary occurrence and the proposition is false. Confusion of primary and secondary occurrences is a ready source of fallacies where descriptions are concerned.

Descriptions occur in mathematics chiefly in the form of *descriptive functions,* *i.e.* " the term having the relation R to *y*," or " the R of *y* " as we may say, on the analogy of " the father of *y* " and similar phrases. To say " the father of *y* is rich," for example, is to say that the following propositional function of *c*: " *c* is rich, and ' *x* begat *y* ' is always equivalent to ' *x* is *c*,' " is " sometimes true," *i.e.* is true for at least one value of *c*. It obviously cannot be true for more than one value.

The theory of descriptions, briefly outlined in the present chapter, is of the utmost importance both in logic and in theory of knowledge. But for purposes of mathematics, the more philosophical parts of the theory are not essential, and have therefore been omitted in the above account, which has confined itself to the barest mathematical requisites.

7

Synonymity

by BENSON MATES

Reprinted from *University of California Publications in Philosophy*, 25 (1950).

SYNONYMITY

BENSON MATES

I

I SHALL BEGIN my paper by attempting to show, in a rough way at least, that a discussion of synonymity is germane to the general topic of these lectures, namely, meaning and interpretation. The connection between synonymity and meaning is perhaps too clear to require much comment: two linguistic expressions are synonymous if and only if they have the same meaning. The relation between synonymity and interpretation is only slightly less obvious. I shall try to explicate it by offering definitions of certain important terms which commonly occur, or ought to occur, in discussions of this subject.

The first of these terms is "language." By "language," in its most general sense, I wish to denote any aggregate of objects which are themselves meaningful or else are such that certain combinations of them are meaningful. It will be seen at once that this definition assigns a very wide meaning to the term "language" and furthermore that it suffers from all the vagueness and ambiguity which attaches to the word "meaningful." Nevertheless, I think that it leads to a usage quite in agreement with ordinary usage. Thus we may first of all observe that all the ordinary conversational languages, for example the English language or the German, come under the definition given. Each of them can be regarded as an aggregate of objects which are meaningful singly or at least in combinations. Likewise, written English, spoken English, the King's English, and plain English would all be languages according to the definition just given.

As one can determine by consulting the dictionary, however, the denotation of the word "language" is much wider than these examples indicate. We must not suppose, for instance, that only human beings can use language, since in one proper sense of the term it refers to activities of the lower animals as well. For example, there is said to be a "language of the birds." Here the meaningful objects are the various characteristic sounds that birds make under given circumstances. Nor, again, must we suppose that the elements of a language are always either inscriptions or sounds. There is, for instance, "the language of the face," or "the language of looks and glances." In this case the meaningful elements are evidently certain positions of the physiognomy. Again, the phrase "language of the heart" presumably refers to a language whose elements are certain patterns of behavior which are supposed to denote the presence of certain emotions. But even these examples do not show the full extent of the term "language" in ordinary discourse. It is by no means necessary that the elements of the language be the results of human or animal activity. Thus, certain clever men are said to be able to read "the language of the stars," and poets and philosophers have a great deal to say about "the language of nature." What is common to all these, it seems to me, is that in each there is an aggregate of objects—whether they be marks, sounds, gestures, looks, or stars—and these objects or certain combinations of these objects are meaningful.

The next important term for which I shall offer a preliminary definition is the term "translation." A body of discourse A is a translation of another body of discourse B if and only if there is a correspondence between the meaningful parts of A and those of B such that corresponding parts are synonymous. What kind of correspondence this is, in general, it is difficult to say. At present, I am merely trying to indicate the connection between the notions of translation and synonymity, and I claim for the foregoing definition only the merit that its consequences are to a great extent in accord with the ordinary usage of the word "translation." Consider, for example, the problem of translating a book from German into English. This amounts to the problem of producing an English version which faithfully reproduces the sense of the original, that is, of producing a book which contains, for every meaningful expression in the German original, a synonymous expression in English, and conversely. Words, sentences, or whole paragraphs may be taken as the smallest meaningful expressions to be translated, depending upon the translator's judgment of how the sense of the original can best be reproduced in the translation.[1]

The term "translation" is most frequently applied when the

---

[1] In general we may say that a translation is relatively literal if it is so constructed that for every important word in the original text there is a synonymous expression in the translation, while it would be considered relatively free if whole paragraphs were the smallest parts for which synonymous expressions were provided.

two texts occur in languages that are entirely disjoint from one another, as for example German and English. However, it may equally well be applied when one of the two languages is contained in the other or even when the two languages are identical. Consider the task of popularizing a technical treatise—of putting it into plain English. It seems to me that the popularization will be a translation of the technical treatise in essentially the same sense in which a German version would be a translation of it. We are given a language—German, or plain English, as the case may be,—and the problem is to find, for every expression or group of expressions in the technical treatise, a synonymous expression or group of expressions in the given language. The process of popularization, therefore, may be regarded as a process of translating the technical treatise out of the whole English language (considered as containing the technical terms) into that part of the English language which we have been calling "plain English." It may also occur that the languages concerned are identical or nearly so. For example, it is perfectly in accord with correct usage to speak of translating poetry into prose. Here the problem is to find nonpoetic expressions which are synonymous with the meaningful expressions occurring in some poem, and both the poem and the prose may of course be written in the same language.

The last term for which I shall give a preliminary definition is "interpretation." A body of discourse A is an interpretation of a body of discourse B if and only if A is a translation of B and the constituent expressions of A are better understood than those of B. Thus, according to me, every interpretation is a translation.[2] Further, since the degree to which a language is understood varies from person to person, what would be an interpretation for one person might not be an interpretation for someone else.

I shall now set forth a series of considerations which will serve both to explain my definition of "interpretation" and to argue that it accords well with established usage. Let us first give attention to the meaning of the related term, "interpret." We may say that a person x interprets a given body of discourse A to a person y if and only if x translates A into a body of discourse which y understands better than he understands A. This general statement obvi-

---

[2] I do not think that the interpretation of calculi is a type of interpretation under discussion in these lectures; at any rate, I have not attempted to define "interpretation" in such a way as to cover that usage of the term.

ously holds when the languages concerned are ordinary natural languages, for example French and German; and indeed the term "interpreter" is ordinarily applied to a person who translates discourse from one such language into another for the benefit of someone who is not able to understand the first. But it is equally true that the statement holds when the languages concerned are systems of meaningful objects of any sort whatever. To interpret a poem for someone is usually to translate the poem into linguistic expressions which he can understand better than he understands the poem. Sometimes the translator may find it desirable to use gestures, signs, tears, and other devices in addition to the meaningful expressions of the conversational language. We shall then regard the language into which the translation is made as a rather complex language, consisting not only of written or spoken expressions but also of these various other occurrences. In like manner the astrologer may properly be said to interpret the positions of the heavenly bodies. He and his clients regard the positions of these objects as meaningful symbols, that is, as elements in a language which the astrologer can understand but the clients cannot. His function is to interpret discourse in this language to the others, which is to say, to translate messages out of the language of the heavens into a language which the others can understand.[3]

Almost all the other situations which would ordinarily be regarded as instances of interpretation will satisfy the definition proposed above. When the psychiatrist interprets dreams he treats the dreams or certain important constituents of them as meaningful expressions in a kind of language which he, by means of a great deal of training, finds it possible to understand. He is able to tell the uninitiated person what the dreams mean, that is, he can translate certain significant elements in what we may call "the language of dreams" into sentences occurring in a more readily intelligible language. Likewise, the person who interprets a painting regards the painting and possibly also various parts of it as somehow meaningful, and he attempts by the use of the

---

[3] It is interesting and important to observe that even though the clientele do not understand the language of the stars, it is quite possible for them to determine that they have not been provided with an adequate interpretation. It is to be assumed, of course, that the pronouncements of the stars are true; hence, any adequate translation of these pronouncements must at least consist of true sentences. Thus the astrology business is not quite as safe as it might at first seem to be.

meaningful expressions of some language, usually supplemented by an assortment of meaningful gestures, and so on, to accomplish a translation of the painting into forms of expression which are more readily understandable to the person for whose benefit the interpretation is made.

As I see it, therefore, most situations to which the word "interpretation" can properly be applied have the following characteristics. First of all, there are two bodies of discourse, which may occur in any language or languages, in the broad sense of "language" explained above. Secondly, there is a person who understands only one of these bodies of discourse, which is to say that the constituent expressions of only one of these bodies of discourse are meaningful for him. This is the person for whose benefit the interpretation is carried out. Thirdly, there is a person who understands both bodies of discourse and who is able to translate one into the other. This person is the interpreter. Finally we set these elements in motion: the interpreter translates the discourse which the other person does not understand into discourse which the other person does understand. This is interpretation, considered as a process; and the result of the translation is the interpretation, considered as a product.

There is an important difficulty which ought to be mentioned at this point. It very often happens that when an interpretation is needed there is no capable interpreter at hand to produce it. Any student of the history of philosophy will, unfortunately, be well acquainted with this difficulty; but of course the same situation arises in fields other than philosophy. For example, in wartime we may possess enemy messages in code or cipher but lack a ready means of translating these messages into plain language. If an interpretation is to be found at all, it will be necessary for someone who does not understand the text to make an interpretation for himself. Often this is no easy task, but we know that it can be done. In cryptanalysis the methods which are used depend essentially upon the fact that an adequate interpretation of the cryptic message will be part-by-part synonymous with the cryptic message; hence, if the cryptic message is about battleships, the interpretation must be about battleships; if the cryptic message contains true sentences, the interpretation must contain true sentences; if the cryptic message expresses information that would be of interest to the persons for whom it was intended, the interpretation must likewise express information that would interest those persons, and so forth. Thus by the use of data concerning the circumstances under which the message was sent, together with further data about the methods likely to have been used by the cryptographer who wrote the message, it is possible to arrive at a probable interpretation. It is clear that similar considerations enable us to find more or less probable interpretations for obscure passages in philosophical discourse. We know that an adequate interpretation would preserve sense; this requires that it take true sentences over into true ones and false into false; it also requires. that valid arguments be interpreted by valid arguments, and invalid arguments by invalid ones. Usually we also possess some knowledge of the rules of syntax for the language in which the obscure passage is stated; here we have a great advantage over the cryptanalyst. For example, we may often safely assume that, within limits, a given expression should always be translated by the same expression. Frequently we have also a good deal of other knowledge about our author's views and capability, and often we have the opinions of other men on how the passage should be interpreted. By means of all these data we construct a more or less adequate interpretation.

I shall not try to anticipate all the objections which may be made to the foregoing definition of "interpretation," but there are two points which I am prompted to set forth. In the first place, although the definition offered above leads to a very broad usage of "interpretation," it requires that interpretation be sharply distinguished from description. This will appear clearly in an example. Suppose that Jones is an interpreter for the Army in Germany. The prisoner, looking out the window, remarks, "Es schneit," and Jones is asked for an interpretation. He replies as follows: "He uttered a German sentence consisting of two words, the first of which was 'es' and the second, 'schneit.'" I think we may confidently say that although Jones has even given a description of what was said, he has certainly not given an adequate interpretation of what was said. This case is typical; in general, a description of an aggregate of objects is by no means the same as an interpretation of those objects. Thus, even if it could be shown that it is impossible to report what one perceives without describing something, it would not follow that it is impossible to report what one perceives without interpreting something.

The second point which I wish to make is this: from the earliest times, men have tended to confuse interpretation with explanation. If we believe in progress, we shall say that this confusion was more prevalent in ancient times than it is now. At any rate, it will be less offensive to illustrate the matter in connection with antiquity. The history of natural philosophy in the ancient world shows that attempts to explain natural phenomena took two easily distinguishable forms. Sometimes the explanations were explanations in the scientific sense of the term; that is, from a relatively well-established generalization there was deduced a sentence expressing the state of affairs to be explained. More often, however, the explanations were what we would call "interpretations." The phenomenon to be explained was regarded as possessing a meaning with which it had been endowed by some supernatural being, and the explanation consisted in reading off this meaning. Thus, for example, some would explain an eclipse of the sun by saying, "The gods are displeased with men"; others by saying, "The moon has come between the earth and the sun." The former explanation seems based on the assumption that the eclipse is a meaningful symbol by which the gods intend to reveal their displeasure. This sort of explanation might better be called "interpretation," it seems to me.[4] The naturalistic explanation, on the other hand, does not rest upon any assumption that the eclipse is a symbol or portent which the gods or anyone else has endowed with meaning. It corresponds more exactly to what would now be denoted by the word "explanation." There were thus two quite distinct types of explanation, one of which was a type of interpretation and one of which was not. This may account for some of the present-day confusion between the notions of interpretation and explanation and for much of the ambiguity in the English word "interpretation."

---

[4] In fact, it *was* called *interpretatio* by the ancients. Thus, Mercury was called *interpres divum*—interpreter of things divine—because he understood the decrees of Jove and Apollo, not to mention a wide assortment of other omens, including the tripods, laurel, and stars, as well as the sounds (*linguas*) and flights of birds. See Virgil, *Aeneid*, 4, 356; 3, 359.

II

The preceding section has shown that the notion of synonymity is involved in the notions of meaning and interpretation. The question which naturally arises next is, "What can be offered by way of a definition of 'synonymity'?" From what has been said it appears that if one could find a precise and plausible definition for this term, then it would be a relatively simple matter to construct satisfactory definitions for the other important terms which we have been discussing. That circumstance alone would make explicating the notion of synonymity a worthwhile task for philosophers, but it is also true that the notion deserves to be investigated in its own right because of the key role which it plays in many philosophical discussions. This key role is often disguised through the fact that there are many different ways of saying that two expressions are synonymous. One group of circumlocutions consists of those having the form 'to say A is only to say B';[5] for example, "if by 'good' you mean pleasure, then to say that pleasure is good is only to say that pleasure is pleasure." Another way of claiming synonymity is to use expressions like 'A; in other words, B'—for instance, "Jones is a positivist; in other words, Jones regards the sentences of metaphysics as pseudo-object sentences." Still other ways make use of the formula 'when I say A, I only mean B,' and there are further types too numerous to mention. The notion of synonymity seems also to be involved in the well-worn notions of analytic and synthetic sentences, real definitions, analysis, and in much of the other conceptual apparatus of philosophers. Thus there is no doubt that this notion, however vague it may be, is of considerable philosophical importance, and a good definition of it is greatly to be desired.[6]

This being so, the appropriate thing for me to do is to produce such a definition or at least to make an attempt to do so. I am sorry to have to confess not only that I have no definition to propose but also that it seems to me doubtful that any adequate definition of "synonymity"—at least for languages sufficiently complex to

---

[5] Single quotation marks, when they enclose expressions containing variables, are to be regarded as quasi-quotation marks. See W. V. Quine, *Mathematical Logic* (New York, Norton, 1940), pp. 33 ff.

[6] As I use the terms, "to find a plausible definition of the term," "to explicate the notion," and "to define the notion" denote the same process.

make the problem interesting—will ever be found by means of the usual armchair methods of philosophizing. We need empirical research regarding the ordinary language in order to determine which expressions are in fact synonymous, and with the help of these data it may be possible to find an acceptable definition of "synonymity" for some language which has a determinate structure and which closely resembles the ordinary language.

Yet it is important to observe that this very research could hardly be carried out unless we possessed in advance a sufficiently precise characterization of synonymity to enable us to decide under what conditions we would regard two expressions as synonymous for a given person. Otherwise, we would be forced to ask questions of the form 'Are A and B synonymous?'; and the answers would depend not only upon whether or not the subjects regarded the expressions as synonymous, but also upon how they understood the term "synonymous." The case is analogous to the following. Suppose that we wanted to determine whether John Smith is color-blind. We would not do this by asking him the question, "Are you color-blind?" for his answers would depend upon how *he* interpreted the term "color-blind," whereas we wish to know whether he is color-blind in *our* sense of the term. Consequently, we would ask such questions as "Do you see a number on this page?" and would employ some such criterion as "Smith is color-blind if and only if he does not see the number '7' on this page of the test book." In the same way, we need a criterion of the form 'A and B are synonymous if and only if ...' in order to be able to investigate which terms are actually synonymous.

Accordingly, I propose the following statement as a condition of adequacy for definitions of "synonymity" and as a guide for conducting research to determine which expressions are in fact synonymous for given persons: *Two expressions are synonymous in a language L if and only if they may be interchanged in each sentence in L without altering the truth value of that sentence.* That we ordinarily intend to use the word "synonymity" in such a way as to satisfy this condition will be argued in the sequel; first, allow me to make two remarks concerning its application. It is plain, no doubt, that this condition refers only to synonymity between expressions which occur in the same language. We shall need a different and more general criterion for the synonymity of expressions occurring in different languages.[7] Secondly, I intend this condition to apply only to languages which are not semantically closed, that is, to languages which do not contain names of their own expressions and semantical terms like "true," "denotes," and so forth. In particular, it is important that the language L not contain the semantical term "synonymous in L."

It is easy to see that if two expressions are synonymous in a language L, then they may be interchanged in any sentence in L without altering the truth value of that sentence. For, following Frege, we may say that the meaning of a sentence is a function of the meanings of the terms which occur in the sentence; from this it follows that if, in a given sentence, we replace a term by an expression which is synonymous with that term, then the resulting sentence is synonymous with (has the same meaning as) the original sentence. Further, it is clear that synonymous sentences have the same truth value. Hence, synonymous expressions may be interchanged without affecting the meaning or the truth value of sentences in which they occur.

Next, it requires to be shown that, if two expressions can be interchanged in each sentence in L without altering the truth value of that sentence, then they are synonymous. Let us first consider the case in which L contains a modal operator and allows for indirect discourse. Thus L will contain such expressions as 'A says that B,' 'A believes that B,' 'It is necessary that if A believes that B, then A believes that C.' In this case we may establish that interchangeability is a sufficient condition for synonymity by the following considerations. Let us begin with a true assertion from arithmetic:

(1) $$9 = 9.$$

If we replace either occurrence of "9" in this sentence by any expression A such that 'A = 9' is true, then the result will again be true.

---

[7] I assume that we are dealing with a language in which the formation rules do not prevent the interchange of expressions of the same type. Thus, the fact that "humanity" and "human" are not interchangeable in English does not indicate a difference in meaning, for syntax alone prevents their interchange. Now although the union of two languages is always a language, it is not generally the case that the union of two languages of the sort under consideration is a language of the sort under consideration. This is why we shall need a different criterion for the synonymity of expressions occurring in different languages.

Next, consider the true sentence,

(2) $N(9 = 9)$.[8]

Here we may obtain a false result if we replace an occurrence of
"9" by an occurrence of some other expression on the basis of a
true identity sentence. Thus "N(the number of the planets = 9)"
is false. However, if we replace an occurrence of "9" by any expression A such that 'A = 9' is logically true, the result will again
be true. Now, suppose that the following sentence is true:

(3)   Jones believes that $9 = 9$.

In this case, replacing an occurrence of "9" by even a logically
equivalent expression—e.g., by "3²"—may lead to falsehood. There
is no guarantee that it *will* lead to falsehood, but we can see that
even if in fact Jones happens to believe both that $9 = 9$ and that
$9 = 3^2$, it is at least possible for him to believe one without believing the other.[9] In other words, the true sentence:

(4) N(Jones believes that $9 = 9$ if and only if Jones believes that
    $9 = 9$),

will become false if the last occurrence of "9" is replaced by an
occurrence of the logically equivalent expression "3²." Thus logical equivalence of expressions is not sufficient to guarantee interchangeability in a language of the type we are now considering.

That nothing short of synonymity will guarantee interchangeability in a language of this type follows from the fact that the
truth value of a sentence 'Jones believes that A' depends not upon
the truth value of the constituent A but upon its meaning. If A
is replaced by any other expression not having the same meaning,
the truth value of 'Jones believes that A' *may* be changed, which
implies that the truth value of 'N(Jones believes that A if and only
if Jones believes that A)' *will* be changed. Consequently, if two sentences A and B are not synonymous, they will not be interchange-

---

[8] I write 'Np' as an abbreation for 'It is necessary that p.'

[9] This assertion may of course be doubted. If it is false, then the cogency
of my argument is destroyed; and I am aware that there is at least one interpretation of belief sentences such that it is false. Thus, suppose that "9" and
"3²" are both abbreviations for descriptive phrases and have what Russell
calls "primary occurrences" in the sentences "Jones believes that $9 = 9$" and
"Jones believes that $9 = 3^2$." Then the two sentences just mentioned are logically equivalent. Nevertheless, I think that in the usual sense of "belief" the
two sentences are logically independent; I therefore reject the proposed interpretation as paradoxical.

able in all sentences of our language. Similar considerations lead
to the further conclusion that if any two sentence constituents x
and y are not synonymous, then they will not be interchangeable
in the true sentence,

(5) N(Jones believes that $\ldots x \ldots$ if and only if Jones believes
that $\ldots x \ldots$).

On the basis of this we may assert that if two expressions can be
interchanged in all sentences of L without altering truth values,
then they are synonymous. Hence, the proposed condition holds for
languages containing modal operators and indirect discourse.

However, when the condition is applied to extensional languages,
or to languages which are extensional except for the presence of
modal operators, the results obtained are paradoxical. In languages
of this sort all equivalent (or, respectively, logically equivalent)
expressions would be synonymous, a result which is in violent
conflict with ordinary usage of the term "synonymous." It seems
to me that the reason for this conflict is simple; in its ordinary
usage, the term "synonymous" is applied to the ordinary language,
or at least to languages which are such as to permit modal sentences
and indirect discourse. Thus, if we consider the question whether
"2" and "4/2" are synonymous, we shall probably regard the language of arithmetic as a part of the ordinary language and decide
the question in the negative, which would be in complete agreement with our criterion.

On the other hand, there are good reasons for making synonymity relative to the language in which the terms occur. Suppose that
we have a language L and we wish to say something in L which
will establish that two expressions in L are not synonymous. The
only way to do this is to find some true sentence in L which would
not be true if the terms were synonymous. For example, "2" and
"4/2" could be shown nonsynonymous by the true sentence, "Someone might believe that $1 + 1 = 2$ without believing that $1 + 1 = 4/2$."
Now, given any pair of equivalent expressions in an extensional
language L_1, it will be impossible to find in L_1 any true sentence
indicating that the expressions are not synonymous; hence, for all
that can be said in an extensional language, any two equivalent
expressions are synonymous. Likewise, given any pair of logically
equivalent expressions in a modal language L_2, it will not be possi-

ble to find a true sentence in L_2 that would be false if the expressions were not synonymous. Therefore, logically equivalent expressions will be synonymous, for all that can be said in L_2 to the contrary.[10] In general, it seems natural to regard two expressions as synonymous in a language if there is no way in the language of distinguishing between their meanings. Thus it is natural to regard synonymity of terms as relative to the language in which the terms occur.

I shall conclude my discussion of the proposed condition of adequacy by offering some comments on other people's views.

Quine has discussed problems very closely related to those at hand, and no one can fail to be instructed by what he says.[11] However, it seems to me that his choice of terminology may lead one to suppose that what is essentially a question of synonymity is instead a question of designation. The following specific example (his own) will be of use in clarifying the point. Consider the sentences:

(6) Philip believes that Tegucigalpa is in Nicaragua.

(7) Tegucigalpa is the capital of Honduras.

Substitution into (6) on the basis of (7) gives

(8) Philip believes that the capital of Honduras is in Nicaragua.

Now apparently (6) and (8) are not logically equivalent. Quine seeks to explain this by asserting that the occurrence of "Tegucigalpa" in (6)) is not "purely designative" and by claiming that only purely designative occurrences of names are subject to substitutivity on the basis of a true identity sentence. But this explanation is not a good one, as will appear from the following parallel case:

(9) Philip believes that $2^{10} < 1000$.

(10) $2^{10} = 1024$.

(11) Philip believes that $1024 < 1000$.

---

[10] But, of course, for any two terms which are not logically equivalent it will be possible in the modal language to find a true sentence which would not be true if they were synonymous. For example, though "morning star" and "evening star" are equivalent, the negation of "N(morning star = evening star)" is a true sentence which indicates that these terms are not synonymous.

[11] See "Notes on Existence and Necessity," *Journal of Philosophy*, XL (1943), 113–127.

If we grant that (9) and (11) need not be equivalent, it is evident that the expression "2^{10}," like "Tegucigalpa," is subject to substitutivity in some contexts and not in others. Hence, in order to apply Quine's mode of explanation here we shall have to say that some occurrences of "2^{10}" are purely designative and some are not. This, unfortunately, commits us to a kind of Platonism which no one is more anxious than Quine to avoid. He apparently wishes to assert that expressions like "2^{10}" *never* occur designatively, for he is of the opinion that there are no such things as numbers. Now if they never occur designatively, substitution on the basis of a true identity sentence will never be possible. But we know that it is possible. Hence, this sort of explanation is difficult to combine with nominalism. I should make it clear, however, that I do not object to Quine's view because it clashes with nominalism; my objection is rather that this particular problem may be treated independently of the nominalism-realism dispute. The sentences (6)–(8) and (9)–(11) show us that substitution on the basis of a true identity sentence cannot be made in a context governed by "believes that." We can discover and utilize this fact without ever taking up the question whether number expressions or any other expressions designate anything.

C. I. Lewis has explicated synonymity in such a way that synthetic sentences are synonymous if and only if they are logically equivalent.[12] It is easy to see that this is not in agreement with our criterion. For example, consider the sentences:

(12) Jones believes that he has one nose.

(13) Jones believes that the number of his noses is equal to $-(e^{\pi i})$.

It will probably be generally agreed that these sentences might well have opposite truth values; if this is possible, then the synthetic subsentences, though they are logically equivalent, are not synonymous according to our criterion. The example chosen need not have been so extreme. In the physical sciences there are many pairs of synthetic sentences which are logically equivalent to each other but which, unfortunately, are not interchangeable in belief contexts, as any teacher will confirm.

Arne Ness, in connection with some very important empirical

---

[12] See "The Modes of Meaning," *Philosophy and Phenomenological Research*, IV (1943–1944), 236–250; and *An Analysis of Knowledge and Valuation* (La Salle, Ill., Open Court, 1946), p. 86.

research he is doing on the subject of synonymity, has mentioned several possible definitions of the term.[13] Some of these do not satisfy our criterion. According to one, for example, two sentences would be synonymous if and only if the same states of affairs would confirm or disconfirm the propositions which they express. According to this, it seems to me, all logically equivalent sentences would be synonymous; but we have seen that logical equivalence is not a strong enough condition for interchangeability in a language containing indirect discourse. According to another possibility mentioned by Ness, two sentences are synonymous if every sentence derivable from one is derivable from the other, and conversely. Now the exact meaning of this depends upon how the word "derivable" is interpreted, but if logically equivalent sentences are derivable from one another, then logically equivalent sentences would be synonymous under this definition, too. Consequently, both of these possibilities for defining "synonymity" would have to be rejected as inadequate, if our criterion of adequacy were accepted.

Carnap has proposed the concept of intensional isomorphism as an approximate explicatum for synonymity.[14] It seems to me that this is the best proposal that has been made by anyone to date. However, it has, along with its merits, some rather odd consequences. For instance, let "D" and "D'" be abbreviations for two intensionally isomorphic sentences. Then the following sentences are also intensionally isomorphic:

(14) Whoever believes that D, believes that D.

(15) Whoever believes that D, believes that D'.

But nobody doubts that whoever believes that D believes that D. Therefore, nobody doubts that whoever believes that D believes that D'. This seems to suggest that, for any pair of intensionally isomorphic sentences—let them be abbreviated by "D" and "D',"— if anybody even doubts that whoever believes that D believes that D', then Carnap's explication is incorrect. What is more, *any* adequate explication of synonymity will have this result, for the validity of the argument is not affected if we replace the words "intensionally isomorphic" by the word "synonymous" throughout.

---

[13] See *Interpretation and Preciseness*, I: *Survey of Basic Concepts* (mim., Oslo, 1947).

[14] See *Meaning and Necessity* (Univ. of Chicago Press, 1947), pp. 56 ff.

III

Interpretation is a matter of prime importance to philosophers in at least two respects. In the first place, every philosopher who deserves the name wants to understand the writings of his fellows and predecessors, and this often requires the utmost in careful and skilled interpretation. Secondly, many of the problems which philosophers seek to solve are themselves problems of interpretation or else correspond to such problems in certain characteristic ways. Both of these respects will be discussed in the present section.

Philosophical writing seems to me to have a pair of characteristics which are especially significant in the present connection. One is that it is argumentative. Very little of what would be regarded as genuine philosophical writing consists of mere musings. On the contrary, philosophers (*qua* philosophers) are nearly always trying to argue in behalf of some thesis. Often the arguments are difficult to follow; often, when they can be understood, they are seen to be invalid. Nevertheless, it seems correct to say that philosophical writing is largely argumentative.

The other characteristic to which I wish to draw attention (and to which I fear I am drawing attention) is that of relative unclarity. Whether the fault be with the subject matter or with the philosophers or with both, ·e must grant that the products are often the very reverse of lucid. I do not mention this in order to derogate from the value of philosophical writing, nor on the other hand do I bring it up in order to suggest that philosophers are persons who think deeply and whose communications are consequently not easy to understand; I only mention the relative opaqueness of philosophical writing as a matter of fact.

As a result of these two factors we often become aware, in reading the discourse of some philosopher, that he is presenting an argument in behalf of some thesis, but at the same time we are unable to understand either the thesis or the argument well enough to decide questions of truth and validity. Thus arises the need for an interpretation. We require a translation of the obscure discourse into a body of discourse which is probably much longer than the original but which consists of expressions more readily intelligible to us than the original expressions were. After the interpretation has been constructed we are better able to decide upon the truth and validity of the original discourse. Then we are at least able to make comments of the following form: 'If by A he means B, then what he says is true (or false), or his argument is valid (or invalid).' In my opinion this is the form in which philosophical criticism ought always to be made, but usually, of course, the hypothesis 'If by A he means B' is omitted.

In this procedure the chances of failing to do justice to the author under examination are very great, and the greatest danger lies in assuming that the interpretation which is the basis of the criticism is a good one. It will be instructive to examine some particular instances of philosophical criticism, with a view toward seeing in detail how errors of interpretation can lead to injustice in criticism. The first case to be presented is artificial and much simplified; yet it will be serious enough, no doubt, to provoke comment.

Suppose that in the writings of some philosopher we find this strange argument:

1) Socrates is human.
2) Human is human.
3) For every A, B, C: if A is C and B is C, then A resembles B with respect to being C.
4) Therefore, Socrates resembles human with respect to being human.[15]

In behalf of the premises of his argument, the author might offer some such considerations as the following. That Socrates is human is asserted as a matter of fact. The statement "Human is human" is an instance of "A is A," and hence is not only true but is necessarily true. The third premise is to be regarded as analytic because of the meaning of "resembles," but it may at least be illustrated by examples. So, if Socrates is a philosopher and Plato is a philosopher, then Socrates resembles Plato (with respect to being a philosopher); likewise, if lead is heavy and gold is heavy, then lead resembles gold (with respect to being heavy). Also, if Mark Twain is the author of *Innocents Abroad* and Samuel Clemens is the author of *Innocents Abroad,* then Mark Twain resembles Samuel Clemens[16] with respect to authoring this book.

---

[15] I do not propose this argument as a model of English composition, but rather as an example of discourse for which an interpretation is needed.

[16] This last is obviously an extreme case, in which the resemblance is very close! But the mere fact that we would ordinarily make the stronger statement, that Mark Twain *is* Samuel Clemens, should not lead us to suppose that the weaker statement, that Mark Twain *resembles* Samuel Clemens, is either

Given these considerations in behalf of the truth of the premises, and given the obvious fact that the argument is valid in form, we are apparently forced to accept the conclusion, which seems to express the Platonic view that Socrates resembles the Idea of Human, that is, that he resembles humanity itself. But there are certain obvious objections to the argument; and let us consider these. (I shall ignore the syntactical strangeness of the conclusion and of the second premise, since this seems to be due to a purely accidental feature of the English language, namely, that there are two terms, "humanity" and "human," which express the same property but which are such that syntax forbids their interchange.)

Probably the most serious objection that would be raised could be stated as follows. The word "is," as it appears in this argument, is ambiguous. Sometimes it means the same as the phrase "has the property," and thus when the philosopher says "Socrates is human" he means that Socrates has the property Human. But sometimes "is" means the same as "is identical with," so that the sentence "Human is human" means that the property Human is identical with the property Human. Now the third premise is plausible only so long as the word "is" retains the same meaning at both of its occurrences in the statement. Thus, the argument is either invalid or one of its premises is false.

Let us examine this objection more closely. It rests upon an interpretation of the original argument, that is, upon a translation of its four sentences into the following four sentences:

1) Socrates has the property Human.
2) The property Human is identical with the property Human.
3) For every A, B, C: if A has the property C and B has the property C, then A resembles B with respect to having the property C.
4) Therefore, Socrates resembles the property Human with respect to having the property Human.

But the argument, as thus interpreted, involves a clear *non sequitur,* and this fact is supposed to show that the original argument is really defective even though it appears to be a valid argument with true premises.

---

false or meaningless. Thus, if I see someone on the street and say to my companion, "Whoever that is, he certainly resembles President Truman," my assertion will not be false or nonsensical if it turns out that the man actually is President Truman.

In a similar way, other interpretations of the same argument
lead to the conclusion that it is unacceptable, either because it
is invalid or because at least one of its premises is false. For instance, if we resolutely translate 'A is B' everywhere into 'A has
the property B,' we get the following interpretation:

1) Socrates has the property Human.
2) Human has the property Human.
3) For every A, B, C: if A has the property C and B has the property C,
   then A resembles B with respect to having the property C.
4) Therefore, Socrates resembles Human with respect to having the property Human.

In this interpretation the argument is valid and the first and third
premises seem acceptable enough, but serious difficulties stand in
the way of our assenting to the second premise. As Russell says in
criticizing Plato: "I can say 'Socrates is human,' 'Plato is human,'
and so on. In all these statements, it may be assumed that the word
'human' has exactly the same meaning. But whatever it means, it
means something which is not of the same kind as Socrates, Plato,
and the rest of the individuals who compose the human race.
'Human' is an adjective; it would be nonsense to say 'human is
human.' "[17] Here Russell is evidently thinking of "Human is human" as meaning that the property Human has the property
Human, and not as an instance of the theorem "$\phi \hat{z} = \phi \hat{z}$."

If, then, we agree to the first interpretation of the argument, we
shall say that the author has committed the fallacy of using the
same term in different senses at certain crucial places in the argument, thus rendering the argument invalid; and if we agree to
the second interpretation, we may say that the author "has no
understanding of philosophical syntax," and that the second
premise is false or meaningless. Thus, under either interpretation, we shall deny that the conclusion is established as true by
this argument.

Now, in my opinion, the dangers in such a critical procedure are
quite evident but usually ignored. In the case at hand, none of the
considerations advanced are sufficient to justify condemnation of
the argument. For in spite of the fact that there are two interpretations of "is" such that the argument is not conclusive under
either of these interpretations, it remains to be shown that no

---

[17] *A History of Western Philosophy* (New York, Simon & Schuster, 1945),
p. 127.

plausible interpretation can be found in which the premises are true and the argument valid. This last would not be an easy thing to do, and it is probable that very few critics would wish to postpone criticism of a piece of philosophical writing until it had been ascertained that there was no plausible interpretation under which that piece of writing would be acceptable. Usually the procedure of critics is quite the reverse; each thinks that he knows well enough how the English language is used—that is, each acts as though *his* interpretation or interpretations were the only ones possible,—and consequently if the passage under scrutiny doesn't make sense when interpreted in his particular way, he judges that it doesn't make sense at all.

Hence, to return to the argument which we are using as an example, we must consider the possibility that neither of the two interpretations proposed is faithful to the sense of the original text. This amounts to considering the possibility that besides the predicative sense of the word "is," in which it always expresses a relation between things of different type, and the identity sense of the word, in which it always expresses a relation between things of the same type, there may be another more general sense of "is" such that the argument is valid when the occurrences of "is" are understood in this sense. "Well!" the objectors will immediately reply, "if there is such a sense, what is it?"

Before attempting to answer this question, let us try to decide what kind of answer is wanted. Probably no one expects the word "is" to be defined ostensively. This being so, we may fairly take the question to be a request for an English expression that is synonymous with "is." The objectors have suggested that the phrase "has the property" is synonymous with "is" in some of its occurrences, and that the phrase "is identical with" is synonymous with it in its other occurrences, and now they expect us either to accept their interpretations as final or else to set forth a phrase which is clearly meaningful and which can be regarded as synonymous with "is" in all or nearly all of its occurrences. But we may observe at once that the possibility of doing this depends in part upon the richness of English. It depends upon whether the English language happens to contain an expression which is synonymous with "is." Whether or not it does so is a purely contingent matter. If it should be the case that it does not, this would not suffice to show that there is no single sense which the word possesses in all its occurrences. As many writers have pointed out, there are in general strong reasons against the existence of synonymous expressions in a conversational language. Usually we simply do not need two expressions with the same meaning, and if there are any synonyms at all, this may be ascribed more to the ancestry of the language than to its utility. Consequently, anyone who asks what the sense of a linguistic expression is ought to be aware that there is no good reason for supposing the question answerable. If he does succeed in getting a satisfactory definition, he may thank fortune; if he does not, his only recourse is to discover the meaning of the expression from observing how it is used.

Let us now attempt to find an interpretation such that under this interpretation the argument in question is translated into a valid argument with true premises. We may proceed as follows. Generic terms like "Human" are commonly regarded as having classes for their extensions and properties for their intensions. Suppose that proper names, for example "Socrates," were also regarded in this way; then the extension of "Socrates" would be the unit class of Socrates and the intension would be the defining characteristic of Socrates. This supposition, no doubt, would represent the height of Platonism. Individuals would turn out to be abstract entities, and thus we would have to imagine it possible for us not only to see an abstract entity but even to be one! But whether or not this interpretation is Platonistic is irrelevant to the present discussion (though I shall here express my confidence that if every individual suddenly turned into his unit class, no one would notice the difference). The problem at hand is merely to construct an interpretation. Accordingly, supposing that we understand proper names as indicated, let us interpret "is" by the phrase "is included in." The argument then becomes:

1) Socrates is included in Human.
2) Human is included in Human.
3) For every A, B, C: if A is included in C and B is included in C, then A resembles B with respect to being included in C.
4) Therefore, Socrates resembles Human with respect to being included in Human.

The premises are true, since both the unit class of Socrates and the class Human are included in the class Human, and since it is not implausible to interpret "resembles" in such a way that (3) holds. Further, the argument is of valid form; therefore, we may say that under the interpretation offered, the argument is a valid argument with true premises.

I hope that the point of this fantastic example is clear. The original argument contained "Socrates is human" as its first premise. We must not suppose that the author necessarily meant what we would express by the sentence "the individual Socrates had the property Human." He may have meant what we would express by "the unit class of Socrates is included in the class Human" or "the defining property of Socrates is included in the property Human." It seems to me, therefore, that if an author's arguments become invalid under a given interpretation, common sense requires that not only the capability of the author but also the correctness of the interpretation come under suspicion.

For a second and less artificial example of philosophical argument based on questionable interpretation, I shall turn again to some aspects of the nominalism of Quine. According to Quine, it is possible to determine that a man is a "platonist" by examining how he uses variables of quantification. The term "platonist" in this sense refers to anyone who supposes that universals exist. Quine's criterion seems to be as follows: whoever applies quantifiers to object variables presupposes that there are such entities as objects; whoever applies quantifiers to class variables presupposes that there are such entities as classes; etc.[18] In behalf of this method of ascertaining ontological commitments, Quine says:

The quantifier '(Ex)' means 'there is an entity x such that,' and the quantifier '(x)' means 'every entity x is such that.' The bound variables of a theory range over all the entities of which the theory treats. That classical mathematics treats of universals, or affirms that there are universals, means simply that classical mathematics requires universals as values of its bound variables. When we say, e.g., that

$$(Ex) \ (x \text{ is prime and } 5 < x < 11)$$

we are saying that *there is* something which is prime and between 5 and 11; and this entity is in fact the number 7, a universal, if such there be.[19]

It seems quite clear, therefore, that Quine's view rests upon the assumption that sentences beginning with the existential quanti-

---

[18] Provided, of course, that the quantifiers are part of the primitive notation of the language. See "Designation and Existence," *Journal of Philosophy*, XXXVI (1939), 701–709; "On Universals," *Journal of Symbolic Logic*, XII (1947), 74–84; and the article cited in note 11 above.

[19] "On Universals," p. 75.

fier "(Ex)" are to be interpreted by sentences beginning with the phrase "there is an entity x such that." As far as I can see, this assumption is without justification. In the first place, if we examine the actual usage of mathematicians and logicians, we find that the existential quantifier is read in many different ways: "there exists an x such that," "for some x," "for some values of 'x,'" etc. These various phrases may or may not be intended by their users as always introducing ontological assertions. But in the second place, it is possible to interpret existential quantifiers in such a way that no ontological commitments are involved, save possibly commitments to the existence of expressions in the language. For instance, the sentence "(Ex) (x is prime and $5 < x < 11$)" may be interpreted by the sentence "there is a constant such that the sentence which results from substituting this constant for 'x' in the matrix 'x is prime and $5 < x < 11$' is true." Thus one might well use the existential quantifier on number variables without committing himself to the view that there are such things as numbers. This method of interpreting existential quantifiers is well known, and, to be sure, it involves certain difficulties. For example, if there is something for which there is no constant in the object language, then it is possible for "(Ex) (x is mortal)" to be false even if something is mortal. But these difficulties can be remedied to a great extent; anyhow, the interpretation is not so patently untenable that some other interpretation can be accepted as self-evidently correct. The point here, as in the other example, is that it is philosophically dangerous to assume that a given interpretation is the correct one.

This completes what I have to say concerning the interpretation of philosophical writing. The other topic of the present section is the relation between certain problems of philosophy and problems of interpretation. I shall begin by giving two examples of how philosophical problems may be expressed as problems of interpretation.

The thesis of phenomenalism might be stated roughly as follows: for every sentence about material things there exists another sentence which is about sense contents and which is synonymous with it. Possibly a better formulation of the thesis could be obtained if we specified, by lists or otherwise, two sets of terms, to be called "material-object terms" and "sense-data terms," respectively. Then we could restate the thesis in the following way: for every sentence containing a material-object term there is a synonymous sentence which contains only sense-data terms together with certain logical constants. In a corresponding way, the naturalistic position in ethics might be expressed by the statement: for every sentence containing an ethical term there is a synonymous sentence containing only terms of the approved, naturalistic variety. Again, we would have somehow to specify the set of ethical terms and the set of naturalistic terms, perhaps by lists. Presumably the terms "good," "bad," "right," "wrong," and the like, would be on the ethical list, and the naturalistic list would contain such words as "pleasure," "approval," "utility," "happiness," and the like.

Now it is important to be very clear about what does and what does not follow from the fact that these positions may be stated in the way described. For instance, does it follow that phenomenalism and naturalism are "purely verbal" theses? It certainly does not. For to find an adequate method of translating sentences containing the word "good" is no more and no less difficult than to find a so-called real definition of good, and to decide whether there is an adequate method of translating material-object sentences into sense-data sentences is exactly as difficult as to solve the metaphysical problem of whether phenomenalism is true. Again, the procedure used by Socrates in his attempt to discover a real definition of piety is essentially the same procedure that one would have to use in order to discover a complex expression synonymous with the word "piety." In general, it seems to me, we do not get rid of philosophical problems by representing them as problems of translation or interpretation; the situation is rather that the solution of either version of the problem always involves the solution of the other version.

This raises the following question: if a linguistic problem corresponding to a given philosophical problem cannot be solved unless the latter is solved, what is the use of giving attention to the linguistic version? The answer is that the linguistic version often serves to clarify the nature of the problem and to show, unfortunately, that the original problem was even more complicated than had been supposed. Consider, for example, the following linguistic version of the thesis usually called "hedonism": for every sentence containing the term "good" there is a synonymous sentence which does not contain "good" or any other ethical term, but which does contain the term "pleasure." If we investigate the problem by means of this formulation we are led to make certain distinctions which are, in my opinion, very important. We see at once that the decision whether a certain type of hedonism is true will involve deciding whether certain sentences are synonymous. Since synonymity is relative to a language, we shall need to specify some language, or, what comes to the same thing, we shall need to specify what *degree* of synonymity is required.[20] Thus, suppose that we are interested in the synonymity or lack of synonymity of the expressions "good" and "productive of pleasure." If we deal only with extensional contexts, then we can establish that these terms are synonymous if we can establish that whatever is good is productive of pleasure and whatever is productive of pleasure is good. If we speak with reference to a language which is extensional except for the presence of the modal operator "it is necessary that . . . ," then to show that the two terms are synonymous we shall have to establish not only that all good things are pleasant, and conversely, but also that it is impossible for something to be good without being pleasant, or to be pleasant without being good. If, as is more likely, we speak with reference to a language containing indirect discourse, then even though the predicators "good" and "productive of pleasure" were logically equivalent, they might not be synonymous. Thus, when the problem of whether or not this form of hedonism is true is stated as a problem of interpretation, it becomes clear that there are at least three distinguishable problems masquerading as one. It is important to be aware of this, since when we examine the writings of ethicists on hedonism, we find that those who support it usually try to show that the expressions are synonymous in the first sense (i.e., that "good" and "productive of pleasure" apply to the same things), while those who attack it try to show that the expressions are not synonymous in the second or third senses (i.e., that it is possible for something to be good and not pleasant, or that we may believe something to

---

[20] I say that two terms are synonymous to a low degree in the natural language if they are synonymous in the largest extensional sublanguage of the natural language; they are synonymous to a higher degree if they are synonymous in the largest sublanguage which is extensional except for containing modal operators; and they are synonymous to the highest degree if they are synonymous in the natural language taken as a whole.

be good without believing it pleasant). Thus these opponents hold positions which are perfectly compatible—if, I hasten to add, I have interpreted them correctly.

In this way, the linguistic version of a philosophical problem may be a useful heuristic device for attacking the problem, just as in deciding certain questions of geography it is useful to translate them into questions regarding the positions of marks on a map. But just as it would be ludicrous to suppose that maps constitute the entire subject matter of geography, so also it would be a great mistake to suppose that philosophy is or ought to be nothing more than the study of language. I trust that what I have said here has served to illustrate, if not to establish, the truth of that conclusion.

8

The Criterion of
Significance

by PAUL MARHENKE

Reprinted from *Proceedings and Addresses of The American Philosophical Association*, 23 (1950).

The Criterion of Significance[1]

PAUL MARHENKE

A CRITERION OF SIGNIFICANCE IS A STATEMENT TO THE EFFECT THAT A sentence is significant if it satisfies such and such conditions, and that it is meaningless if it does not satisfy the specified conditions. When one examines the various formulations of this criterion, it is not always clear whether the criterion is intended as a definition of the term 'significant sentence,' or whether it is intended as a generalization about significant sentences. If the criterion is intended as a definition the conditions referred to are the defining properties of a significant sentence. Thus, a sentence is often said to be significant if and only if it expresses a proposition. This formulation of the criterion is perhaps intended as a definition of the term "significant sentence," rather than as a generalization about significant sentences. If the criterion is intended as a generalization, it specifies some property that belongs to all significant sentences and only to such sentences. When the criterion of significance is formulated as the thesis that a sentence is significant if and only if it is verifiable, this thesis is perhaps intended as a generalization about significant sentences rather than as a definition.

The formulation of a criterion of significance in the sense of a generalization about significant sentences can get under way only if we already know how to distinguish between significant and meaningless sentences. Assuming that we know how to divide any given group of sentences into significant and meaningless sentences, the initial step in the formulation of this generalization is the ascertainment of the common properties of the sentences in the two groups. And assuming that these have been found, we may next find it possible to select a subset of the common properties of the significant sentences which is not also a subset of the common properties of the meaningless sentences. This subset can then be used in the formulation of a criterion of significance, and any sentence that was not used in the formulation of the criterion can be subjected to the test provided by the criterion. The sentence is significant if it has all the properties belonging to the subset, otherwise meaningless.

---

[1]Presidential address delivered before the twenty-third annual meeting of the Pacific Division of the American Philosophical Association at Mills College, Oakland, California, December 27, 28, 29, 1949.

It is theoretically possible to find a correct generalization of this sort, if we know how to distinguish between significant and meaningless sentences. We can make this distinction if we have a definition of significance, and if we can determine for every sentence whether or not it has the defining properties of a significant sentence. But we can also make this distinction if the notion of significance is taken as primitive. To be sure, it may not be possible to determine by simple inspection whether or not a given sentence is significant. But we may nevertheless be able to make this determination indirectly by showing that the sentence can or cannot be transformed into a significant sentence. The criterion we use in making this determination may be formulated in several alternative ways. (1) A sentence is significant if and only if it is translatable into a significant sentence. (2) A sentence is significant if and only if it is a member of a class of synonymous sentences. (3) A sentence is significant if and only if it is well-formed or transformable into a well-formed sentence. This criterion presupposes that certain sentences are known to be significant. Now if we have a definition of significance or a criterion of the sort just described, we can separate sense from nonsense, and we can next attack the problem of finding a criterion of significance in the sense of a generalization that is true of significant sentences and only of such sentences. If we are successful in finding one or more generalizations of this kind, we can subsequently degrade one of these generalizations to the status of a definition. Once the common properties of significant and meaningless sentences have been ascertained, we may find that the notion of significance is definable, even if our original classification of sentences into significant and meaningless was made on the supposition that significance is a primitive notion.

It would be very desirable if we had a criterion of significance either in the sense of a definition or in the sense of a true generalization about all significant sentences. But such a definition or generalization has not yet been found. It will be maintained in this paper that the criteria of significance that have been proposed suffer from two defects. (1) If they are intended as definitions of significance they are either inadequate or else reducible to the criterion for which significance is a primitive notion. (2) If they are intended as generalizations about the class of significant sentences, they are false. It will be maintained instead that the criterion of significance in its present form amounts, roughly speaking, to the statement that a sentence is significant if and only if it is transformable into a significant sentence. This is the criterion which is in fact always used when we seek to determine whether or not a sentence is significant.

In order to see how we arrive at the decision that a sentence is significant or meaningless, let us review first some of the necessary conditions that do not presuppose the notion of significance. For this purpose we need to consider only declarative sentences. Sentences other than declarative may be ignored, because an imperative, optative, or interrogative sentence is significant or meaningless only if its declarative prototype is significant or meaningless. A declarative sentence in a natural language, such as English, is a string of words such that every word, with the possible exception of certain proper names, belongs to the language in question. If the string includes words, aside from proper names, that do not belong to the language, it is not a sentence in that language, unless the definitions of these words have also been supplied, i.e., unless these words can be replaced by their defined equivalents. Though every sentence is a string of words, not every string of words is a sentence, for a sentence may be either grammatical or ungrammatical, and some strings of words are neither. A sentence is ungrammatical if it resembles, in a certain degree, a correctly constructed sentence. How great a departure from the grammatical norm is permissible before a string of words ceases to be an ungrammatical sentence we do not need to decide; we may suppose that any string of words is an acceptable sentence if a grammarian finds it possible to restore it to grammatical correctness. Now, though compliance with the rules of grammar is not a necessary condition of significance, the transformability of an ungrammatical sentence into one that is grammatically sound is a necessary condition of significance. A string of words that fails to satisfy this condition is not a sentence and hence meaningless. In other words, if a sentence is significant, it must be constructed in accordance with the grammatical rules or else it must be transformable into a sentence that satisfies these rules. A string of words may also fail to be a sentence under the foregoing characterization if there is a violation of the rules of orthography. If a string of this nature can not be transformed into a sentence, grammatical or ungrammatical, by restoring the offending words to orthographic perfection, it is meaningless. In other words, if a sentence is significant, the words of the sentence satisfy the rules of orthography or else it is transformable into a sentence whose component words do satisfy these rules.

The two conditions mentioned are, I think, sufficiently trivial to be acceptable as necessary conditions of significance without further argument. These conditions assure us only that a string of words that resists grammatical and orthographic correction is nonsensical. If a sentence is significant, the grammatical and orthographic defects can always be removed, provided we know what the intended meaning is. We shall therefore use the term 'sentence' henceforth as a synonym for the term 'grammatically correct sentence.' Since a sentence may be grammatically and orthographically correct without being significant, a significant sentence has to satisfy further conditions that are stronger than these two. The necessary condition of significance I propose to examine next is as trivial as these two, but, I think, will not be found acceptable without argument.

The condition I have in mind is one that is imposed whenever we encounter a sentence whose significance we question. If a sentence is significant, we require that it be translatable into the ordinary idiom. The ordinary idiom may be characterized, somewhat vaguely it must be admitted, as the idiom we use in communicating with one another. It is the idiom in which most conversations are conducted and in which almost all books are written. Translatability into this idiom is a necessary condition of significance, because we have but one recourse when we are asked to clarify the meaning of a sentence that is not in this idiom. It would not be to the purpose to answer the question by translating the sentence into another sentence of the same idiom, for its meaning, if it has one, would not thereby become any clearer. The problem can be met only, if at all, by translating the sentence into the ordinary idiom. But since translatability into this idiom is only a necessary condition of significance, there is no guarantee that the result of the translation is a significant sentence. Russell's nonsense sentence "Quadruplicity drinks procrastination" is a sentence in the ordinary idiom. The sentence happens to be formulated in English, but it is a simple matter to produce its translation in the ordinary idiom of French or German. Moreover, this sentence can easily be transformed into another sentence in the ordinary idiom of English by replacing "Quadruplicity" and "Procrastination" by their defined equivalents. These translations are of course in every instance as nonsensical as the original sentence.

The objection may now be made that the requirement of translatability into the ordinary idiom is too strong, and that this requirement should be replaced by the weaker condition of translatability into some other idiom. It is undeniable that often only this weaker condition is imposed when a sentence is put to the test of significance. A metaphysician, for instance, may satisfy himself that the statements of a rival metaphysician are intelligible only if he finds it possible to translate them into his own idiom. However, if a sentence is translatable into the private idiom of a metaphysician, it is also translatable into the public idiom in which communication takes place. Once we grant that a sentence is significant only if it is translatable into some other idiom, we also grant that it is significant only if it is translatable into the ordinary idiom. For if the sentence is found translatable because its meaning is known, then this meaning can also be expressed in the ordinary idiom. The objection is therefore without force. Many commentators on the works of metaphysicians appear to take the view, as a matter of fact, that the stronger condition is a necessary condition of significance. Thus, when McTaggart reaches Hegel's statement that "the Various is the Difference which is merely posited, the Difference which is no Difference," he offers the following translation into the ordinary idiom:

What is meant by this? I conceive that he means that in this category there is no special connexion of any thing with any other thing. The relation may fairly be said to be one of Indifference, if no thing has any connection with one other except that which it has to all others. And this Indifference, I conceive, arises as follows. We are now dealing with Likenesses and Unlikenesses. But everything is, as we have seen, Unlike every other thing. And it is also Like every other thing, for in any possible group we can, as we have seen, find a common quality. Thus under this category everything has exactly the same relation to everything else. For it is both Like and Unlike everything else.[2]

The works of Hegel have attracted commentators because this philosopher has written thousands of sentences that are not in the ordinary idiom. The commentators attempt to extract the cognitive meaning of these sentences by translating them into a more familiar idiom, though often with results that are satisfactory, as regards intelligibility, only to themselves. Hegel's famous statement "Being and Nothing are one and the same" is undeniably in need of clarification, as Hegel himself admitted. But his own explanation is not in the ordinary idiom, since Hegel uses the terms "the being" and "the nothing" as designative expressions, while the ordinary idiom does not countenance the use of these expressions as designative. It would be unreasonable to conclude, on this ground alone, that the statement is nonsense. But if it is

---

[2]McTaggart, A Commentary on Hegel's Logic, p. 112.

not, its cognitive content can not be appraised until it is translated into the ordinary idiom.

There is a widespread conviction, which is particularly prevalent among logical positivists, that metaphysical statements, such as the one we quoted from Hegel's Logic, are nonsense. In defense of metaphysics it is often said that such statements are intelligible, but that they create the impression that they are unintelligible, because they are expressed in an unfamiliar idiom. Their meaning is revealed only to those who have mastered the idiom. To the uninitiated they appear to be unintelligible, because their meaning is obscure and recondite. If this is the correct explanation of the belief that metaphysical statements are unintelligible, the charge of unintelligibility can easily be disproved by translating these statements into the ordinary idiom. Anyone who has mastered the esoteric idiom and knows what is being said is *ipso facto* in a position to communicate his knowledge in the language he shares with the rest of us. The requirement of translatability is often rejected on the ground that a sentence can not always be translated without loss or change of meaning. Thus it has often been alleged that a work such as Hegel's *Wissenschaft der Logik* is untranslatable. If this allegation means that this work can not be translated literally into French or English without first inventing an esoteric French or English vocabulary, it is unquestionably correct. No one knows how to translate this work literally into the ordinary idiom of these languages, just as no one knows how to translate it literally into the ordinary idiom of the German language. But if the allegation means that one can say things in German that can not be said in another language, it can easily be refuted. For as soon as one has said what can be said only in German, the required translation can at once be produced. The objection therefore has no merit whatsoever. If the proposed translation of a sentence is rejected as inaccurate or incorrect, it is always possible to improve or correct it. A translation that fails to duplicate the meaning of the original sentence can always be corrected as soon as the difference in meaning is known. There is of course a trivial sense in which no sentence is translatable into a sentence either of the same or of a different language. For the causal and particularly the emotive effects of a sentence are different from the effects of its translation, these differences being determined, in part at least, by the differences in the words alone. Translatability of a sentence requires only that its cognitive meaning be reproducible, if it has one; it does not require that its effects on a hearer or reader be reproducible as well.

One who attempts the solution of the problem of translating a work on metaphysics into the ordinary idiom has to be able to eliminate the technical terms that are used in the work, and, if their definitions have not been given, he has to be able to reconstruct these through an investigation of the sentential contexts in which these terms occur. The technical terms are the terms that are not found in the ordinary vocabulary, and, besides these, all the terms that occur in sentential contexts in which they never occur in the ordinary idiom. He must also be able to replace the terms that are used metaphorically by terms that have literal meaning, for the proposed translation is intended to duplicate only the cognitive meanings of the sentences and not also their emotive or poetic overtones. The problem of translating a work on metaphysics is thus in some respects similar to the problem of deciphering a work that has been written in code. The problem of breaking the code is attacked by taking a part of the work and then replacing the code words by words that have the effect of breaking this part up into intelligible sentences. The correct key has been found if the remaining parts of the work likewise break up into intelligible sentences by using this key. But if the key makes nonsense of the remainder, and this is perhaps the fate of most keys to the secrets of metaphysics, we have nevertheless no guarantee that the correct key has not been found, since translatability is only a necessary condition of significance. The correct key turns sentence into sentence and hence nonsense into nonsense.

That translatability is at least a necessary condition of significance is shown by the fact that we answer a question of the form "What does the sentence S mean?" by producing some sentence we believe to be synonymous with S. If you do not know what a given sentence means you ask someone who does know, and he answers you by translating the sentence into one that has the same meaning. This question is answered in exactly the same way in which a dictionary answers the question "What does the word W mean?" The dictionary specifies the meaning of a given word by means of other words. Hence, if you are ignorant of the meannigs of all words, the dictionary is of no help, and similarly, if you are ignorant of the meanings of all sentences, the meaning of a given sentence can not be explained to you. The procedure we use in explaining the meaning of a sentence suggests that a necessary and sufficient condition of significance is obtained by simply strengthening the requirement of translatability: a sentence is significant if and only if it is translatable into a significant sentence. In one sense of the term "criterion" this condition is of course not a criterion of significance. For if a criterion is formulated with the intention of providing us with a method by which we can determine whether or not a given sentence is significant, then the notion of significance can not itself be used in the formulation of such a criterion. A criterion must enable us to make this determination without the prior knowledge that any sentence is significant or meaningless. We shall now turn to the examination of two formulations of the criterion that appear to answer to this description. One of these specifies the necessary and sufficient condition of significance by means of the concept of a proposition: a sentence is significant if and only if it expresses a proposition. The other specifies it by means of the concept of verifiability: a sentence is significant if and only if it is verifiable.

The first of these formulations is based on the view that a significant sentence is related to an entity which is the significance or meaning of the sentence. This entity is the proposition expressed by the sentence. The existence of the entity demanded by this view can of course be guaranteed by defining the phrase "the proposition expressed by S" by means of the phrase "the class of sentences that are synomymous with S." However, the proponents of the view under consideration do not reckon with the possibility of defining the former phrase by means of terms that refer to linguistic entities; they assume, rather, that this phrase designates an extra-linguistic entity. Some philosophers believe that the propositions expressed by sentences are psychical or psychophysical occurrences, others that they are of the nature of Platonic universals and thus non-physical and non-psychical. Now if there are propositions and if sentences express them, and if we can identify the proposition a sentence expresses whenever such a sentence is significant, then we can decide whether or not a given sentence is significant without the prior knowledge that it is significant or meaningless. But if we are forced to make this decision independently of the fact, if it is a fact, that the sentence does or does not express a proposition, it is useless to tell us that all significant sentences and only such sentences express propositions. For this characteristic of significant sentences can not be used to distinguish sense from nonsense, if we do not know how to determine whether a sentence possesses it.

The most recent version of the view that propositions are psychophysical entities is due to Russell. Propositions, according to Russell, are to be defined as "psychological and physiological occurrences of certain sorts—complex images, expectations, etc. Such occurrences are expressed by sentences.[3] But nonsense can also cause the occurrence of complex images and expectations, and it therefore becomes necessary to differentiate the kinds of images and expectations that are expressed by significant from the images and expectations that are expressed by meaningless sentences. Russell dismisses this problem with the declaration that "the exact psychological definition of propositions is irrelevant to logic and theory of knowledge."[4] Russell finds it necessary to look for an extra-linguistic entity as the significance of a sentence in the first instance, because he thinks that the syntactical rules of significance are arbitrary unless we can find a reason for them. Apparently he thinks that this reason is to be found in the psychological and physiological occurrences that are expressed by sentences. Now perhaps there is a difference between the psychological and physiological effects that are expressed by significant and by meaningless sentences, but if there is one Russell has certainly not found it. The problem whose solution is to lead him to the discovery of the proposition is formulated by Russell in two ways. (1) "What do we believe when we believe some thing?" (2) "When a number of people all believe that there is going to be an explosion, what have they in common?" There is only one conceivable kind of answer that can be given to the first question, and that is the kind of answer that is customarily given. Depending on what we take to be the import of the question "What do you believe when you believe there is going to be an explosion?", we give one or the other of the following answers: (1) There is going to be an explosion; (2) I believe there is going to be an explosion; (3) When I believe there is going to be an explosion, I believe there is going to be an explosion. In each case the answer is given by formulating a sentence. To the second question "What is common to a number of people who believe that there is going to be an explosion?", Russell proposes the following answer: "A certain state of tension, which will be discharged when the explosion occurs, but, if their belief was false, will continue for some time, and then give place to surprise."[5] But this answer can not be quite correct. We can not rest satisfied with it because the psychological and physiological states of people who hear about an impending explosion are not the same. Even when the conditions are otherwise the same, people react in different ways to such information. And when the conditions are not the same, the state of tension aroused in a man who knows he is within one hundred yards

---

[3]Russell, An Inquiry into Meaning and Truth, p. 237.
[4]*Loc cit.*, p. 237.　　　　　　[5]Inquiry, p. 223.

of the impending explosion is quite different from the state of tension of a man who knows that the site of the explosion is one hundred miles away. Russell is quite well aware of such differences, but he thinks that they are probably only differences of degree.[6] As a matter of fact, the degree of the state of tension may be so low that the state is undetectable, again by his own admission: "When I believe something less exciting—that tomorrow's 'Times' will contain a weather forecast, or that Caesar crossed the Rubicon—I cannot observe any such occurrences in myself."[7] But if the state of tension may be of such low degree as to be undetectable, this state of tension, i.e., the proposition expressed by a sentence, can not be used for differentiating between sense and nonsense. Every significant sentence may express a proposition, as Russell claims, but this fact does not help us to distinguish significant from nonsensical sentences. The majority of sentences that come before us are too uninteresting and too unexciting; if any of them do express propositions these are too feeble to be observable. Russell's justification of the rules of syntax must hence be considered as a failure. In view of Russell's demand for a justification of these rules, he might have been expected to show that a given sentence is significant by showing that it expresses a proposition. But he never actually uses this procedure. Instead he shows that a sentence is significant by showing that it can be transformed into a significant sentence, i.e., into a sentence that is constructed in accordance with the syntactical rules.

The view that propositions are non-physical and non-psychic entities is the orthodox form of the proposition theory. The chief defect of this theory is that it forces us to hold that propositions belong to a realm of being that is inaccessible to inspection. A sentence does not come before us with the proposition it expresses, if the sentence is significant. Hence how are we going to determine, in the instance of a given sentence, whether or not it expresses a proposition, and, if we decide that it does, how are we going to determine the proposition it expresses? When we are in doubt whether a given sentence is significant, the doubt can not be removed by finding out whether or not it expresses a proposition. The criterion of significance of the proposition theory is formally similar to the criterion we use in determining whether or not a man is married. In the instance of a man, we can remove any doubt regarding his marital status by producing his wife. When we are in

---

[6]Cf. Inquiry, p. 225.
[7]Inquiry, p. 224.

doubt whether a sentence is significant, the doubt can not be similarly resolved by producing the proposition it expresses. In order to resolve the doubt concerning a sentence, we are limited to an examination of the sentence and its logical relations to other sentences.

There is a variant of the criterion of significance of the proposition theory that appears to be immune at least to the objection that propositions are removed to an inaccessible realm of being. This variant may be formulated as follows: a sentence is significant if and only if the sentence would designate a fact if the sentence were true. Aside from the fact that this criterion presupposes that we can know, independently of the condition stipulated by the criterion, that a sentence is significant, this being contained in the supposition that the sentence is true, this formulation of the criterion is objectionable on the following additional grounds. The view that sentences are designative expressions and that they designate facts is presumably based on the analogy between proper names and noun-clauses, i.e., clauses in which sentences occur as fragmentary expressions. But this analogy is defective. On the one hand, a proper name can not be eliminated from a sentence without replacing it by an expression, another proper name for instance, that performs the same semantical function. Noun-clauses, on the other hand, are not resistant to elimination. A sentence containing a noun-clause can usually be replaced by a synonymous sentence without replacing this noun-clause by another noun-clause. We have therefore no more reason to suppose that sentences designate facts than that they express propositions. The criterion moreover forces us to distinguish the facts designated by true sentences from the would-be facts designated by false sentences. These would-be facts are indistinguishable from the propositions which the proponents of this theory of significance would like to repudiate. If sentences are designative expressions, then false sentences certainly do not designate facts, if facts, whatever they may be, belong to the accessible realm of being. We can no more provide a false sentence with a fact, than we can provide a spinster with a husband by defining this personage as the man she would have been married to if she had married him.

If propositions were given with the sentences that express them, the criterion of significance of the proposition theory would be an adequate test of significance. But since only one member of this relation is ever given, this criterion must be rejected as inadequate. If the criterion is taken as a definition, it is inadequate, because the defining property can not be used in the identification of sentences as significant or meaningless. And if it is taken as a generalization, it is at best an untestable hypothesis. On the proposition theory the decision that a sentence is significant should be based on the antecedent ground that the sentence expresses a proposition. Instead, the doctrine of the proposition theory that certain sentences express propositions is based on the antecedent ground that these sentences are significant.

We come now to the much debated verifiability criterion of logical positivism. This criterion has appeared in innumerable formulations in the last twenty-five years, but we shall limit this examination to the more or less official versions of Schlick and of Carnap. An early formulation of the criterion is given by Schlick in the following terms: "It is impossible to specify the meaning of an assertion otherwise than by describing the state of affairs that must obtain if the assertion is to be true."[8] From this formulation it appears that a sentence is significant if it is translatable into a significant sentence. To take only one example, let us apply Schlick's test to the sentence "Caesar crossed the Rubicon." In the instance of this sentence we can all doubtlessly describe the state of affairs that must have obtained if the sentence is true. Presumably what is here wanted as a description of the state of affairs is not the sentence "Caesar crossed the Rubicon," though this sentence describes the state of affairs in question quite adequately, but rather some other sentence which uses a different set of words but describes the same state of affairs. We may offer the sentence "Caesar went from one bank of the Rubicon to the other" as a description of the state of affairs that must have obtained if and only if Caesar crossed the Rubicon. According to Schlick's own statement, then, the criterion of significance amounts to the assertion that a sentence is significant if it is possible to formulate another sentence which is synonymous with the given sentence. Schlick himself does not say that the second sentence must be significant, but this is of course included in the demand that this sentence be the description of a state of affairs.

Schlick appears to think that the criterion he has formulated is equivalent to the following: A sentence is significant if and only if it is possible to specify for every descriptive word that occurs in it a definitional chain (or a set of such chains) whose last link is an ostensive definition. For he says: "In order to find the meaning of a sentence we have to transform it by the introduction of successive definitions

---

[8]Erkenntnis, v. 3, p. 6.
[9]*Loc. cit.*, p. 7.

until finally it contains only words that are not further defined, but whose meanings can be given only by direct ostension."[9] We have observed previously that the condition that is here formulated is only a necessary condition of significance, unless we add the further proviso that the transformed sentence be significant. That the criterion as it stands is only a necessary condition of significance becomes obvious when we consider that Russell's nonsense sentence "Quadruplicity drinks procrastination" can easily be transformed into a sentence that contains only ostensively defined terms. But this sentence is not thereby transformed into a significant sentence.

Schlick's second formulation of the criterion may be rendered as follows: A sentence is significant if and only if it is possible to specify the circumstances under which the sentence is true.[10] This formulation is evidently equivalent to the first. For the specification of the circumstances under which a sentence is true is effected by means of sentences. The only circumstance that is at all relevant to the truth of the sentence "Caesar crossed the Rubicon" is the circumstance that Caesar did cross the Rubicon, and the only method known to man of specifying this circumstance is the formulation of a sentence such as the sentence "Caesar crossed the Rubicon" or of some other sentence synonymous with this sentence. There is another version of the foregoing formulation of the criterion in which the notion of verifiability is used. A sentence is significant if and only if it is verifiable, and it is verifiable if it is possible to give a description of the conditions under which it is true as well as of those under which it is false.[11] The property of verifiability that is mentioned in this formulation has nothing to do with verification. To say that a sentence is verifiable is simply a shorthand way of saying that it is possible to give a description of the conditions under which the sentence is true and false respectively.

Schlick's third formulation of the criterion also makes use of the notion of verifiability. But here we get a different account of what is meant by "verifiability." A sentence is significant if and only if it is verifiable, and to say that it is verifiable is to say that it is logically possible to verify it. Schlick says that "a fact or a process is logically possible if it can be *described*, i.e., if the sentence which is supposed to describe it obeys the rules of grammar we have stipulated in our language."[12] If Schlick were now called upon to show that a given sen-

---

[10]*Loc. cit.*, p. 7.
[11]Schlick, Gesammelte Aufsaetze, p. 340.
[12]*Loc. cit.*, p. 348.

tence is verifiable, we would expect him to show that the procedure of verifying the sentence is logically possible, i.e., that the procedure of verifying the sentence can be described. But this he fails to do. He considers the sentence "Rivers flow uphill," but instead of demonstrating the logical possibility of verifying this sentence, he demonstrates the logical possibility of rivers flowing uphill. It is logically possible that rivers flow uphill, because the sentence is not self-contradictory. Schlick does not say how he determines that a sentence is not self-contradictory. He apparently holds that this determination is made by examining its logical form. However, a sentence that is not self-contradictory in form may nevertheless be nonsensical. Neither the sentence S nor the sentences that describe the procedure of verifying S may have the logical form of a contradiction. But this is no guarantee that these sentences are not nonsense. Schlick's test therefore comes to nothing, because in order to apply it we must know in advance that the sentence S is significant.

Verifiability is a dispositional property of a sentence. The decision that a given sentence is verifiable is based on exactly the same sort of considerations on which one bases the decision that a sample of a given substance has a specified dispositional property. Let us take an example. The label on a bottle identifies its contents as ether and it adds the warning that ether is highly inflammable. This dispositional property is attributed to the sample before us, because of the law that ether is easily set on fire when exposed to an open flame. The law asserts an invariable connection between the defining properties of ether and another property. The dispositional property of inflammability is correctly attributed to the contents of the bottle if (i) the law is correct and (ii) the bottle contains ether. We show that a given sentence has the property of verifiability in exactly the same way. We establish (i) a law to the effect that sentences of a specified kind have invariably been verified under specified circumstances and (ii) that the sentence before us is a sentence of this kind. These two conditions are undoubtedly satisfied by sentences of many different kinds. Sentences about last year's arrivals and departures of ships in San Francisco Harbor are verifiable in the sense specified, because we can verify a sentence of this kind whenever we please by looking up the shipping news in a newspaper. Sentences about next week's weather are also verifiable in this sense, because sentences of this kind are invariably verified simply by waiting until next week's weather is here to be scrutinized. Though verifiability in this sense is a sufficient condition of significance, it is certainly not a necessary condition. If it were a necessary condition, we would have to know that every significant sentence is verifiable. There is no law to the effect that significant sentences have always been verified whenever we chose to ascertain whether one of these sentences is true. The sentence "Caesar was shaved by his barber on the morning of the day he crossed the Rubicon" is significant, but not verifiable. There are a great many sentences about Caesar, but very few of these have ever been verified. Now if the term "verifiability" is understood in the foregoing sense, Schlick's statement[13] that one can not start verifying a sentence until one has established the possibility of its verification, i.e., its verifiability, is exactly parallel to the statement that one can not start burning the ether in the bottle until one has esablished its inflammability. The demand that we first establish that a sentence is verifiable before we start verifying it is as ridiculous as the demand that we first establish that a substance is inflammable before we start burning it. If no one had ever set any substance on fire he would never have learned that some substances are inflammable, and if no one had ever verified a sentence he would never have learned that some sentences are verifiable.

The criterion of significance has so far been formulated by Schlick simply as a test of significance. We must now consider a formulation of the criterion which does not merely specify the conditions a significant sentence must satisfy, but beyond this tells us what the meaning of the sentence is. The formulation reads as follows: "Stating the meaning of a sentence amounts to stating the rules according to which the sentence is to be used, and this is the same as stating the way in which it can be verified. The meaning of a proposition is the method of its verification."[14] One wonders whether Schlick, and with him many other logical positivists who have repeated the slogan that the meaning of a sentence is the method of its verification, was quite clear in his own mind as to the meaning of the term 'method' when the meaning of a sentence is identified with the method of its verification. A method of verification is a procedure one selects for the purpose of verifying a sentence. Thus I verify the sentence "This is vinegar" by smelling the bottle or by reading the label. But the sentence obviously does not mean smelling the bottle or reading the label. It might be objected that this interpretation of the slogan is a gross misinterpreta-

---

[13]*Loc. cit.,* p. 347.
[14]*Loc. cit.,* p. 340.

tion. That this objection is without force becomes quite plain when Schlick takes occasion to refute an opponent who maintains that statements about the future are meaningless under the verifiability criterion on the ground that such statements are not verifiable. In this refutation Schlick is fully conscious of the meaning of the term "method of verification." He repels the attack and wins an easy victory by telling the opponent that statements about the future are verified by waiting for the event to happen and that waiting is a legitimate method of verification.[15] Schlick apparently never noticed that all statements about future events must be synonymous, if we should choose to verify them by waiting, and if the meaning of a statement is identical with the method of its verification.

In so far as Schlick has established a connection between the meaning of a sentence and its verifiability, he uses the term "verifiable" simply as a synonym for "transformable into a significant sentence." If, however, the term "verifiability" is understood in the ordinary sense as the possibility of describing a method by which the truth-value of a sentence may be ascertained, then verifiability is not a test of significance. For a method of testing, i.e., the test sentences, can be formulated only if we know the meaning of the sentence we are going to test. In other words, the decision that the sentence is significant must be made in advance of the testing.

Carnap's formulation of the verifiability criterion is essentially the same as Schlick's, and we shall therefore deal with it rather briefly. Although Carnap has repudiated the criterion in its original form on the ground that sentences are only confirmable and not verifiable, he nevertheless agrees with Schlick that the meaning of a sentence is linked to its verification. The answers to the two questions "What is the meaning of the sentence S?" and "How is the sentence S verified?", he says, are closely connected. Regarding this connection he makes the following guarded statement: "In a certain sense, there is only one answer to the two questions. If we know what it would be for a given sentence to be found true, then we would know what its meaning is. And if for two sentences the conditions under which we would have to take them as true are the same, then they have the same meaning. Thus the meaning of a sentence is in a certain sense identical with the way we determine its truth or falsehood."[16] Let us ask whether what

---

[15]*Loc. cit.*, p. 445.
[16]Philosophy of Science, v. 3, p. 420.

Carnap says about the close connection between the answers to the two questions "What is the meaning of the sentence S?" and "How is the sentence S verified?" is true. If someone were to ask me these questions with reference to the sentence "Caesar transivit Rubiconem flumen" my answers would be far from identical. I would answer the first question by translating it into English, and the second by referring my interlocutor to a book on Roman history. It can not have been Carnap's intention to maintain the absurd thesis that the answers one ordinarily gives to these two questions are the same or even closely connected. We must therefore suppose that he had a different type of answer in mind when he wrote that the answers to the two questions are in a certain sense identical. In order to discover the type of answer Carnap requires, let us frame the question about the verification of a sentence in the idiom he proposes: "What would it be for the sentence 'The dog lies under the table' to be found true?" I can think of only one answer: "That would be to find the dog lying under the table." If a sentence is true and if I find it true, I can report to you what I found true only by means of a sentence, either by means of the sentence I found true or a synonymous sentence. Hence, if Carnap means that a sentence is verifiable, and therefore significant if it is possible to specify the conditions under which the sentence is true, his criterion of significance is identical with the criterion of translatability, since the specification of these conditions consists in the formulation of another sentence, synonymous with the given sentence. But if Carnap means that a sentence is significant if and only if it is possible to find evidence which either confirms or refutes the sentence, then the thesis that meaning and verifiability are identical or closely connected must be rejected. For I can not know that something is evidence for or against a sentence unless I know what the sentence means.

Carnap follows Schlick also in producing a variant of the slogan that the meaning of a sentence is the method of its verification. "The meaning of a sentence," he says, "is in a certain sense identical with the way in which we determine its truth or falsehood." Carnap never reveals whether the identity hinges on the sense we give to "way" or whether it hinges on the sense we give to "meaning," or whether perhaps it hinges on some peculiar sense of both of these terms. In any case, if "way" is understood in the same way in which Schlick understands "method" then the slogan is nonsense. But if Carnap means that a sentence is significant if and only if a test method can be formulated by which the sentence can be confirmed or refuted, then the slogan is merely false, on the ground that the formulation of such a method presupposes that the meaning of the sentence is known.

We have seen that the logical positivists use the term "verifiable" in both an improper and a proper sense. In the improper sense, a sentence is said to be verifiable when it is possible to transform the sentence into a significant sentence. In the proper sense it is said to be verifiable when it is possible to formulate the observation sentences that would verify the sentence if the sentence were true. But the possibility of formulating these observation sentences presupposes that the decision that the sentence is significant has already been made. You can not devise an observation test until you know the meaning of the sentence you are going to test.

That the question whether a sentence is verifiable can be raised only after the decision that the sentence is significant has already been made becomes especially clear when one examines Ayer's definition of the term "verifiable": the sentence S is verifiable if and only if there is some sentence R and an observation sentence O such that O is deducible from S and R, but is not deducible from S alone nor from R alone. This definition presupposes that the sentences S, R, and O are all significant, for the rules of deduction apply to significant sentences only. If, however, the rules of deduction apply to nonsense also, then every sentence is verifiable and hence significant under the definition Ayer proposes. Ayer has sought to remedy this defect by revising the definition. But the revised form suffers from the same defect as the original: either the sentence that is tested by means of the criterion is known to be significant independently of the criterion or else every sentence is significant.[17]

If a sentence can not be shown to be significant otherwise than by showing that it is convertible into a significant sentence, we may expect this criterion to be used as the test of significance even by those philosophers whose official criterion would indicate a different procedure. This expectation is fully confirmed by an examination of the text. Russell never demonstrates that an apparently nonsensical sentence is significant by finding the proposition the sentence expresses. He always makes this demonstration by showing that the sentence is transformable into a significant sentence. Thus he decides that the sentence "The sound of a trombone is blue" is significant, because this sentence asserts the identity of two objects that have different names. The sentence is

---

[17]Ayer, *Language, Truth and Logic,* p. 11 sq.

thus merely false, but not nonsensical. Again he shows that the paradox to which the sentence "I am lying" gives rise, on the hypothesis that it is significant, can be avoided, if this sentence is regarded as an infinite conjunction of the sentences "I am asserting a false sentence of the first order," "I am asserting a false sentence of the second order," etc. The resulting translation is again merely false.[18] In one of his examples Russell considers the result of translating the sentence "Quadruplicity drinks procrastination" when the word "Quadruplicity" is replaced by its defined equivalent "That property of a propositional function which consists in being true for exactly four values of the variable," and he wonders how we know that the resulting translation is nonsense.[19] On his own theory it should not be too difficult to remove any doubt on this subject: you investigate the body and find out whether the resulting sentence expresses a proposition. If you fail to detect the complex images and expectations which are the components of propositions, you may be sure that the sentence is nonsense. Russell never avails himself of this procedure. The procedure would indeed be quite useless, even if it were feasible to investigate the body, since nonsense is as prolific in the production of complex images and expectations as the soundest sense.

Carnap holds that a sentence is significant when it is possible to formulate an observation sentence by which the sentence in question can be tested. But he never uses this test when he determines whether or not a sentence is significant. Like Russell he uses the test of translatability. Carnap shows how this test operates in his paper on the repudiation of metaphysics. In this paper he is concerned with showing that a great many of the sentences that occur in Heidegger's *Was ist Metaphysik?* are pseudo-sentences. These sentences are shown to be pseudo-sentences, not by applying the criterion of verifiability, or, as Carnap now prefers, of confirmability, but by showing that these sentences can not be transformed into significant sentences of the ordinary idiom.

In order to see on what grounds the metaphysical sentences of Heidegger are repudiated, it is necessary to translate some of these sentences into English. If we have to do violence to the English language in making these translations, this is unavoidable, since Heidegger had to do violence to the German language when he constructed the

---

[18]Inquiry, p. 218.

[19]Inquiry, p. 222.

originals. Heidegger begins by defining the domain of metaphysics. Science, he says, is concerned with the exploration of the real and aside from that with nothing. He then immediately asks the question which is the theme of his paper "How about this nothing?" Since science has preëmpted the realm of the real, there is nothing left for metaphysics but the exploration of the nothing. The question is then followed by sentences of which the following are typical:

Why are we concerned about this nothing? The nothing is rejected by science and sacrificed as the unreal. Science wants to have nothing to do with the nothing. What is the nothing? Does the nothing exist only because the not, i.e., negation, exists? Or do negation and the not exist only because the nothing exists? We maintain: The nothing is more primitive than the not and negation. We know the nothing. The nothing is the simple negation of the totality of being. Anxiety reveals the nothing. The nothing itself nots.

Carnap shows that none of these sentences can be transformed into significant sentences of the natural language. For in this idiom the word "nothing" is not used as a name. When it appears to be used as a name in a sentence, as for instance in the sentence "Outside there is nothing," the sentence is always transformable into the negation of an existential statement. Everyone of Heidegger's sentences in which "the nothing" is used as a designative expression is accordingly nonsensical, since these sentences are not transformable into sentences of this kind. Furthermore, even if it were assumed that the phrase "the nothing" is used as a descriptive phrase in Heidegger's sentence "The nothing exists," the contextual definition of this phrase would have to be so formulated as to yield the sentence "The nothing does not exist" as a logical consequence. Finally, Carnap points out that Heidegger introduces the meaningless verb "to not." This neologism,—the original is likewise a neologism—, appears in Heidegger's sentences without having been previously defined and can therefore not be eliminated from the sentences in which it occurs. The sentence "The nothing nots" is therefore nonsensical for a two-fold reason. Carnap concludes that Heidegger's sentences can not be constructed in a logically correct language.

A sentence is thus condemned as nonsensical by Carnap not because it is not verifiable, but because it can not be transformed into a significant sentence of the natural language or of a logically correct language which takes the place of the latter. The criterion Carnap actually uses may thus be formulated as follows: A sentence is significant if and only if it is transformable into a significant sentence of standard logical form. A sentence is of standard logical form when it is either a simple sentence or else constructible from sentences of that kind by truth-functional composition and quantification, and it is moreover significant if and only if the simple components from which the sentence is constructed are themselves significant. The conditions a sentence in standard logical form must satisfy in order to be significant are thus specified in such a way that one can decide in a finite number of steps whether or not the sentence is significant. In other words, when we examine a sentence in standard logical form with the view of determining whether it satisfies the conditions of a significant sentence, we are finally led back to the simple sentences from which the given sentence was constructed. And unless these are significant, the original sentence is not significant.

In the absence of a criterion of significance, either in the sense of a definition or a generalization, we are forced, at the present time, to take significance, with respect to simple sentences, e.g., atomic sentences, as a primitive notion. The decision whether or not a sentence not of this form is significant is made by a recursion procedure. For the simple sentences to which we are led by this procedure we have no test of significance. The criterion of significance for sentences of this form has yet to be discovered.

University of California

9

Problems and Changes
in the Empiricist
Criterion of Meaning

by CARL G. HEMPEL

Reprinted from *Revue internationale de Philosophie,* 11 (1950).

Problems and Changes
in the Empiricist Criterion of Meaning

by Carl G. HEMPEL

1. *Introduction*

The fundamental tenet of modern empiricism is the view that all non-analytic knowledge is based on experience. Let us call this thesis the principle of empiricism. [1] Contemporary logical empiricism has added [2] to it the maxim that a sentence makes a cognitively meaningful assertion, and thus can be said to be either true or false, only if it is either (1) analytic or self-contradictory or (2) capable, at least in principle, of experiential test. According to this so-called *empiricist criterion of cognitive meaning, or of cognitive significance,* many of the formulations of traditional metaphysics and large parts of epistemology are devoid of cognitive significance—however rich some of them may be in non-cognitive import by virtue of their emotive appeal or the moral inspiration they offer. Similarly certain doctrines which have been, at one time or another, formulated within empirical science or its border disciplines are so contrived as to be incapable of test by any conceivable evidence; they are therefore qualified as pseudo-

[1] This term is used by Benjamin (2) in an examination of the foundations of empiricism. For a recent discussion of the basic ideas of empiricism see Russell (27), Part Six.

[2] In his stimulating article, Positivism, W. T. Stace argues, in effect, that the testability criterion of meaning is not logically entailed by the principle of empiricism. (See (29), especially section 11.) This is correct: According to the latter, a sentence expresses knowledge only if it is either analytic or corroborated by empirical evidence; the former goes further and identifies the domain of cognitively significant discourse with that of potential knowledge; i. e., it grants cognitive import only to sentences for which—unless they are either analytic or contradictory—a test by empirical evidence is conceivable.

hypotheses, which assert nothing, and which therefore have no explanatory or predictive force whatever. This verdict applies, for example, to the neo-vitalist speculations about entelechies or vital forces, and to the "telefinalist hypothesis" propounded by Lecomte du Noüy. [1]

The preceding formulations of the principle of empiricism and of the empiricist meaning criterion provide no more, however, than a general and rather vague characterization of a basic point of view, and they need therefore to be elucidated and amplified. And while in the earlier phases of its development, logical empiricism was to a large extent preoccupied with a critique of philosophic and scientific formulations by means of those fundamental principles, there has been in recent years an increasing concern with the positive tasks of analyzing in detail the logic and methodology of empirical science and of clarifying and restating the basic ideas of empiricism in the light of the insights thus obtained. In the present article, I propose to discuss some of the problems this search has raised and some of the results it seems to have established.

2. *Changes in the testability criterion of empirical meaning*

As our formulation shows, the empiricist meaning criterion lays down the requirement of experiential testability for those among the cognitively meaningful sentences which are neither analytic nor contradictory; let us call them sentences with empirical meaning, or empirical significance. The concept of testability, which is to render precise the vague notion of being based—or rather baseable—on experience, has undergone several modifications which reflect an increasingly refined analysis of the structure of empirical knowledge. In the present section, let us examine the major stages of this development.

For convenience of exposition, we first introduce three auxiliary concepts, namely those of observable characteristic, of observation predicate, and of observation sentence. A property or a relation of physical objects will be called an *observable characteristic* if, under suitable circumstances, its presence or absence in a given instance can be ascertained

[1] Cf. (19), Ch. XVI.

through direct observation. Thus, the terms "green", "soft", "liquid", "longer than", designate observable characteristics, while "bivalent", "radioactive", "better electric conductor", and "introvert" do not. Terms which designate observable characteristics will be called _observation predicates_. Finally, by an _observation sentence_ we shall understand any sentence which—correctly or incorrectly—asserts of one or more specifically named objects that they have, or that they lack, some specified observable characteristic. The following sentences, for example, meet this condition: "The Eiffel Tower is taller than the buidings in its vicinity", "The pointer of this instrument does not cover the point marked '3' on the scale", and even, "The largest dinosaur on exhibit in New York's Museum of Natural History had a blue tongue"; for this last sentence assigns to a specified object a characteristic—having a blue tongue—which is of such a kind that under suitable circumstances (e.g., in the case of my Chow dog) its presence or absence can be ascertained by direct observation. Our concept of observation sentence is intended to provide a precise interpretation of the vague idea of a sentence asserting something that is "in principle" ascertainable by direct observation, even though it may happen to be actually incapable of being observed by myself, perhaps also by my contemporaries, and possibly even by any human being who ever lived or will live. Any evidence that might be adduced in the test of an empirical hypothesis may now be thought of as being expressed in observation sentences of this kind.[1]

We now turn to the changes in the conception of testability, and thus of empirical meaning. In the early days of the Vienna Circle, a sentence was said to have empirical

how _"?_
"name"

---

[1] Observation sentences of this kind belong to what Carnap has called the thing-language (cf., e. g., (7), pp. 52-53). That they are adequate to formulate the data which serve as the basis for empirical tests is clear in particular for the intersubjective testing procedures used in science as well as in large areas of empirical inquiry on the common-sense level. In epistemological discussions, it is frequently assumed that the ultimate evidence for beliefs about empirical matters consists in perceptions and sensations whose description calls for a phenomenalistic type of language. The specific problems connected with the phenomenalistic approach cannot be discussed here; but it should be mentioned that at any rate all the critical considerations presented in this article in regard to the testability criterion are applicable, _mutatis mutandis_, to the case of a phenomenalistic basis as well.

meaning if it was capable, at least in principle, of complete verification by observational evidence; i.e., if observational evidence could be described which, if actually obtained, would conclusively establish the truth of the sentence.[1] With the help of the concept of observation sentence, we can restate this requirement as follows: A sentence S has empirical meaning if and only if it is possible to indicate a finite set of observation sentences, O_1, O_2, ..., O_n, such that if these are true, then S is necessarily true, too. As stated, however, this condition is satisfied also if S is an analytic sentence or if the given observation sentences are logically incompatible with each other. By the following formulation, we rule these cases out and at the same time express the intended criterion more precisely:

---

[1] Originally, the permissible evidence was meant to be restricted to what is observable by the speaker and perhaps his fellow-beings during their life times. Thus construed, the criterion rules out, as cognitively meaningless, all statements about the distant future or the remote past, as has been pointed out, among others, by Ayer in (1), Chapter I; by Pap in (21), Chapter 13, esp. pp. 333 ff.; and by Russell in (27), pp. 445-447. This difficulty is avoided, however, if we permit the evidence to consist of any finite set of "logically possible observation data", each of them formulated in an observation sentence. Thus, e. g., the sentence S_1, "The tongue of the largest dinosaur in New York's Museum of Natural History was blue or black" is completely verifiable in our sense; for it is a logical consequence of the sentence S_2, "The tongue of the largest dinosaur in New York's Museum of Natural History was blue"; and this is an observation sentence, as has been shown above.

And if the concept of *verifiability in principle* and the more general concept of *confirmability in principle*, which will be considered later, are construed as referring to *logically possible evidence* as expressed by observation sentences, then it follows similarly that the class of statements which are verifiable, or at least confirmable, in principle includes such assertions as that the planet Neptune and the Antarctic Continent existed before they were discovered, and that atomic warfare, if not checked, may lead to the extermination of this planet. The objections which Russell (cf. (27), pp. 445 and 447) raises against the verifiability criterion by reference to those examples do not apply therefore if the criterion is understood in the manner here suggested. Incidentally, statements of the kind mentioned by Russell, which are not actually verifiable by any human being, were explicitly recognized as cognitively significant already by Schlick (in (28), Part V), who argued that the impossibility of verifying them was "merely empirical". The characterization of verifiability with the help of the concept of observation sentence as suggested here might serve as a more explicit and rigorous statement of that conception.

in Ayer, the obs.-sent. & the consequent, & the cpt of antecedent. is always pptn putative pptn

(2.1) *Requirement of complete verifiability in principle:*

A sentence has empirical meaning if and only if it is not analytic and follows logically from some finite and logically consistent class of observation sentences.[1]

This criterion, however, has several serious defects. The

---

[1] As has frequently been emphasized in empiricist literature, the term "verifiability" is to indicate, of course, the conceivability, or better, the logical possibility of evidence of an observational kind which, if actually encountered, would constitute conclusive evidence for the given sentence; it is not intended to mean the technical possibility of performing the tests needed to obtain such evidence, and even less does it mean the possibility of actually finding directly observable phenomena which constitute conclusive evidence for that sentence—which would be tantamount to the actual existence of such evidence and would thus imply the truth of the given sentence. Analogous remarks apply to the terms "falsifiability" and "confirmability". This point has been disregarded in some recent critical discussions of the verifiability criterion. Thus, e. g., Russell (cf. (27), p. 448) construes verifiability as the actual existence of a set of conclusively verifying occurrences. This conception, which has never been advocated by any logical empiricist, must naturally turn out to be inadequate since according to it the empirical meaningfulness of a sentence could not be established without gathering empirical evidence, and moreover enough of it to permit a conclusive proof of the sentences in question! It is not surprising, therefore, that his extraordinary interpretation of verifiability leads Russell to the conclusion: "In fact, that a proposition is verifiable is itself not verifiable" (*l. c.*) Actually, under the empiricist interpretation of complete verifiability, any statement asserting the verifiability of some sentence S whose text is quoted, is either analytic or contradictory; for the decision whether there exists a class of observation sentences which entail S, i. e., whether such observation sentences can be formulated, no matter whether they are true or false— that decision is a matter of pure logic and requires no factual information whatever.

A similar misunderstanding is in evidence in the following passage in which W. H. Werkmeister claims to characterize a view held by logical positivists : "A proposition is said to be 'true' when it is verifiable in principle'; i. e., when we know the conditions which, when realized, will make 'verification' possible (cf. Ayer)." (cf. (31), p. 145). The quoted thesis, which, again, was never held by any logical positivist, including Ayer, is in fact logically absurd. For we can readily describe conditions which, if realized, would verify the sentence "The outside of the Chrysler Building is painted a bright yellow"; but similarly, we can describe verifying conditions for its denial; hence, according to the quoted principle, both the sentence and its denial would have to be considered true. Incidentally, the passage under discussion does not accord with Werkmeister's perfectly correct observation, *l. c.*, p. 40, that verifiability is intended to characterize the meaning of a sentence—which shows that verifiability is meant to be a criterion of cognitive significance rather than of truth.

first of those here to be mentioned has been pointed out by various writers:

(a) The verifiability requirement rules out all sentences of universal form and thus all statements purporting to express general laws; for these cannot be conclusively verified by any finite set of observational data. And since sentences of this type constitute an integral part of scientific theories, the verifiability requirement must be regarded as overly restrictive in this respect. Similarly, the criterion disqualifies all sentences such as "For any substance there exists some solvent", which contain both universal and existential quantifiers (i.e., occurrences of the terms "all" and "some" or their equivalents); for no sentences of this kind can be logically deduced from any finite set of observation sentences.

Two further defects of the verifiability requirement do not seem to have been widely noticed:

(b) Suppose that S is a sentence which satisfies the proposed criterion, whereas N is a sentence such as "The absolute is perfect", to which the criterion attributes no empirical meaning. Then the alternation SvN (i.e., the expression obtained by connecting the two sentences by the word "or"), likewise satisfies the criterion; for if S is a consequence of some finite class of observation sentences, then trivially SvN is a consequence of the same class. But clearly, the empiricist criterion of meaning is not intended to countenance sentences of this sort. In this respect, therefore, the requirement of complete verifiability is too inclusive.

(c) Let "P" be an observation predicate. Then the purely existential sentence "$(Ex)P(x)$" ("There exists at least one thing that has the property P") is completely verifiable, for it follows from any observation sentence asserting of some particular object that it has the property P. But its denial, being equivalent to the universal sentence "$(x) \backsim P(x)$" ("Nothing has the property P") is clearly not completely verifiable, as follows from comment (a) above. Hence, under the criterion (2.1), the denials of certain empirically—and thus cognitively—significant sentences are empirically meaningless; and as they are neither analytic nor contradictory, they are cognitively meaningless. But however we may delimit the domain of significant discourse, we shall have to insist that if a sentence falls within that domain, then so must its denial. To put the matter more explicitly: The sentences to be qualified as cognitively meaningful are precisely those which can be significantly said to be either true or false. But then, adherence to (2.1) would engender a serious dilemma, as is shown by the consequence just mentioned: We would either have to give up the fundamental logical principle that if a sentence is true or false, then its denial is false or true, respectively (and thus cognitively significant); or else, we must deny, in a manner reminiscent of the intuitionistic conception of logic and mathematics, that "$(x) \backsim P(x)$" is logically equivalent to the negation of "(Ex) P (x)". Clearly, the criterion (2.1), which has disqualified itself on several other counts, does not warrant such drastic measures for its preservation; hence, it has to be abandoned.[1]

Strictly analogous considerations apply to an alternative criterion, which makes complete falsifiability in principle the defining characteristic of empirical significance. Let us formulate this criterion as follows: A sentence has empirical meaning if and only if it is capable, in principle, of complete refutation by a finite number of observational data; or, more precisely:

[1]

(2.2) *Requirement of complete falsifiability in principle:*
A sentence has empirical meaning if and only if its denial is

---

[1] The arguments here adduced against the verifiability criterion also prove the inadequacy of a view closely related to it, namely that two sentences have the same cognitive significance if any set of observation sentences which would verify one of them would also verify the other, and conversely. Thus, e. g., under this criterion, any two general laws would have to be assigned the same cognitive significance, for no general law is verified by any set of observation sentences. The view just referred to must be clearly distinguished from a position which Russell examines in his critical discussion of the positivistic meaning criterion. It is "the theory that two propositions whose verified consequences are identical have the same significance" ((27), p. 448). This view is untenable indeed, for what consequences of a statement have actually been verified at a given time is obviously a matter of historical accident which cannot possibly serve to establish identity of cognitive significance. But I am not aware that any logical positivist ever subscribed to that "theory".

not analytic and follows logically from some finite logically consistent class of observation sentences.[1]

This criterion qualifies a sentence as empirically meaningful if its denial satisfies the requirement of complete verifiability; as is to be expected, it is therefore inadequate on similar grounds as the latter:

(*a*) It rules out purely existential hypotheses, such as "There exists at least one unicorn", and all sentences whose formulation calls for mixed—i.e., universal and existential—quantification; for none of these can possibly be conclusively falsified by a finite number of observation sentences.

(*b*) If a sentence S is completely falsifiable whereas N is a sentence which is not, then their conjunction, S.N (i.e., the expression obtained by connecting the two sentences by the word "and") is completely falsifiable; for if the denial of S is entailed by some class of observation sentences, then the denial of S.N is, *a fortiori*, entailed by the same class. Thus, the criterion allows empirical signifiance to many sentences which an adequate empiricist criterion should rule out, such as, say "All swans are white and the absolute is perfect."

(c) If "P" is an observation predicate, then the assertion that all things have the property P is qualified as significant, but its denial, being equivalent to a purely existential hypothesis, is disqualified (cf. (*a*)). Hence, criterion (2.2) gives rise to the same dilemma as (2.1).

In sum, then, interpretations of the testability criterion in terms of complete verifiability or of complete falsifiability are inadequate because they are overly restrictive in one direction and overly inclusive in another, and because both of them require incisive changes in the fundamental principles of logic.

Several attempts have been made to avoid these difficulties by construing the testability criterion as demanding merely a partial and possibly indirect confirmability of empirical hypotheses by observational evidence.

---

[1] The idea of using theoretical falsifiability by observational evidence as the "criterion of demarcation" separating empirical science from mathematics and logic on the one hand and from metaphysics on the other is due to K. Popper (cf. (22), section 1-7 and 19-24; also see (23), vol. II, pp. 282-285). Whether Popper would subscribe to the proposed restatement of the falsifiability criterion, I do not know.

(2.3)   A formulation suggested by Ayer[1] is characteristic of these attempts to set up a clear and sufficiently comprehensive criterion of confirmability.   It states, in effect, that a sentence S has empirical import if from S in conjunction with suitable subsidiary hypotheses it is possible to derive observation sentences which are not derivable from the subsidiary hypotheses alone.

This condition is suggested by a closer consideration of the logical structure of scientific testing; but it is much too liberal as it stands.   Indeed, as Ayer himself has pointed out in the second edition of his book, *Language, Truth, and Logic,*[2] his criterion allows empirical import to any sentence whatever.   Thus, e.g., if S is the sentence "The absolute is perfect", it suffices to choose as a subsidiary hypothesis the sentence "If the absolute is perfect then this apple is red" in order to make possible the deduction of the observation sentence "This apple is red," which clearly does not follow from the subsidiary hypothesis alone.[3]

---

[1] (1), Ch. I.—The case against the requirements of verifiability and of falsifiability, and favor of a requirement of partial confirmability and disconfirmability is very clearly presented also by Pap in (21), Chapter 13.

[2] (1), 2d ed., pp. 11-12.

[3] According to Stace (cf. (29), p. 218), the criterion of partial and indirect testability, which he calls the positivist principle, presupposes (and thus logically entails) another principle, which he terms the *Principle of Observable Kinds*: "A sentence, in order to be significant, must assert or deny facts which are of a kind or class such that it is logically possible directly to observe some facts which are instances of that class or kind. And if a sentence purports to assert or deny facts which are of a class or kind such that it would be logically impossible directly to observe any instance of that class or kind, then the sentence is non-significant." I think the argument Stace offers to prove that this principle is entailed by the requirement of testability is inconclusive (mainly because of the incorrect tacit assumption that "on the transformation view of deduction", the premises of a valid deductive argument must be necessary conditions for the conclusion (*l. c.*, p. 225)). Without pressing this point any further, I should like to add here a remark on the principle of observable kinds itself. Professor Stace does not say how we are to determine what "facts" a given sentence asserts or denies, or inded whether it asserts or denies any "facts" at all. Hence, the exact import of the principle remains unclear. No matter, however, how one might choose the criteria for the factual reference of sentences, this much seems certain: If a sentence expresses any fact at all, say *f*, then it satisfies the requirement laid down in the first sentence of the principle; for we can always form a class containing *f* together with the fact expressed by some observation

(2.4)   To meet this objection, Ayer has recently proposed a modified version of his testability criterion.   The modification restricts, in effect, the subsidiary hypotheses mentioned in (2.3) to sentences which are either analytic or can independently be shown to be testable in the sense of the modified criterion. [1]

But it can readily be shown that this new criterion, like the requirement of complete falsifiability, allows empirical significance to any conjunction S.N, where S satisfies Ayer's criterion while N is a sentence such as "The absolute is perfect," which is to be disqualified by that criterion.   Indeed: whatever consequences can be deduced from S with the help of permissible subsidiary hypotheses can also de deduced from S.N by means of the same subsidiary hypotheses, and as Ayer's new criterion is formulated essentially in terms of the deducibility of a certain type of consequence from the given sentence, it countenances S.N together with S.   Another difficulty has been pointed out by Professor A. Church, who has shown [2] that if there are any three observation sentences none of which alone entails any of the others, then it follows for any sentence S whatsoever that either it or its denial has empirical import according to Ayer's revised criterion.

3.   *Translatability into an empiricist language as a new criterion of cognitive meaning*

I think it is useless to continue the search for an adequate criterion of testability in terms of deductive relationships to observation sentences.   The past development of this search—of which we have considered the major stages—seems to warrant the expectation that as long as we try to set up a criterion of testability for individual sentences in a natural language, in terms of logical relationship to observation sentences, the result will be either too restrictive or too inclusive,

sentence of our choice, which makes *f* a member of a class of facts at least one of which is capable, in principle, of direct observation. The first part of the principle of observable kinds is therefore all-inclusive, somewhat like Ayer's original formulation of the empiricist meaning criterion.

[1] This restriction is expressed in recursive form and involves no vicious circle. For the full statement of Ayers's criterion, see (1), 2d edition, p. 13.

[2] Church (11).

or both. In particular it appears likely that such criteria would allow empirical import, in the manner of (2.1)(b) or of (2.2)(b), either to any alternation or to any conjunction of two sentences of which at least one is qualified as empirically meaningful; and this peculiarity has undesirable consequences because the liberal grammatical rules of English as of any other natural language countenance as sentences certain expressions ("The absolute is perfect" was our illustration) which even by the most liberal empiricist standards make no assertion whatever; and these would then have to be permitted as components of empirically significant statements.

The predicament would not arise, of course, in an artificial language whose vocabulary and grammar were so chosen as to preclude altogether the possibility of forming sentences of any kind which the empiricist meaning criterion is intended to rule out. Let us call any such language an *empiricist language*. This reflection suggests an entirely different approach to our problem: Give a general characterization of the kind of language that would qualify as empiricist, and then lay down the following

(3.1) *Translatability criterion of cognitive meaning:* A sentence has cognitive meaning if and only if it is translatable into an empiricist language.

This conception of cognitive import, while perhaps not explicitly stated, seems to underlie much of the more recent work done by empiricist writers; as far as I can see it has its origin in Carnap's essay, *Testability and Meaning* (especially part IV).

As any language, so also any empiricist language can be characterized by indicating its vocabulary and the rules determining its logic; the latter include the syntactical rules according to which sentences may be formed by means of the given vocabulary. In effect, therefore, the translatability criterion proposes to characterize the cognitively meaningful sentences by the vocabulary out of which they may be constructed, and by the syntactical principles governing their construction. What sentences are singled out as cognitively significant will depend, accordingly, on the choice of the vocabulary and of the construction rules. Let us consider a specific possibility:

(3.2) We might qualify a language L as empiricist if it satisfies the following conditions:

(a) *The vocabulary of L* contains:

(1) The customary locutions of logic which are used in the formulation of sentences; including in particular the expressions "not", "and", "or", "if... then...", "all", "some", "the class of all things such that...", "... is an element of class...";

(2) Certain *observation predicates.* These will be said to constitute the basic empirical vocabulary of L;

(3) Any expression definable by means of those referred to under (1) and (2).

(b) *The rules of sentence formation for L* are those laid down in some contemporary logical system such as *Principia Mathematica.*

Since all defined terms can be eliminated in favor of primitives, these rules stipulate in effect that a language L is empiricist if all its sentences are expressible, with the help of the usual logical locutions, in terms of observable characteristics of physical objects. Let us call any language of this sort a thing-language in the narrower sense. Alternatively, the basic empirical vocabulary of an empiricist language might be construed as consisting of phenomenalistic terms, each of them referring to some aspect of the phenomena of perception or sensation. The construction of adequate phenomenalistic languages, however, presents considerable difficulties [1], and in recent empiricism, attention has been focussed primarily on the potentialities of languages whose basic empirical vocabulary consists of observation predicates; for the latter lend themselves more directly to the description of that type of intersubjective evidence which is invoked in the test of scientific hypotheses.

If we construe empiricist languages in the sense of (3.2), then the translatability criterion (3.1) avoids all of the shortcomings pointed out in our discussion of earlier forms of the testability criterion:

---

[1] Important contributions to the problem have been made by Carnap (5) and by Goodman (15).

(*a*) Our characterization of empiricist languages makes explicit provision for universal and existential quantification, i.e., for the use of the terms "all" and "some"; hence, no type of quantified statement is generally excluded from the realm of cognitively significant discourse;

(*b*) Sentences such as "The absolute is perfect" cannot be formulated in an empiricist language (cf. (*d*) below); hence there is no danger that a conjunction or alternation containing a sentence of that kind as a component might be qualified as cognitively significant;

(*c*) In a language L with syntactical rules conforming to *Principia Mathematica*, the denial of a sentence is always again a sentence of L. Hence, the translatability criterion does not lead to the consequence, which is entailed by both (2.1) and (2.2), that the denials of certain significant sentences are non-significant;

(*d*) Despite its comprehensiveness, the new criterion does not attribute cognitive meaning to *all* sentences; thus, e.g., the sentences "The absolute is perfect" and "Nothingness nothings" cannot be translated into an empiricist language because their key terms are not definable by means of purely logical expressions and observation terms.

4. *The problem of disposition terms and of theoretical constructs*

Yet, the new criterion is still too restrictive—as are, incidentally, also its predecessors—in an important respect which now calls for consideration. If empiricist languages are defined in accordance with (3.2), then, as was noted above, the translatability criterion (3.1) allows cognitive import to a sentence only if its constitutive empirical terms are explicitly definable by means of observation predicates. But as we shall argue presently, many terms even of the physical sciences are not so definable; hence the criterion would oblige us to reject, as devoid of cognitive import, all scientific hypotheses containing such terms—an altogether intolerable consequence.

The concept of temperature is a case in point. At first glance, it seems as though the phrase "Object x has a temperature of c degrees centigrade", or briefly "$T(x) = c$" could be defined by the following sentence, (D): $T(x) = c$ if and only if the following condition is satisfied: If a thermometer is in contact with x, then it registers c degrees on its scale.

Disregarding niceties, it may be granted that the definiens given here is formulated entirely in reference to observables. However, it has one highly questionable aspect: In *Principia Mathematica* and similar systems, the phrase "if p then q" is construed as being synonymous with "not p or q"; and under this so-called material interpretation of the conditional, a statement of the form "if p then q" is obviously true if (though not only if) the sentence standing in the place of "p" is false. If, therefore, the meaning of "if... then..." in the definiens of (D) is understood in the material sense, then that definiens is true if (though not only if) x is an object not in contact with a thermometer—no matter what numerical value we may give to c. And since the definiendum would be true under the same circumstances, the definition (D) would qualify as true the assignment of any temperature value whatsoever to any object not in contact with a thermometer! Analogous considerations apply to such terms as "electrically charged", "magnetic", "intelligent", "electric resistance", etc., in short to all disposition terms, i.e., terms which express the disposition of one or more objects to react in a determinate way under specified circumstances: A definition of such terms by means of observation predicates cannot be effected in the manner of (D), however natural and obvious a mode of definition this may at first seem to be. [1]

There are two main directions in which a resolution of the difficulty might be sought. On the one hand, it could be argued that the definition of disposition terms in the manner of (D) is perfectly adequate provided that the phrase "if... then..." in the definiens is construed in the sense it is obviously intended to have, namely as implying, in the case of (D), that even if x is not actually in contact with a thermometer, still if it *were* in such contact, then the thermometer *would* register c degrees. In sentences such as this, the phrase "if... then..." is said to be used counterfactually; and it is in this "strong" sense, which implies a counterfactual conditional,

[1] This difficulty in the definition of disposition terms was first pointed out and analyzed by Carnap (in (6); see esp. section 7).

that the definiens of (D) would have to be construed. This suggestion would provide an answer to the problem of defining disposition terms if it were not for the fact that no entirely satisfactory account of the exact meaning of counterfactual (1950) conditionals seems to be available at present. Thus, the first way out of the difficulty has the status of a program rather than that of a solution. The lack of an adequate theory of counterfactual conditionals is all the more deplorable as such a theory is needed also for the analysis of the concept of general law in empirical science and of certain related ideas. A clarification of this cluster of problems constitutes at present one of the urgent desiderata in the logic and methodology of science. [1]

An alternative way of dealing with the definitional problems raised by disposition terms was suggested, and developed in detail, by Carnap. It consists in permitting the introduction of new terms, within an empiricist language, by means of so-called reduction sentences, which have the character of partial or conditional definitions. [2] Thus, e.g., the concept of temperature in our last illustration might be introduced by means of the following reduction sentence, (R): If a thermometer is in contact with an object x, then $T(x) = c$ if and only if the thermometer registers c degrees.

This rule, in which the conditional may be construed in the material sense, specifies the meaning of "temperature", i.e., of statements of the form "$T(x) = c$", only partially, namely in regard to those objects which are in contact with a ✓ thermometer; for all other objects, it simply leaves the meaning of "$T(x) = c$" undetermined. The specification of the meaning

[1] The concept of strict implication as introduct by C. I. Lewis would be of no avail for the interpretation of the strong "if... then..." as here understood, for it refers to a purely logical relationship of entailment, whereas the concept under consideration will, in general, represent a nomological relationship, i. e., one based on empirical laws. For recent discussions of the problems of counterfactuals and laws, see Langford (18); Lewis (20), pp. 210-230; Chisholm (10); Goodman (14); Reichenbach (26), Chapter VIII; Hempel and Oppenheim (16), Part III; Popper (24).

[2] Cf. Carnap (6); a brief elementary exposition of the central idea may be found in Carnap (7), Part III. The partial definition (R) formulated above for the expression "$T(x) = c$" illustrates only the simplest type of reduction sentence, the so-called bilateral reduction sentence.

of "temperature" may then be gradually extended to cases not covered in (R) by laying down further reduction sentences, which reflect the measurement of temperature by devices other than thermometers. *Still won't cover; do objects have temperatures, if not being measured at the moment?*

Reduction sentences thus provide a means for the precise formulation of what is commonly referred to as operational definitions[1]. At the same time, they show that the latter are not definitions in the strict sense of the word, but rather partial specifications of meaning.

The preceding considerations suggest that in our characterization (3.2) of empiricist languages we broaden the provision *a* (3) by permitting in the vocabulary of L all those terms whose meaning can be specified in terms of the basic empirical vocabulary by means of definitions or reduction sentences. Languages satisfying this more inclusive criterion will be referred to as thing-languages in the wider sense.

If the concept of empiricist language is broadened in this manner, then the translatability criterion (3.1) covers—as it should—also all those statements whose constituent empirical terms include "empirical constructs", i.e., terms which do not designate observables, but which can be introduced by reduction sentences on the basis of observation predicates.

Even in this generalized version, however, our criterion of cognitive meaning may not do justice to advanced scientific theories, which are formulated in terms of "theoretical constructs", such as the terms "absolute temperature", "gravitational potential", "electric field", "ψ function", etc. There are reasons to think that neither definitions nor reduction sentences are adequate to introduce these terms on the basis of observation predicates. Thus, e.g., if a system of reduction sentences for the concept of electric field were available, then —to oversimplify the point a little—it would be possible to describe, in terms of observable characteristics, some necessary and some sufficient conditions for the presence, in a given region, of an electric field of any mathematical description, however complex. Actually, however, such criteria can at best be given only for some sufficiently simple kinds of fields.

---

[1] On the concept of operational definition, which was developed by Bridgman, see, for example, Bridgman (3, 4) and Feigl (12).

Now theories of the advanced type here referred to may be considered as hypothetico-deductive systems in which all statements are logical consequences of a set of fundamental assumptions. Fundamental as well as derived statements in such a system are formulated either in terms of certain theoretical constructs which are not defined within the system and thus play the rôle of primitives, or in terms of expressions defined by means of the latter. Thus, in their logical structure such systems equal the axiomatized uninterpreted systems studied in mathematics and logic. They acquire applicability to empirical subject matter, and thus the status of theories of empirical science, by virtue of an empirical interpretation. The latter is effected by a translation of some of the sentences of the theory—often derived rather than fundamental ones— into an empiricist language, which may contain both observation predicates and empirical constructs. And since the sentences which are thus given empirical meaning are logical consequences of the fundamental hypotheses of the theory, that translation effects, indirectly, a partial interpretation of the latter and of the constructs in terms of which they are formulated. [1] *Then what? test them?*

of Ayer again

In order to make translatability into an empiricist language an adequate criterion of cognitive import, we broaden therefore the concept of empiricist language so as to include thing-languages in the narrower and in the wider sense as well as all interpreted theoretical systems of the kind just referred to. [2] With this understanding, (3.1) may finally serve as a general criterion of cognitive meaning.

CGH:

But now an obvious patchwork of arbitrarily restricted realms of discourse, merely best means to pre-assigned end.

[1] The distinction between a formal deductive system and the empirical theory resulting from it by an interpretation has been elaborated in detail by Reichenbach in his penetrating studies of the relations between pure and physical geometry; cf., e. g., Reichenbach (25). The method by means of which a formal system is given empirical content is characterized by Reichenbach as "coordinating definition" of the primitives in the theory by means of specific empirical concepts. As is suggested by our discussion of reduction and the interpretation of theorical constructs, however, the process in question may have to be construed as a partial interpretation of the non-logical terms of the system rather than as a complete definition of the latter in terms of the concepts of a thing-language.

[2] These systems have not been characterized here as fully and as precisely as would be desirable. Indeed, the exact character of the

"We want modern science & math to be meaningful, nothing else! Now, how do we define 'meaning' for this purpose?"

5. *On "the meaning" of an empirical statement*

In effect, the criterion thus arrived at qualifies a sentence as cognitively meaningful if its non-logical constituents refer, directly or in certain specified indirect ways, to observables. But it does not make any pronouncement on what "the meaning" of a cognitively significant sentence is, and in particular it neither says nor implies that that meaning can be exhaustively characterized by what the totality of possible tests would reveal in terms of observable phenomena. Indeed, *the content of a statement with empirical import cannot, in general, be exhaustively expressed by means of any class of observation sentences.*

For consider first, among the statements permitted by our criterion, any purely existential hypothesis or any statement involving mixed quantification. As was pointed out earlier, under $(2.2)(a)$, statements of these kinds entail no observation sentences whatever; hence their content cannot be expressed by means of a class of observation sentences.

And secondly, even most statements of purely universal form (such as "All flamingoes are pink") entail observation sentences (such as "That thing is pink") only when combined with suitable other observation sentences (such as "That thing is a flamingo").

This last remark can be generalized: The use of empirical hypotheses for the prediction of observable phenomena requires, in practically all cases, the use of subsidiary empirical hypotheses [1]. Thus, e.g., the hypothesis that the agent of tuberculosis is rod-shaped does not by itself entail the consequence that upon looking at a tubercular sputum specimen through a microscope, rod-like shapes will be observed: a large number of subsidiary hypotheses, including the theory

empirical interpretation of theoretical constructs and of the theories in which they function is in need of further investigation. Some problems which arise in this connection—such as whether, or in what sense, theoretical constructs may be said to denote—are obviously also of considerable epistemological interest. Some suggestions as to the interpretation of theoretical constructs may be found in Carnap (8), section 24, and in Kaplan (17); for an excellent discussion of the epistemological aspects of the problem, see Feigl (13).

[1] This point is clearly taken into consideration in Ayer's criteria of cognitive significance, which were discussed in section 2.

of the microscope, have to be used as additional premises in deducing that prediction.

Hence, what is sweepingly referred to as "the (cognitive) meaning" of a given scientific hypothesis cannot be adequately characterized in terms of potential observational evidence alone, nor can it be specified for the hypothesis taken in isolation: In order to understand "the meaning" of a hypothesis within an empiricist language, we have to know not merely what observation sentences it entails alone or in conjunction with subsidiary hypotheses, but also what other, non-observational, empirical sentences are entailed by it, what sentences in the given language would confirm or disconfirm it, and for what other hypotheses the given one would be confirmatory or disconfirmatory. In other words, the cognitive meaning of a statement in an empiricist language is reflected in the totality of its logical relationships to all other statements in that language and not to the observation sentences alone. In this sense, the statements of empirical science have a surplus meaning over and above what can be expressed in terms of relevant observation sentences. [1]

6. *The logical status of the empiricist criterion of meaning*

What kind of a sentence, it has often been asked, is the empiricist meaning criterion itself? Plainly it is not an empirical hypothesis; but it is not analytic or self-contradictory either; hence, when judged by its own standard, is it not devoid of cognitive meaning? In that case, what claim of soundness or validity could possibly be made for it?

One might think of construing the criterion as a definition which indicates what empiricists propose to understand by a cognitively significant sentence; thus understood, it would not have the character of an assertion and would be neither true nor false. But this conception would attribute to the criterion a measure of arbitrariness which cannot be reconciled with the heated controversies it has engendered and even less with the fact, repeatedly illustrated in the present article, that the changes in its specific content have always been deter-

---

[1] For a fuller discussion of the issues here involved cf. Feigl (13) and the comments on Feigl's position which will be published together with that article.

mined by the objective of making the criterion a more adequate index of cognitive import. And this very objective illuminates the character of the empiricist criterion of meaning: It is intended to provide a clarification and *explication* of the idea of a sentence which makes an intelligible assertion.[1] This idea is admittedly vague, and it is the task of philosophic explication to replace it by a more precise concept. In view of this difference of precision we cannot demand, of course, that the "new" concept, the explicatum, be strictly synonymous with the old one, the explicandum.[2] How, then, are we to judge the adequacy of a proposed explication, as expressed in some specific criterion of cognitive meaning?

First of all, there exists a large class of sentences which are rather generally recognized as making intelligible assertions, and another large class of which this is more or less generally denied. We shall have to demand of an adequate explication that it take into account these spheres of common usage; hence an explication which, let us say, denies cognitive import to descriptions of past events or to generalizations expressed in terms of observables has to be rejected as inadequate. As we have seen, this first requirement of adequacy has played an important rôle in the development of the empiricist meaning criterion.

But an adequate explication of the concept of cognitively significant statement must satisfy yet another, even more important, requirement: Together with the explication of certain other concepts, such as those of confirmation and of probability, it has to provide the framework for a general theoretical account of the structure and the foundations of scientific knowledge. Explication, as here understood, is not a mere description of the accepted usages of the terms under consider-

[1] In the preface to the second edition of his book, Ayer takes a very similar position: he holds that the testability criterion is a definition which, however, is not entirely arbitrary, because a sentence which did not satisfy the criterion "would not be capable of being understood in the sense in which either scientific hypotheses or common-sense statements are habitually understood" ((1), p. 16).

[2] Cf. Carnap's characterization of explication in his article (9), which examines in outline the explication of the concept of probability. The Frege-Russell definition of integers as classes of equivalent classes, and the semantical definition of truth—cf. Tarski (30)—are outstanding examples of explication. For a lucid discussion of various aspects of logical analysis see Pap (21), Chapter 17.

ation: it has to go beyond the limitations, ambiguities, and inconsistencies of common usage and has to show how we had better construe the meanings of those terms if we wish to arrive at a consistent and comprehensive theory of knowledge. This type of consideration, which has been largely influenced by a study of the structure of scientific theories, has prompted the more recent extensions of the empiricist meaning criterion. These extensions are designed to include in the realm of cognitive significance various types of sentences which might occur in advanced scientific theories, or which have to be admitted simply for the sake of systematic simplicity and uniformity, [1] but on whose cognitive significance or non-significance a study of what the term "intelligible assertion" means in everyday discourse could hardly shed any light at all.

As a consequence, the empiricist criterion of meaning, like the result of any other explication, represents a linguistic proposal which itself is neither true nor false, but for which adequacy is claimed in two respects: First in the sense that the explication provides a reasonably close *analysis* of the commonly accepted meaning of the explicandum—and this claim implies an empirical assertion; and secondly in the sense that the explication achieves a "*rational reconstruction*" of the explicandum, i.e., that it provides, together perhaps with other explications, a general conceptual framework which permits a consistent and precise restatement and theoretical systematization of the contexts in which the explicandum is used—and this claim implies at least an assertion of a logical character.

Though a proposal in form, the empiricist criterion of meaning is therefore far from being an arbitrary definition; it is subject to revision if a violation of the requirements of adequacy, or even a way of satisfying those requirements more fully, should be discovered. Indeed, it is to be hoped that

---

[1] Thus, e. g., our criterion qualifies as significant certain statements containing, say, thousands of existential or universal quantifiers—even though such sentences may never occur in every-day nor perhaps even in scientific discourse. For indeed, from a systematic point of view it would be arbitrary and unjustifiable to limit the class of significant statements to those containing no more than some fixed number of quantifiers. For further discussion of this point, cf. Carnap (6), sections 17, 24, 25.

before long some of the open problems encountered in the analysis of cognitive significance will be clarified and that then our last version of the empiricist meaning criterion will be replaced by another, more adequate one.

Yale University.

Bibliographic references

(1) AYER, A. J., *Language, Truth and Logic*, Oxford Univ. Press, 1936; 2nd ed., Gollancz, London, 1946.

(2) BENJAMIN, A. C., *Is empiricism self-refuting?* (*Journal of Philos.*, vol. 38, 1941).

(3) BRIDGMAN, P. W., *The Logic of Modern Physics*, The Macmillan Co., New York, 1927.

(4) BRIDGMAN, P. W., *Operational analysis* (*Philos. of Science*, vol. 5, 1938).

(5) CARNAP, R., *Der logische Aufbau der Welt*, Berlin, 1928.

(6) CARNAP, R., *Testability and meaning* (*Philos. of Science*, vol. 3, 1936, and vol. 4, 1937).

(7) CARNAP, R., *Logical foundations of the unity of science*, In: *Internat. Encyclopedia of Unified Science*, I, 1; Univ. of Chicago Press, 1938.

(8) CARNAP, R., *Foundations of logic and mathematics. Internat. Encyclopedia of Unified Science*, I, 3; Univ. of Chicago Press, 1939.

(9) CARNAP, R., *The two concepts of probability* (*Philos. and Phenom. Research*, vol. 5, 1945).

(10) CHISHOLM, R. M., *The contrary-to-fact conditional* (*Mind*, vol. 55, 1946).

(11) CHURCH, A., Review of (1), 2nd. ed. (*The Journal of Symb. Logic*, vol. 14, 1949, pp. 52-53).

(12) FEIGL, H., *Operationism and scientific method* (*Psychol. Review*, vol. 52, 1945). (Also reprinted in Feigl and Sellars, *Readings in Philosophical Analysis*, New York, 1949.)

(13) FEIGL, H., *Existential hypotheses; realistic vs. phenomenalistic interpretations*, (*Philos. of Science*, vol. 17, 1950).

(14) GOODMAN, N. *The problem of counterfactual conditionals* (*Journal of Philos.*, vol. 44, 1947).

(15) GOODMAN, N., *The Structure of Appearance*, To be published soon, probably by Harvard University Press.

(16) HEMPEL, C. G., and OPPENHEIM, P., *Studies in the logic of explanation* (*Philos. of Science*, vol. 15, 1948).

(17) KAPLAN, A., *Definition and specification of meaning* (*Journal of Philos.*, vol. 43, 1946).

(18) LANGFORD, C. H., Review in *The Journal of Symb. Logic*, vol. 6 (1941), pp. 67-68.

(19) LECOMTE DU NOÜY, *Human Destiny*, New York, London, Toronto, 1947.

(20) LEWIS, C. I., *An Analysis of Knowledge and Valuation*, Open Court Publ., La Salle, Ill., 1946.

(21) PAP, A., *Elements of Analytic Philosophy*, The Macmillan Co., New York, 1949.

(22) POPPER, K., *Logik der Forschung*, Springer, Wien, 1935.

(23) POPPER, K., *The Open Society and its Enemies*, 2 vols., Routledge, London, 1945.

(24) POPPER, K., *A note on natural laws and so-called "contrary-to-fact conditionals"* (*Mind*, vol. 58, 1949).

(25) REICHENBACH, H., *Philosophie der Raum-Zeit-Lehre*, Berlin, 1928.

(26) REICHENBACH, H., *Elements of Symbolic Logic*, The Macmillan Co., New York, 1947.

(27) RUSSELL, B., *Human Knowledge*, Simon and Schuster, New York, 1948.

(28) SCHLICK, M., *Meaning and Verification* (*Philos. Review*, vol. 45, 1936). (Also reprinted in FEIGL and SELLARS, *Readings in Philosophical Analysis*, New York, 1949).

(29) STACE, W. T., *Positivism* (*Mind*, vol. 53, 1944).

(30) TARSKI, A., *The semantic conception of truth and the foundations of semantics* (*Philos. and Phenom. Research*, vol. 4, 1944) (Also reprinted in FEIGL and SELLARS, *Readings in Philosophical Analysis*, New York, 1949.)

(31) WERKMEISTER, W. H., *The Basis and Structure of Knowledge*, Harper, New York and London, 1948.

(32) WHITEHEAD, A. N., and RUSSELL, B., *Principia Mathematica*, 3 vols., 2nd ed., Cambridge, 1925-1927.

10

On What There Is

by **WILLARD V. QUINE**

Reprinted from *Review of Metaphysics*, 2 (1948).

ON WHAT THERE IS *

A curious thing about the ontological problem is its simplicity. It can be put in three Anglo-Saxon monosyllables : "What is there ?" It can be answered, moreover, in a word — "Everything" — and everyone will accept this answer as true. However, this is merely to say that there is what there is. There remains room for disagreement over cases; and so the issue has stayed alive down the centuries.

Suppose now that two philosophers, McX and I, differ over ontology. Suppose McX maintains there is something which I maintain there is not. McX can, quite consistently with his own point of view, describe our difference of opinion by saying that I refuse to recognize certain entities. I should protest of course that he is wrong in his formulation of our disagreement, for I maintain that there are no entities, of the kind which he alleges, for me to recognize; but my finding him wrong in his formulation of our disagreement is unimportant, for I am committed to considering him wrong in his ontology anyway.

When I try to formulate our difference of opinion, on the other hand, I seem to be in a predicament. I cannot admit that there are some things which McX countenances and I do not, for in admitting that there are such things I should be contradicting my own rejection of them.

It would appear, if this reasoning were sound, that in any ontological dispute the proponent of the negative side suffers the disadvantage of not being able to admit that his opponent disagrees with him.

This is the old Platonic riddle of non-being. Non-being must in some sense be, otherwise what is it that there is not ? This tangled doctrine might be nicknamed *Plato's beard;* historically it has proved tough, frequently dulling the edge of Occam's razor.

---

* This is a revised version of a paper which was presented before the Graduate Philosophy Club of Yale University on May 7, 1948. The latter paper, in turn, was a revised version of one which was presented before the Graduate Philosophical Seminary of Princeton University on March 15.

It is some such line of thought that leads philosophers like McX to impute being where they might otherwise be quite content to recognize that there is nothing. Thus, take Pegasus. If Pegasus *were* not, McX argues, we should not be talking about anything when we use the word; therefore it would be nonsense to say even that Pegasus is not. Thinking to show thus that the denial of Pegasus cannot be coherently maintained, he concludes that Pegasus is.

McX cannot, indeed, quite persuade himself that any region of space-time, near or remote, contains a flying horse of flesh and blood. Pressed for further details on Pegasus, then, he says that Pegasus is an idea in men's minds. Here, however, a confusion begins to be apparent. We may for the sake of argument concede that there is an entity, and even a unique entity (though this is rather implausible), which is the mental Pegasus-idea; but this mental entity is not what people are talking about when they deny Pegasus.

McX never confuses the Parthenon with the Parthenon-idea. The Parthenon is physical; the Parthenon-idea is mental (according any way to McX's version of ideas, and I have no better to offer). The Parthenon is visible; the Parthenon-idea is invisible. We cannot easily imagine two things more unlike, and less liable to confusion, than the Parthenon and the Parthenon-idea. But when we shift from the Parthenon to Pegasus, the confusion sets in — for no other reason than that McX would sooner be deceived by the crudest and most flagrant counterfeit than grant the non-being of Pegasus.

The notion that Pegasus must be, because it would otherwise be nonsense to say even that Pegasus is not, has been seen to lead McX into an elementary confusion. Subtler minds, taking the same precept as their starting point, come out with theories of Pegasus which are less patently misguided than McX's, and correspondingly more difficult to eradicate. One of these subtler minds is named, let us say, Wyman. Pegasus, Wyman maintains, has his being as an unactualized possible. When we say of Pegasus that there is no such thing, we are saying, more precisely, that Pegasus does not have the special attribute of actuality. Saying that Pegasus is not actual is on a par, logically, with saying that the Parthenon is not red; in

Meinong?

either case we are saying something about an entity whose ✓
being is unquestioned.

Wyman, by the way, is one of those philosophers who
have united in ruining the good old word 'exist'. Despite his
espousal of unactualized possibles, he limits the word 'existence' to actuality — thus preserving an illusion of ontological
agreement between himself and us who repudiate the rest of
his bloated universe. We have all been prone to say, in our
common-sense usage of 'exist', that Pegasus does not exist,
meaning simply that there is no such entity at all. If Pegasus
existed he would indeed be in space and time, but only because
the word 'Pegasus' has spatio-temporal connotations, and not
because 'exists' has spatio-temporal connotations. If spatio-
temporal reference is lacking when we affirm the existence of
the cube root of 27, this is simply because a cube root is not a
spatio-temporal kind of thing, and not because we are being
ambiguous in our use of 'exist'. However, Wyman, in an ill-
conceived effort to appear agreeable, genially grants us the
non-existence of Pegasus and then, contrary to what *we* meant
by non-existence of Pegasus, insists that Pegasus *is*. Existence
is one thing, he says, and subsistence is another. The only
way I know of coping with this obfuscation of issues is to *give*
Wyman the word 'exist'. I'll try not to use it again; I still
have 'is'. So much for lexicography; let's get back to Wyman's
ontology.

Wyman's overpopulated universe is in many ways un-
lovely. It offends the aesthetic sense of us who have a taste
for desert landscapes, but this is not the worst of it. Wyman's
slum of possibles is a breeding ground for disorderly elements.
Take, for instance, the possible fat man in that doorway; and,
again, the possible bald man it that doorway. Are they the
same possible man, or two possible men ? How do we decide ?
How many possible men are there in that doorway ? Are
there more possible thin ones than fat ones ? How many of
them are alike ? Or would their being alike make them one ?
Are no *two* possible things alike ? Is this the same as saying
that it is impossible for two things to be alike ? Or, finally, is
the concept of identity simply inapplicable to unactualized possibles ? But what sense can be found in talking of entities

which cannot meaningfully be said to be identical with themselves and distinct from one another? These elements are well nigh incorrigible. By a Fregean therapy of individual concepts, some effort might be made at rehabilitation; but I feel we'd do better simply to clear Wyman's slum and be done with it.

Possibility, along with the other modalities of necessity and impossibility and contingency, raises problems upon which I do not mean to imply that we should turn our backs. But we can at least limit modalities to whole statements. We may impose the adverb 'possibly' upon a statement as a whole, and we may well worry about the semantical analysis of such usage; but little real advance in such analysis is to be hoped for in expanding our universe to include so-called *possible entities*. I suspect that the main motive for this expansion is simply the old notion that Pegasus, e.g., must be because it would otherwise be nonsense to say even that he is not.

Still, all the rank luxuriance of Wyman's universe of possibles would seem to come to naught when we make a slight change in the example and speak not of Pegasus but of the round square cupola on Berkeley College. If, unless Pegasus were, it would be nonsense to say that he is not, then by the same token, unless the round square cupola on Berkeley College were, it would be nonsense to say that it is not. But, unlike Pegasus, the round square cupola on Berkeley College cannot be admitted even as an unactualized *possible*. Can we drive Wyman now to admitting also a realm of unactualizable impossibles? If so, a good many embarrassing questions could be asked about them. We might hope even to trap Wyman in contradictions, by getting him to admit that certain of these entities are at once round and square. But the wily Wyman chooses the other horn of the dilemma and concedes that it is nonsense to say that the round square cupola on Berkeley College is not. He says that the phrase 'round square cupola' is meaningless.

Wyman was not the first to embrace this alternative. The doctrine of the meaninglessness of contradictions runs away back. The tradition survives, moreover, in writers such as Wittgenstein who seem to share none of Wyman's motivations.

Still I wonder whether the first temptation to such a doctrine may not have been substantially the motivation which we have observed in Wyman. Certainly the doctrine has no intrinsic appeal; and it has led its devotees to such quixotic extremes as that of challenging the method of proof by *reductio ad absurdum* — a challenge in which I seem to detect a quite striking *reductio ad absurdum eius ipsius*.

Moreover, the doctrine of meaninglessness of contradictions has the severe methodological drawback that it makes it impossible, in principle, ever to devise an effective test of what is meaningful and what is not. It would be forever impossible for us to devise systematic ways of deciding whether a string of signs made sense — even to us individually, let alone other people — or not. For, it follows from a discovery in mathematical logic, due to Church, that there can be no generally applicable test of contradictoriness.

I have spoken disparagingly of Plato's beard, and hinted that it is tangled. I have dwelt at length on the inconveniences of putting up with it. It is time to think about taking steps.

Russell, in his theory of so-called singular descriptions, showed clearly how we might meaningfully use seeming names without supposing that the entities allegedly named be. The names to which Russell's theory directly applies are complex descriptive names such as 'the author of *Waverly*', 'the present King of France', 'the round square cupola on Berkeley College'. Russell analyzes such phrases systematically as fragments of the whole sentences in which they occur. The sentence 'The author of *Waverly* was a poet', e.g., is explained as a whole as meaning 'Someone (better : something) wrote *Waverly* and was a poet, and nothing else wrote *Waverly*'. (The point of this added clause is to affirm the uniqueness which is implicit in the word 'the', in '*the* author of *Waverly*'.) The sentence 'The round square cupola on Berkeley College is pink' is explained as 'Something is round and square and is a cupola on Berkeley College and is pink, and nothing else is round and square and a cupola on Berkeley College'.

The virtue of this analysis is that the seeming name, a descriptive phrase, is paraphrased *in context* as a so-called incomplete symbol. No unified expression is offered as an analysis of the descriptive phrase, but the statement as a whole which was the context of that phrase still gets its full quota of meaning — whether true or false.

The unanalyzed statement 'The author of *Waverly* was a poet' contains a part, 'the author of *Waverly*', which is wrongly supposed by McX and Wyman to demand objective reference in order to be meaningful at all. But in Russell's translation, 'Something wrote *Waverly* and was a poet and nothing else wrote *Waverly*', the burden of objective reference which had been put upon the descriptive phrase is now taken over by words of the kind that logicians call bound variables, variables of quantification : namely, words like 'something', 'nothing', 'everything'. These words, far from purporting to be names specifically of the author of *Waverly*, do not purport to be names at all; they refer to entities generally, with a kind of studied ambiguity peculiar to themselves. These quantificational words or bound variables are of course a basic part of language, and their meaningfulness, at least in context, is not to be challenged. But their meaningfulness in no way presupposes there being either the author of *Waverly* or the round square cupola on Berkeley College or any other specifically preassigned objects.

Where descriptions are concerned, there is no longer any difficulty in affirming or denying being. 'There *is* the author of *Waverly*' is explained by Russell as meaning 'Someone (or, more strictly, something) wrote *Waverly* and nothing else wrote *Waverly*'. 'The author of *Waverly* is not' is explained, correspondingly, as the alternation 'Either each thing failed to write *Waverly* or two or more things wrote *Waverly*.' This alternation is false, but meaningful; and it contains no expression purporting to designate the author of *Waverly*. The statement 'The round square cupola on Berkeley College is not' is analyzed in similar fashion. So the old notion that statements of non-being defeat themselves goes by the board. When a statement of being or non-being is analyzed by Russell's theory of descriptions, it ceases to contain any expression which even purports to name the alleged entity whose being is in question, so that the meaningfulness of the statement no longer can be thought to presuppose that there be such an entity.

Now what of 'Pegasus'? This being a word rather than a descriptive phrase, Russell's argument does not immediately apply to it However, it can easily be made to apply. We have only to rephrase 'Pegasus' as a description, in any way that seems adequately to single out our idea : say 'the winged horse that was captured by Bellerophon'. Substituting such a phrase for 'Pegasus', we can then proceed to analyze the statement 'Pegasus is', or 'Pegasus is not', precisely on the analogy of Russell's analysis of 'The author of *Waverly* is' and 'The author of *Waverly* is not'.

In order thus to subsume a one-word name or alleged name such as 'Pegasus' under Russell's theory of description, we must of course be able first to translate the word into a description. But this is no real restriction, If the notion of Pegasus had been so obscure or so basic a one that no pat translation into a descriptive phrase had offered itself along familiar lines, we could still have availed ourselves of the following artificial and trivial-seeming device : we could have appealed to the *ex hypothesi* unanalyzable, irreducible attribute of *being Pegasus*, adopting, for its expression, the verb 'is-Pegasus', or 'pegasizes'. The noun 'Pegasus' itself could then be treated as derivative, and identified after all with a description : 'the thing that is-Pegasus', 'the thing that pegasizes'.

If the importing of such a predicate as 'pegasizes' seems to commit us to recognizing that there is a corresponding attribute, pegasizing, in Plato's heaven or in the mind of men, well and good. Neither we nor Wyman nor McX have been contending, thus far, about the being or non-being of universals, but rather about that of Pegasus. If in terms of pegasizing we can interpret the noun 'Pegasus' as a description subject to Russell's theory of descriptions, then we have disposed of the old notion that Pegasus cannot be said not to be without presupposing that in some sense Pegasus is.

ie, can handle all denials of ∃x.

Our argument is now quite general. McX and Wyman supposed that we could not meaningfully affirm a statement of the form 'So-and-so is not', with a simple or descriptive singular noun in place of 'so-and-so', unless so-and-so be . This supposition is now seen to be quite generally groundless, since the singular noun in question can always be expanded into a singular description, trivially or otherwise, and then analyzed out à la Russell.

We cannot conclude, however, that man is henceforth free of all ontological commitments. We commit ourselves outright to an ontology containing numbers when we say there are prime numbers between 1000 and 1010; we commit ourselves to an ontology containing centaurs when we say there are centaurs; and we commit ourselves to an ontology containing Pegasus when we say Pegasus is. But we do not commit ourselves to an ontology containing Pegasus or the author of *Waverly* or the round square cupola on Berkeley College when we say that Pegasus or the author of *Waverly* or the cupola in question is not. We need no longer labor under the delusion that the meaningfulness of a statement containing a singular term presupposes an entity named by the term. A singular term need not name to be significant.

An inkling of this might have dawned on Wyman and McX even without benefit of Russell if they had only noticed — as so few of us do — that there is a gulf between *meaning* and *naming* even in the case of a singular term which *is* genuinely a name of an object. Frege's example will serve : the phrase 'Evening Star' names a certain large physical object of spherical form, which is hurtling through space some scores of millions of miles from here. The phrase 'Morning Star' names the same thing, as was probably first established by some observant Babylonian. But the two phrases cannot be regarded as having the same meaning; otherwise that Babylonian could have dispensed with his observations and contented himself with reflecting on the meanings of his words. The meanings, then, being different from one another, must be other than the named object, which is one and the same in both cases.

Confusion of meaning with naming not only made McX think he could not meaningfully repudiate Pegasus; a continuing confusion of meaning with naming no doubt helped engender his absurd notion that Pegasus is an idea, a mental entity. The structure of his confusion is as follows. He confused the alleged *named object* Pegasus with the *meaning* of the word 'Pegasus', therefore concluding that Pegasus must be in order that the word have meaning. But what sorts of things are meanings? This is a moot point; however, one might quite plausibly explain meanings as ideas in the mind, supposing we can make clear sense in turn of the idea of ideas in the mind. Therefore Pegasus, initially confused with a meaning, ends up as an idea in the mind. It is the more remarkable that Wyman, subject to the same initial motivation as McX, should have avoided this particular blunder and wound up with unactualized possibles instead.

Now let us turn to the ontological problem of universals : the question whether there are such entities as attributes, relations, classes, numbers, functions. McX, characteristically enough, thinks there are. Speaking of attributes, he says : "There are red houses, red roses, red sunsets; this much is prephilosophical common-sense in which we must all agree. These houses, roses, and sunsets, then, have something in common; and this which they have in common is all I mean by the attribute of redness." For McX, thus, there being attributes is even more obvious and trivial than the obvious and trivial fact of there being red houses, roses, and sunsets. This, I think, is characteristic of metaphysics, or at least of that part of metaphysics called ontology : one who regards a statement on this subject as true at all must regard it as trivially true. One's ontology is basic to the conceptual scheme by which he interprets all experiences, even the most commonplace ones. Judged within some particular conceptual scheme — and how else is judgment possible ? — an ontological statement goes without saying, standing in need of no separate justification at all. Ontological statements follow immediately from all manner of casual statements of commonplace fact, just as — from the point of view, anyway, of McX's conceptual scheme — 'There is an attribute' follows from 'There are red houses, red roses, red sunsets.

Judged in another conceptual scheme, an ontological statement which is axiomatic to McX's mind may, with equal immediacy and triviality, be adjudged false. One may admit that there are red houses, roses, and sunsets, but deny, except as a popular and misleading manner of speaking, that they have anything in common. The words 'houses', 'roses', and 'sunsets' denote each of sundry individual entities which are houses and roses and sunsets, and the word 'red' or 'red object' denotes each of sundry individual entities which are red houses, red roses, red sunsets; but there is not, in addition, any entity whatever, individual or otherwise, which is named by the word 'redness', nor, for that matter, by the word 'household', 'rosehood', 'sunsethood'. That the houses and roses and sunsets are all of them red may be taken as ultimate and irreducible, and it may be held that McX is no better off, in point of real explanatory power, for all the occult entities which he posits under such names as 'redness'.

One means by which McX might naturally have tried to impose his ontology of universals on us was already removed before we turned to the problem of universals. McX cannot argue that predicates such as 'red' or 'is-red', which we all concur in using, must be regarded as names each of a single universal entity in order that they be meaningful at all. For, we have seen that being a name of something is a much more special feature than being meaningful. He cannot even charge us — at least not by *that* argument — with having posited an attribute of pegasizing by our adoption of the predicate 'pegasizes'.

However, McX hits upon a different stratagem. "Let us grant," he says, "this distinction between meaning and naming of which you make so much. Let us even grant that 'is red', pegasizes', etc., are not names of attributes Still, you admit they have meanings. But these *meanings, whether they are named or not, are still universals,* and I venture to say that some of them might even be the very things that I call attributes, or something to much the same purpose in the end."

For McX, this is an unusually penetrating speech; and the only way I know to counter it is by refusing to admit meanings. However, I feel no reluctance toward refusing to admit meanings, for I do not thereby deny that words and statements are meaningful. McX and I may agree to the letter in our classification of linguistic forms into the meaningful and the meaningless, even though McX construes meaningfulness as the *having* (in some sense of 'having') of some abstract entity which he calls a meaning, whereas I do not. I remain free to maintain that the fact that a given linguistic utterance is mean-

C.

behaviorist ploy

ingful (or *significant,* as I prefer to say so as not to invite hypostasis of meanings as entities) is an ultimate and irreducible matter of fact; or, I may undertake to analyze it in terms directly of what people do in the presence of the linguistic utterance in question and other utterances similar to it.

The useful ways in which people ordinarily talk or seem to talk about meanings boil down to two : the *having* of meanings, which is significance, and *sameness* of meaning, or synonymy. What is called *giving* the meaning of an utterance is simply the uttering of a synonym, couched, ordinarily, in clearer language than the original. If we are allergic to meanings as such, we can speak directly of utterances as significant or insignificant, and as synonymous or heteronymous one with another. The problem of explaining these adjectives 'significant' and 'synonymous' with some degree of clarity and rigor — preferably, as I see it, in terms of behavior — is as difficult as it is important. But the explanatory value of special and irreducible intermediary entities called meanings is surely illusory.

Up to now I have argued that we can use singular terms significantly in sentences without presupposing that there be the entities which those terms purport to name. I have argued further that we can use general terms, e.g., predicates, without conceding them to be names of abstract entities. I have argued further that we can view utterances as significant, and as synonymous or heteronymous with one another, without countenancing a realm of entities called meanings. At this point McX begins to wonder whether there is any limit at all to our ontological immunity. Does *nothing* we may say commit us to the assumption of universals or other entities which we may find unwelcome ?

d.

I have already suggested a negative answer to this question, in speaking of bound variables, or variables of quantification, in connection with Russell's theory of descriptions. We can very easily involve ourselves in ontological commitments, by saying, e.g., that *there is something* (bound variable) which *etc.* red houses and sunsets have in common; or that *there is something* which is a prime number between 1000 and 1010. But this is, essentially, the *only* way we can involve ourselves in ontological commitments : by our use of bound variables. The use of alleged names is no criterion, for we can repudiate their namehood at the drop of a hat unless the assumption of a corresponding entity can be spotted in the things we affirm in terms of bound variables. Names are in fact altogether immaterial to the ontological issue, for I have shown, in connection with 'Pegasus' and 'pegasize', that names can be converted to descriptions, and Russell has shown that descriptions can be eliminated. Whatever we say with help of names can be said in a language which shuns names altogether. To be is, purely and simply, to be the value of a variable. In terms of the categories of traditional grammar, this amounts roughly to saying that to be is to be in the range of reference of a pronoun. Pronouns are the basic media of reference; nouns might better have been named pro-pronouns. The variables of quantification, 'something', 'nothing', 'everything', range over our whole ontology, whatever it may be; and we are convicted of a particular ontological presupposition if, and only if, the alleged presuppositum has to be reckoned among the entities over which our variables range in order to render one of our affirmations true.

We may say, e.g., that some dogs are white, and not thereby commit ourselves to recognizing either doghood or whiteness as entities. 'Some dogs are white' says that some things that are dogs are white; and, in order that this statement be true, the things over which the bound variable 'something' ranges must include some white dogs, but need not include doghood or whiteness. On the other hand, when we say that some zoölogical species are cross-fertile, we are committing ourselves to recognizing as entities the several species themselves, abstract though they be. We remain so committed at least until we devise some way of so paraphrasing the statement as to show that the seeming reference to species on the part of our bound variable was an avoidable manner of speaking.

If I have been seeming to minimize the degree to which in our philosophical and unphilosophical discourse we involve ourselves in ontological commitments, let me then emphasize that classical mathematics, as the example of primes between 1000 and 1010 clearly illustrates, is up to its neck in commitments to an ontology of abstract entities. Thus it is that the great mediaeval controversy over universals has flared up anew in the modern philosophy of mathematics. The issue is clearer now than of old, because we now have a more explicit standard whereby to decide what ontology a given theory or form of discourse is committed to : a theory is committed to those and only those entities to which the bound variables of the theory must be capable of referring in order that the affirmations made in the theory be true.

Because this standard of ontological presupposition did not emerge clearly in the philosophical tradition, the modern philosophical mathematicians have not on the whole recognized that they were debating the same old problem of universals in a newly clarified form. But the fundamental cleavages among modern points of view on foundations of mathematics do come down pretty explicitly to disagreements as to the range of entities to which the bound variables should be permitted to refer.

The three main mediaeval points of view regarding universals are designated by historians as *realism, conceptualism, and nominalism.* Essentially these same three doctrines reappear in twentieth-century surveys of the philosophy of mathematics under the new names *logicism, intuitionism, and formalism.*

Realism, as the word is used in connection with the mediaeval controversy over universals, is the Platonic doctrine that universals or abstract entities have being independently of the mind; the mind may discover them but cannot create them. *Logicism,* represented by such latter-day Platonists as Frege, Russell, Whitehead, Church, and Carnap, condones the use of bound variables to refer to abstract entities known and unknown, specifiable and unspecifiable, indiscriminately.

Conceptualism holds that there are universals but they are mind-made. *Intuitionism,* espoused in modern times in one form or another by Poincaré, Brouwer, Weyl, and others, countenances the use of bound variables to refer to abstract entities only when those entities are capable of being cooked up individually from ingredients specified in advance. As Fraenkel has put it, logicism holds that classes are discovered while intuitionism holds that they are invented — a fair statement indeed of the old opposition between realism and conceptualism. This opposition is no mere quibble; it makes an essential difference in the amount of classical mathematics to which one is willing to subscribe. Logicists, or realists, are able on their assumptions to get Cantor's ascending orders of infinity; intuitionists are compelled to stop with the lowest order of infinity, and, as an indirect consequence, to abandon even some of the classical laws of real numbers. The modern controversy between logicism and intuitionism arose, in fact, from disagreements over infinity.

Formalism, associated with the name of Hilbert, echoes intuitionism in deploring the logicist's unbridled recourse to universals. But formalism also finds intuitionism unsatisfactory. This could happen for either of two opposite reasons. The formalist might, like the logicist, object to the crippling of classical mathematics; or he might, like the *nominalists* of old, object to admitting abstract entities at all, even in the restrained sense of mind-made entities. The upshot is the same: the formalist keeps classical mathematics as a play of insignificant notations. This play of notations can still be of utility — whatever utility it has already shown itself to have as a crutch for physicists and technologists. But utility need not imply significance, in any literal linguistic sense. Nor need the marked success of mathematicians in spinning out theorems, and in finding objective bases for agreement with one another's results, imply significance. For, an adequate basis for agreement among mathematicians can be found simply in the rules which govern the manipulation of the notations — these syntactical rules being, unlike the notations themselves, quite significant and intelligible. *

I have argued that the sort of ontology we adopt can be consequential — notably in connection with mathematics, although this is only an example. Now how are we to adjudicate among rival ontologies? Certainly the answer is not provided by the semantical formula "To be is to be the value of a variable"; this formula serves rather, conversely, in testing the conformity of a given remark or doctrine to a prior ontological

---

* See Goodman and Quine, "Steps toward a constructive nominalism," *Journal of Symbolic Logic,* vol. 12 (1947), pp. 97-122.

standard. We look to bound variables in connection with ontology not in order to know what there is, but in order to know what a given remark or doctrine, ours or someone else's, *says* there is; and this much is quite properly a problem involving language. But what there is is another question.

In debating over what there is, there are still reasons for operating on a semantical plane. One reason is to escape from the predicament noted at the beginning of the paper : the predicament of my not being able to admit that there are things which McX countenances and I do not. So long as I adhere to my ontology, as opposed to McX's, I cannot allow my bound variables to refer to entities which belong to McX's ontology and not to mine. I can, however, consistently describe our disagreement by characterizing the statements which McX affirms. Provided merely that my ontology countenances linguistic forms, or at least concrete inscriptions and utterances, I can talk about McX's sentences.

Another reason for withdrawing to a semantical plane is to find common ground on which to argue. Disagreement in ontology involves basic disagreement in conceptual schemes; yet McX and I, despite these basic disagreements, find that our conceptual schemes converge sufficiently in their intermediate and upper ramifications to enable us to communicate successfully on such topics as politics, weather, and, in particular, language. In so far as our basic controversy over ontology can be translated upward into a semantical controversy about words and what to do with them, the collapse of the controversy into question-begging may be delayed. *delaying-action?*

It is no wonder, then, that ontological controversy should tend into controversy over language. But we must not jump to the conclusion that what there is depends on words. Translatability of a question into semantical terms is no indication that the question is linguistic. To see Naples is to bear a name which, when prefixed to the words 'sees Naples', yields a true sentence; still there is nothing linguistic about seeing Naples.

Our acceptance of an ontology is, I think, similar in principle to our acceptance of a scientific theory, say a system of physics : we adopt, at least insofar as we are reasonable, the simplest conceptual scheme into which the disordered fragments of raw experience can be fitted and arranged. Our ontology is determined once we have fixed upon the over-all conceptual scheme which is to accommodate science in the broadest sense; and the considerations which determine a reasonable construction of any part of that conceptual scheme, e.g. the biological or the physical part, are not different in kind from the considerations which determine a reasonable construction of the whole. To whatever extent the adoption of any system of scientific theory may be said to be a matter of language, the same — but no more — may be said of the adoption of an ontology.

But simplicity, as a guiding principle in constructing conceptual schemes, is not a clear and unambiguous idea; and it is quite capable of presenting a double or multiple standard. Imagine, e.g., that we have devised the most economical set of concepts adequate to the play-by-play reporting of immediate experience. The entities under this scheme — the values of bound variables — are, let us suppose, individual subjective events of sensation or reflection. We should still find, no doubt, that a physicalistic conceptual scheme, purporting to talk about external objects, offers great advantages in simplifying our over-all reports. By bringing together scattered sense events and treating them as perceptions of one object, we reduce the complexity of our stream of experience to a manageable conceptual simplicity. The rule of simplicity is indeed our guiding maxim in assigning sense data to objects : we associate an earlier and a later round sensum with the same so-called penny, or with two different so-called pennies, in obedience to the demands of maximum simplicity in our total world-picture.

Here we have two competing conceptual schemes, a phenomenalistic one and a physicalistic one. Which should prevail ? Each has its advantages; each has its special simplicity in its own way. Each, I suggest, deserves to be developed. Each may be said, indeed, to be the more fundamental, though in different senses : the one is epistemologically, the other physically, fundamental.

The physical conceptual scheme simplifies our account of experience because of the way myriad scattered sense events come to be associated with single so-called objects; still there is no likelihood that each sentence about physical objects can actually be translated, however deviously and complexly, into the phenomenalistic language. Physical objects are postulated entities which round out and simplify our account of the flux of experience, just as the introduction of irrational numbers simplifies laws of arithmetic. From the point of view of the conceptual scheme of the elementary arithmetic of rational numbers alone, the broader arithmetic of rational and irrational numbers would have the status of a convenient myth, simpler than the literal truth (namely the arithmetic of rationals) and yet containing that literal truth as a scattered part. Similarly, from a phenomenalistic point of view, the conceptual scheme of physical objects is a convient myth, simpler than the literal truth and yet containing that literal truth as a scattered part.

Now what of classes or attributes of physical objects, in turn? A platonistic ontology of this sort is, from the point of view of a strictly physicalistic conceptual scheme, as much of a myth as that physicalistic conceptual scheme itself was for phenomenalism. This higher myth is a good and useful one, in turn, in so far as it simplifies our account of physics. Since mathematics is an integral part of this higher myth, the utility of this myth for physical science is evident enough. In speaking of it nevertheless as a myth, I echo that philosophy of mathematics to which I alluded earlier under the name of formalism. But my present suggestion is that an attitude of formalism may with equal justice be adopted toward the physical conceptual scheme, in turn, by the pure aesthete or phenomenalist.

The analogy between the myth of mathematics and the myth of physics is, in some additional and perhaps fortuitous ways, strikingly close. Consider, for example, the crisis which was precipitated in the foundations of mathematics, at the turn of the century, by the discovery of Russell's paradox and other antinomies of set theory. These contradictions had to be obviated by unintuitive, *ad hoc* devices; our mathematical mythmaking became deliberate and evident to all. But what of physics? An antinomy arose between the undular and the corpuscular accounts of light; and if this was not as out-and-out a contradiction as Russell's paradox, I suspect that the reason is merely that physics is not as out-and-out as mathematics.

Again, the second great modern crisis in the foundations of mathematics — precipitated in 1931 by Gödel's proof that there are bound to be undecidable statements in arithmetic — has its companion-piece in physics in Heisenberg's indeterminacy principle.

In earlier pages I undertook to show that some common arguments in favor of certain ontologies are fallacious. Further, I advanced an explicit standard whereby to decide what the ontological commitments of a theory are. But the question what ontology actually to adopt still stands open, and the obvious counsel is tolerance and an experimental spirit. Let us by all means see how much of the physicalistic conceptual scheme can be reduced to a phenomenalistic one; still physics also naturally demands pursuing, irreducible *in toto* though it be. Let us see how, or to what degree, natural science may be rendered independent of platonistic mathematics; but let us also pursue mathematics and delve into its platonistic foundations.

From among the various conceptual schemes best suited to these various pursuits, one — the phenomenalistic — claims epistemological priority. Viewed from within the phenomenalistic conceptual scheme, the ontologies of physical objects and mathematical objects are myths. The quality of myth, however, is relative; relative, in this case, to the epistemological point of view. This point of view is one among various, corresponding to one among our various interests and purposes.

WILLARD V. QUINE

Harvard University

11

Empiricism, Semantics, and Ontology

by RUDOLF CARNAP

Reprinted from *Revue internationale de Philosophie*, 11 (1950).

Empiricism, Semantics, and Ontology

by Rudolf CARNAP

1. *The Problem of Abstract Entities*

Empiricists are in general rather suspicious with respect to any kind of abstract entities like properties, classes, relations, numbers, propositions, etc. They usually feel much more in sympathy with nominalists than with realists (in the medieval sense). As far as possible they try to avoid any reference to abstract entities and to restrict themselves to what is sometimes called a nominalistic language, i. e., one not containing such references. However, within certain scientific contexts it seems hardly possible to avoid them. In the case of mathematics, some empiricists try to find a way out by treating the whole of mathematics as a mere calculus, a formal system for which no interpretation is given or can be given. Accordingly, the mathematician is said to speak not about numbers, functions, and infinite classes, but merely about meaningless symbols and formulas manipulated according to given formal rules. In physics it is more difficult to shun the suspected entities, because the language of physics serves for the communication of reports and predictions and hence cannot be taken as a mere calculus. A physicist who is suspicious of abstract entities may perhaps try to declare a certain part of the language of physics as uninterpreted and uninterpretable, that part which refers to real numbers as space-time coordinates or as values of physical magnitudes, to functions, limits, etc. More probably he will just speak about all these things like anybody else but with an uneasy conscience, like a man who in his everyday life does with qualms many things which are not in accord with the high

ofesses on Sundays. Recently the
ties has arisen again in connection
ory of meaning and truth. Some
ertain expressions designate certain
e designated entities they include not
ings but also abstract entities, e. g.,
by predicates and propositions as
[1]. Others object strongly to this
e basic principles of empiricism and
ysical ontology of the Platonic kind.

his article to clarify this controversial
implications of the acceptance of a
ostract entities will first be discussed
own that using such a language does
Platonic ontology but is perfectly
cism and strictly scientific thinking.
on of the role of abstract entities in
ed. It is hoped that the clarification
ul to those who would like to accept
eir work in mathematics, physics,
field; it may help them to overcome

2. Frameworks of Entities

Are there properties, classes, numbers, propositions? In
order to understand more clearly the nature of these and
related problems, it is above all necessary to recognize a
fundamental distinction between two kinds of questions
concerning the existence or reality of entities. If someone
wishes to speak in his language about a new kind of entities,
he has to introduce a system of new ways of speaking, subject
to new rules; we shall call this procedure the construction
of a *framework* for the new entities in question. And now
we must distinguish two kinds of questions of existence:
first, questions of the existence of certain entities of the new
kind *within the framework*; we call them *internal questions*;
and second, questions concerning the existence or reality *of*

[1] The terms "sentence" and "statement" are here used synonymously for declarative (indicative, propositional) sentences.

the framework itself, called *external questions.* Internal questions and possible answers to them are formulated with the help of the new forms of expressions. The answers may be found either by purely logical methods or by empirical methods, depending upon whether the framework is a logical or a factual one. An external question is of a problematic character which is in need of closer examination.

The world of things. Let us consider as an example the simplest framework dealt with in the everyday language: the spatio-temporally ordered system of observable things and events. Once we have accepted this thing-language and thereby the framework of things, we can raise and answer internal questions, e. g., "Is there a white piece of paper on my desk?", "Did King Arthur actually live?", "Are unicorns and centaurs real or merely imaginary?", and the like. These questions are to be answered by empirical investigations. Results of observations are evaluated according to certain rules as confirming or disconfirming evidence for possible answers. (This evaluation is usually carried out, of course, as a matter of habit rather than a deliberate, rational procedure. But it is possible, in a rational reconstruction, to lay down explicit rules for the evaluation. This is one of the main tasks of a pure, as distinguished from a psychological epistemology.) The concept of reality occurring in these internal questions is an empirical, scientific, non-metaphysical concept. To recognize something as a real thing or event means to succeed in incorporating it into the framework of things at a particular space-time position so that it fits together with the other things recognized as real, according to the rules of the framework.

From these questions we must distinguish the external question of the reality of the thing world itself. In contrast to the former questions, this question is raised neither by the man in the street nor by scientists, but only by philosophers. Realists give an affirmative answer, subjective idealists a negative one, and the controversy goes on for centuries without ever being solved. And it cannot be solved because it is framed in a wrong way. To be real in the scientific sense means to be an element of the framework; hence this concept cannot be meaningfully applied to the framework itself. Those who raise the question of the reality of the thing world itself have perhaps in mind not a theoretical question as their formulation seems to suggest, but rather a practical question, a matter of a practical decision concerning the structure of our language. We have to make the choice whether or not to accept and use the forms of expression for the framework in question.

In the case of this particular example, there is usually no deliberate choice because we all have accepted the thing language early in our lives as a matter of course. Nevertheless, we may regard it as a matter of decision in this sense: we are free to choose to continue using the thing language or not; in the latter case we could restrict ourselves to a language of sense-data and other "phenomenal" entities, or construct an alternative to the customary thing language with another structure, or, finally, we could refrain from speaking. If someone decides to accept the thing language, there is no objection against saying that he has accepted the world of things. But this must not be interpreted as if it meant his acceptance of a *belief* in the reality of the thing world; there is no such belief or assertion or assumption, because it is not a theoretical question. To accept the thing world means nothing more than to accept a certain form of language, in other words, to accept rules for forming statements and for testing, accepting, or rejecting them. Thus the acceptance of the thing language leads, on the basis of observations made, also to the acceptance, belief, and assertion of certain statements. But the thesis of the reality of the thing world cannot be among these statements, because it cannot be formulated in the thing language or, it seems, in any other theoretical language.

The decision of accepting the thing language, althoug itself not of a cognitive nature, will nevertheless usually be influenced by theoretical knowledge, just like any other deliberate decision concerning the acceptance of linguistic or other rules. The purposes for which the language is intended to be used, for instance, the purpose of communicating factual knowledge, will determine which factors are relevant for the decision. The efficiency, fruitfulness, and simplicity of the use of the thing language may be among the decisive factors.

And the questions concerning these qualities are indeed of a theoretical nature. But these questions cannot be identified with the question of realism. They are not yes-no questions but questions of degree. The thing language in the customary form works indeed with a high degree of efficiency for most purposes of everyday life. This is a matter of fact, based upon the content of our experiences. However, it would be wrong to describe this situation by saying: "The fact of the efficiency of the thing language is confirming evidence for the reality of the thing world"; we should rather say instead: "This fact makes it advisable to accept the thing language".

The system of numbers. As an example of a framework which is of a logical rather than a factual nature let us take the system of natural numbers. This system is established by introducing into the language new expressions with suitable rules: (1) numerals like "five" and sentence forms like "there are five books on the table"; (2) The general term "number" for the new entities, and sentence forms like "five is a number"; (3) expressions for properties of numbers (e. g., "odd", "prime"), relations (e. g., "greater than"), and functions (e. g., "plus"), and sentence forms like "two plus three is five"; (4) numerical variables ("m","n", etc.) and quantifiers for universal sentences ("for every n, ...") and existential sentences ("there is an n such that ...") with the customary deductive rules.

Here again there are internal questions, e. g., "Is there a prime number greater than hundred?" Here, however, the answers are found, not by empirical investigation based on observations, but by logical analysis based on the rules for the new expressions. Therefore the answers are here analytic, i. e., logically true.

What is now the nature of the philosophical question concerning the existence or reality of numbers? To begin with, there is the internal question which, together with the affirmative answer, can be formulated in the new terms, say, by "There are numbers" or, more explicitly, "There is an n such that n is a number". This statement follows from the analytic statement "five is a number" and is therefore itself analytic. Moreover, it is rather trivial (in contradistinction to a statement like "There is a prime number greater than a million", which is likewise analytic but far from trivial), because it does not say more than that the new system is not empty; but this is immediately seen from the rule which states that words like "five" are substitutable for the new variables. Therefore nobody who meant the question "Are there numbers?" in the internal sense would either assert or even seriously consider a negative answer. This makes it plausible to assume that those philosophers who treat the question of the existence of numbers as a serious philosophical problem and offer lengthy arguments on either side, do not have in mind the internal question. And, indeed, if we were to ask them: "Do you mean the question as to whether the system of numbers, *if* we were to accept it, would be found to be empty or not?", they would probably reply: "Not at all; we mean a question *prior* to the acceptance of the new framework". They might try to explain what they mean by saying that it is a question of the ontological status of numbers; the question whether or not numbers have a certain metaphysical characteristic called reality (but a kind of ideal reality, different from the material reality of the thing world) or subsistence or status of "independent entities". Unfortunately, these philosophers have so far not given a formulation of their question in terms of the common scientific language. Therefore our judgement must be that they have not succeeded in giving to the external question and to the possible answers any cognitive content. Unless and until they supply a clear cognitive interpretation, we are justified in our suspicion that their question is a pseudo-question, that is, one disguised in the form of a theoretical question while in fact it is non-theoretical; in the present case it is the practical problem whether or not to incorporate into the language the new linguistic forms which represent the framework of numbers.

The framework of propositions. New variables, "p", "q", etc., are introduced with a rule to the effect that any (declarative) sentence may be substituted for a variable of this kind; this includes, in addition to the sentences of the original thing language, also all general sentences with variables of any kind which may have been introduced into the language. Further, the general term "proposition" is introduced. "*p* is a proposition" may be defined by "*p* or not *p*" (or by any other sentence form yielding only analytic sentences). Therefore, every sentence of the form "... is a proposition" (where any sentence may stand in the place of the dots) is analytic. This holds, for example, for the sentence:

(*a*)   "Chicago is large is a proposition".

(We disregard here the fact that the rules of English grammar require not a sentence but a that-clause as the subject of another sentence; accordingly, instead of (*a*) we should have to say "That Chicago is large is a proposition".) Predicates may be admitted whose argument expressions are sentences; these predicates may be either extensional (e. g., the customary truth-functional connectives) or not (e. g., modal predicates like "possible", "necessary", etc.). With the help of the new variables, general sentences may be formed, e. g.

(*b*)   "For every *p*, either *p* or not-*p*".

(*c*)   "There is a *p* such that *p* is not necessary and not-*p* is not necessary".

(*d*)   "There is a *p* such that *p* is a proposition".

(*c*) and (*d*) assert internal existence. The statement "There are propositions" may be meant in the sense of (*d*); in this case it is analytic (since it follows from (*a*)) and even trivial. If, however, the statement is meant in an external sense, then it is non-cognitive.

It is important to notice that the system of rules for the linguistic expressions of the propositional framework (of which only a few rules have here been briefly indicated) is sufficient for the introduction of the framework. Any further explanations as to the nature of the propositions (i. e., the elements of the framework indicated, the values of the variables "*p*", "*q*", etc.) are theoretically unnecessary because, if correct, they follow from the rules. For example, are propositions mental events (as in Russell's theory)? A look at the rules shows us that they are not, because otherwise existential statements would be of the form: "If the mental state of the person in question fulfils such and such conditions, then there is a p such that ...". The fact that no references to mental conditions occur in existential statements (like (c), (d), etc.) shows that propositions are not mental entities. Further, a statement of the existence of linguistic entities (e. g., expressions, classes of expressions, etc.) must contain a reference to a language. The fact that no such reference occurs in the existential statements here, shows that propositions are not linguistic entities. The fact that in these statements no reference to a subject (an observer or knower) occurs (nothing like: "There is a p which is necessary for Mr. X"), shows that the propositions (and their properties, like necessity, etc.) are not subjective. Although characterizations of these or similar kinds are, strictly speaking, unnecessary, they may nevertheless be practically useful. If they are given, they should be understood, not as ingredient parts of the system, but merely as marginal notes with the purpose of supplying to the reader helpful hints or convenient pictorial associations which may make his learning of the use of the expressions easier than the bare system of the rules would do. Such a characterization is analogous to an extra-systematic explanation which a physicist sometimes gives to the beginner. He might, for example, tell him to imagine the atoms of a gas as small balls rushing around with great speed, or the electromagnetic field and its oscillations as quasi-elastic tensions and vibrations in an ether. In fact, however, all that can accurately be said about atoms or the field is implicitly contained in the physical laws of the theories in question [1].

[1] In my book *Meaning and Necessity* (Chicago, 1947) I have developed a semantical method which takes propositions as entities designated by sentences (more specifically, as intensions of sentences). In order to facilitate the understanding of the systematic development, I added some informal, extra-systematic explanations concerning the nature of propositions. I said that the term "proposition" "is used neither for a linguistic expression nor for a subjective, mental occurence, but rather for something objective that may or may not be exemplified in nature... We apply the term 'proposition' to any entities of a certain logical type, namely, those that may be expressed by (declarative) sentences in a language" (p. 27). After some more detailed discussions concerning the relation between propositions and facts, and the nature of false propositions, I added: "It has been the purpose of the preceding remarks to facilitate the understanding of our conception of propositions. If, however, a reader should find these explanations more puzzling than clarifying, or even unacceptable, he may disregard them" (p. 31) (that

The framework of thing properties. The thing language contains words like "red", "hard", "stone", "house", etc., which are used for describing what things are like. Now we may introduce new variables, say "*f*", "*g*", etc., for which those words are substitutable and furthermore the general term "property". New rules are laid down which admit sentences like "Red is a property", "Red is a color", "These two pieces of paper have at least one color in common" (i. e., "There is an *f* such that *f* is a color, and ..."). The last sentence is an internal asertion. It is of an empirical, factual nature. However, the external statement, the philosophical statement of the reality of properties—a special case of the thesis of the reality of universals—is devoid of cognitive content.

The frameworks of integers and rational numbers. Into a language containing the framework of natural numbers we may introduce first the (positive and negative) integers as relations among natural numbers and then the rational numbers as relations among integers. This involves introducing new types of variables, expressions substitutable for them and the general terms "integer" and " rational number".

The framework of real numbers. On the basis of the rational numbers, the real numbers may be introduced as classes of a special kind (segments) of rational numbers (according to the method developed by Dedekind and Frege). Here again a new type of variables is introduced, expressions substitutable for them (e. g., "$\sqrt{2}$"), and the general term "real number".

The framework of a spatio-temporal coordinate system for physics. The new entities are the space-time points.

is, disregard these extra-systematic explanations, not the whole theory of the propositions as intensions of sentences, as one reviewer understood). In spite of this warning, it seems that some of those readers who were puzzled by the explanations, did not disregard them but thought that by raising objections against them they could refute the theory. This is analogous to the procedure of some laymen who by (correctly) criticizing the ether picture or other visualizations of physical theories, thought they had refuted these theories. Perhaps the discussions in the present paper will help in clarifying the role of the system of linguistic rules for the introduction of a framework of entities on the one hand, and that of extra-systematic explanations concerning the nature of the entities on the other.

Each is an ordered quadruple of four real numbers, called its coordinates, consisting of three spatial and one temporal coordinates. The physical state of a spatio-temporal point or region is described either with the help of qualitative predicates (e. g., "hot") or by ascribing numbers as values of a physical magnitude (e. g., mass, temperature, and the like). The step from the framework of things (which does not contain space-time points but only extended objects with spatial and temporal relations between them) to the physical coordinate system is again a matter of decision. Our choice of certain features, although itself not theoretical, is suggested by theoretical knowledge, either logical or factual. For example, the choice of real numbers rather than rational numbers or integers as coordinates is not much influenced by the facts of experience but mainly due to considerations of mathematical simplicity. The restriction to rational coordinates would not be in conflict with any experimental knowledge we have, because the result of any measurement is a rational number. However, it would prevent the use of ordinary geometry (which says, e. g., that the diagonal of a square with the side 1 has the irrational value $\sqrt{2}$) and thus lead to great complications. On the other hand, the decision to use three rather than two or four spatial coordinates is strongly suggested, but still not forced upon us, by the result of common observations. If certain events allegedly observed in spiritualistic séances, e. g., a ball moving out of a sealed box, were confirmed beyond any reasonable doubt, it might seem advisable to use four spatial coordinates. Internal questions are here, in general, empirical questions to be answered by empirical investigations. On the other hand, the external questions of the reality of physical space and physical time are pseudo-questions. A question like "Are there (really) space-time points?" is ambiguous. It may be meant as an internal question; then the affirmative answer is, of course, analytic and trivial. Or it may be meant in the external sense: "Shall we introduce such and such forms into our language?"; in this case it is not a theoretical but a practical question, a matter of decision rather than assertion, and hence the proposed formulation would be misleading. Or finally, it may be meant in the following sense: "Are our experiences such that the use of the linguistic forms in question will be expedient and fruitful?" This is a theoretical question of a factual, empirical nature. But it concerns a matter of degree; therefore a formulation in the form "real or not?" would be inadequate.

3. *What does Acceptance of a Framework mean?*

Let us now summarize the essential characteristics of situations involving the introduction of a new framework of entities, characterictics which are common to the various examples outlined above.

The acceptance of a framework of new entities is represented in the language by introduction of new forms of expressions to be used according to a new set of rules. There may be new names for particular entities of the kind in question; but some such names may already occur in the language before the introduction of the new framework. (Thus, for example, the thing language contains certainly words of the type of "blue" and "house" before the framework of properties is introduced; and it may contain words like "ten" in sentences of the form "I have ten fingers" before the framework of numbers is introduced.) The latter fact shows that the occurrence of constants of the type in question—regarded as names of entities of the new kind after the new framework is introduced—is not a sure sign of the acceptance of the framework. Therefore the introduction of such constants is not to be regarded as an essential step in the introduction of the framework. The two essential steps are rather the following. First, the introduction of a general term, a predicate of higher level, for the new kind of entities, permitting us to say of any particular entity that it belongs to this kind (e. g., "Red is a *property*", "Five is a *number*"). Second, the introduction of variables of the new type. The new entities are values of these variables; the constants (and the closed compound expressions, if any) are substitutable for the variables [1]. With the help of the variables, general sentences concerning the new entities can be formulated.

[1] W. V. Quine was the first to recognize the importance of the introduction of variables as indicating the acceptance of entities. "The

After the new forms are introduced into the language, it is possible to formulate with their help internal questions and possible answers to them. A question of this kind may be either empirical or logical; accordingly a true answer is either factually true or analytic.

From the internal questions we must clearly distinguish external questions, i. e., philosophical questions concerning the existence or reality of the framework itself. Many philosophers regard a question of this kind as an ontological question which must be raised and answered *before* the introduction of the new language forms. The latter introduction, they believe, is legitimate only if it can be justified by an ontological insight supplying an affirmative answer to the question of reality. In contrast to this view, we take the position that the introduction of the new ways of speaking does not need any theoretical justification because it does not imply any assertion of reality. We may still speak (and have done so) of "the acceptance of the framework" or "the acceptance of the new entities" since this form of speech is customary; but one must keep in mind that these phrases do not mean for us anything more than acceptance of the new linguistic forms. Above all, they must not be interpreted as referring to an assumption, belief, or assertion of "the reality of the entities". There is no such assertion. An alleged statement of the reality of the framework of entities is a pseudo-statement without cognitive content. To be sure, we have to face at this point an important question; but it is a practical, not a theoretical question; it is the question of whether or not to accept the new linguistic forms. The acceptance cannot be judged as being either true or false because it is not an assertion. It can only be judged as being more or less expedient, fruitful, conducive to the aim for which the language is intended. Judgments of this

ontology to which one's use of language commits him comprises simply the objects that he treats as falling... within the range of values of his variables" ("Notes on Existence and Necessity", *Journal of Philos.*, 40 (1943), pp. 113-127, see p. 118; compare also his "Designation and Existence", *ibid.*, 36 (1939), pp. 701-9, and "On Universals", *Journal of Symbolic Logic*, 12 (1947), pp. 74-84).

kind supply the motivation for the decision of accepting or rejecting the framework. [1]

Thus it is clear that the acceptance of a framework must not be regarded as implying a metaphysical doctrine concerning the reality of the entities in question. It seems to me due to a neglect of this important distinction that some contemporary nominalists label the admission of variables of abstract types as "platonism". [2] This is, to say the least, an extremely misleading terminology. It leads to the absurd consequence, that the position of everybody who accepts the language of physics with its real number variables (as a language of communication, not merely as a calculus) would be called platonistic, even if he is a strict empiricist who rejects platonic metaphysics.

A brief historical remark may here be inserted. The non-cognitive character of the questions which we have called here external questions was recognized and emphasized already by the Vienna Circle under the leadership of Moritz Schlick, the group from which the movement of logical empiricism originated. Influenced by ideas of Ludwig Wittgenstein, the Circle rejected both the thesis of the reality

---

[1] For a closely related point of view on these questions see the detailed discussions in Herbert FEIGL, *Existential Hypotheses*, forthcoming in *Philosophy of Science*, 1950.

[2] Paul BERNAYS, *Sur le platonisme dans les mathématiques* (*L'Enseignement math.*, 34 (1935), pp. 52-69). W. V. QUINE, see footnote p. 65, and a recent paper *On What There Is*, (*Review of Metaphysics*, 2 (1948), pp. 21-38). Quine does not acknowledge the distinction which I emphasize above, because according to his general conception there are no sharp boundary lines between logical and factual truth, between questions of meaning and questions of fact, between the acceptance of a language structure ant the acceptance of an assertion formulated in the language. This conception, which seems to deviate considerably from customary ways of thinking, will be explained in his forthcoming book, *Foundations of Logic*. When Quine in the article mentioned above classifies my logicistic conception of mathematics (derived from Frege and Russell) as "platonic realism" (p. 33), this is meant (according to a personal communication from him) not as ascribing to me agreement with Plato's metaphysical doctrine of universals, but merely as referring to the fact that I accept a language of mathematics containing variables of higher levels. With respect to the basic attitude to take in choosing a language form (an "ontology" in Quine's terminology, which seems to me misleading), there appears now to be agreement between us: "the obvious counsel is tolerance and an experimental spirit" (*op. cit.*, p. 38).

of the external world and the thesis of its irreality as pseudo-statements; [1] the same was the case for both the thesis of the reality of universals (abstract entities, in our present terminology) and the nominalistic thesis that they are not real and that their alleged names are not names of anything but merely *flatus vocis*. (It is obvious that the apparent negation of a pseudo-statement must also be a pseudo-statement.) It is therefore not correct to classify the members of the Vienna Circle as nominalists, as is sometimes done. However, if we look at the basic anti-metaphysical and pro-scientific attitude of most nominalists (and the same holds for many materialists and realists in the modern sense), disregarding their occasional pseudo-theoretical formulations, then it is, of course, true to say that the Vienna Circle was much closer to those philosophers than to their opponents.

4. *Abstract Entities in Semantics*

The problem of the legitimacy and the status of abstract entities has recently again led to controversial discussions in connection with semantics. In a semantical meaning analysis certain expressions in a language are often said to designate (or name or denote or signify or refer to) certain extra-linguistic entities.[2] As long as physical things or events (e. g., Chicago or Caesar's death) are taken as designata (entities designated), no serious doubts arise. But strong objections have been raised, especially by some empiricists, against abstract entities as designata, e. g., against semantical statements of the following kind:

(1) "The word 'red' designates a property of things;"

---

[1] See Carnap, *Scheinprobleme in der Philosophie; das Fremdpsychische und der Realismusstreit*, Berlin, 1928. Moritz Schlick, *Positivismus und Realismus*, reprinted in *Gesammelte Aufsätze*, Wien 1938.

[2] *See Introduction to Semantics*, Cambridge Mass., 1942; *Meaning and Necessity*, Chicago, 1947. The distinction I have drawn in the latter book between the method of the name-relation and the method of intension and extension is not essential for our present discussion. The term "designation" is here used in a neutral way; it may be understood as referring to the name-relation or to the intension-relation or to the extension-relation or to any similar relations used in other semantical methods.

(2) "The word 'color' designates a property of properties of things;"

(3) "The word 'five' designates a number;"

(4) "The word 'odd' designates a property of numbers;"

(5) "The sentence 'Chicago is large' designates a proposition."

Those who criticize these statements do not, of course, reject the use of the expressions in question, like "red" or "five"; nor would they deny that these expressions are meaningful. But to be meaningful, they would say, is not the same as having a meaning in the sense of an entity designated. They reject the belief, which they regard as implicitly presupposed by those semantical statements, that to each expression of the types in question (adjectives like "red", numerals like "five", etc.) there is a particular real entity to which the expression stands in the relation of designation. This belief is rejected as incompatible with the basic principles of empiricism or of scientific thinking. Derogatory labels like "Platonic realism", "hypostatization", or " 'Fido'-Fido principle " are attached to it.   The latter is the name given by Gilbert Ryle [1] to the criticized belief, which, in his view, arises by a naive inference of analogy: just as there is an entity well known to me, viz. my dog Fido, which is designated by the name "Fido", thus there must be for every meaningful expression a particular entity to which it stands in the relation of designation or naming, i. e., the relation exemplified by "Fido"-Fido.   The belief criticized is thus a case of hypostatization, i. e., of treating as names expressions which are not names. While "Fido" is a name, expressions like "red", "five", etc. are said not to be names, not to designate anything.

Our previous discussions concerning the acceptance of frameworks enables us now to clarify the situation with respect to abstract entities as designata. Let us take as an example the statement:

(a) " 'Five' designates a number."

The formulation of this statement presupposes that our

---

[1] G. RYLE, *Meaning and Necessity* (*Philosophy*, 24 (1949), pp. 69-76).

language L contains the forms of expressions corresponding to what we have called the framework of numbers, in particular, numerical variables and the general term "number". If L contains these forms, the following is an analytic statement in L:

(b) "Five is a number."

Further, to make the statement (a) possible, L must contain an expression like "designates" or "is a name of" for the semantical relation of designation. If suitable rules for this term are laid down, the following is likewise analytic :

(c) " 'Five' designates five. "

(Generally speaking, any expression of the form " '...' designates..." is an analytic statement provided the term "..." is a constant in an accepted framework. If the latter condition is not fulfilled, the expression is not a statement.) Since (a) follows from (c) and (b), (a) is likewise analytic.

Thus it is clear that *if* someone accepts the framework of numbers, then he must acknowledge (c) and (b) and hence (a) as true statements. Generally speaking, if someone accepts a framework of entities, then he is bound to admit its entities as possible designata. Thus the question of the admissibility of entities of a certain type or of abstract entities in general as designata is reduced to the question of the acceptability of those entities. Both the nominalistic critics, who refuse the status of designators or names to expressions like "red", "five", etc., because they deny the existence of abstract entities, and the skeptics, who express doubts concerning the existence and demand evidence for it, treat the question of existence as a theoretical question. They do, of course, not mean the internal question; the affirmative answer to *this* question is analytic and trivial and too obvious for doubt or denial, as we have seen. Their doubts refer rather to the framework itself; hence they mean the external question. They believe that only after making sure that there really are entities of the kinds in question are we justified in accepting the framework by incorporating the linguistic forms into our language. However, we have seen that the external question is not a theoretical question but rather the practical question whether or not to accept those linguistic forms. This acceptance is not in need of a theoretical justification (except with respect to expediency and fruitfulness), because it does not imply a belief or assertion. Ryle says that the "Fido"-Fido principle is "a grotesque theory". Grotesque or not, Ryle is wrong in calling it a theory. It is rather the practical decision to accept certain frameworks. Maybe Ryle is historically right with respect to those whom he mentions as previous representatives of the principle, viz. John Stuart Mill, Frege, and Russell. If these philosophers regarded the acceptance of a framework of entities as a theory, an assertion, they were victims of the same old, metaphysical confusion. But it is certainly wrong to regard *my* semantical method as involving a belief in the reality of abstract entities, since I reject a thesis of this kind as a metaphysical pseudo-statement.

The critics of the use of abstract entities in semantics overlook the fundamental difference between the acceptance of a framework of entities and an internal assertion, e. g., an assertion that there are elephants or electrons or prime numbers greater than a million. Whoever makes an internal assertion is certainly obliged to justify it by providing evidence, empirical evidence in the case of electrons, logical proof in the case of the prime numbers. The demand for a theoretical justification, correct in the case of internal assertions, is sometimes wrongly applied to the acceptance of a framework of entities. Thus, for example, Ernest Nagel [1] asks for "evidence relevant for affirming with warrant that there are such entities as infinitesimals or propositions". He characterizes the evidence required in these cases—in distinction to the empirical evidence in the case of electrons—as "in the broad sense logical and dialectical". Beyond this no hint is given as to what might be regarded as relevant evidence. Some nominalists regard the acceptance of abstract entities as a kind of superstition or myth, populating the world with fictitious or at least dubious entities, analogous to the belief in centaurs or demons. This shows again the confusion mentioned, because a superstition or myth is a false (or dubious) internal statement.

---

[1] E. NAGEL, Review of Carnap *Meaning and Necessity* (*Journal of Philos.*, 45 (1948), pp. 467-72).

Let us take as example the natural numbers as cardinal numbers, i. e., in contexts like "Here are three books". The linguistic forms of the framework of numbers, including variables and the general term "number" are generally used in our common language of communication; and it is easy to formulate explicit rules for their use. Thus the logical characteristics of this framework are sufficiently clear (while many internal questions, i. e., arithmetical questions, are, of course, still open). In spite of this, the controversy concerning the external question of the ontological reality of numbers continues. Suppose that one philosopher says: "I believe that there are numbers as real entities. This gives me the right to use the linguistic forms of the numerical framework and to make semantical statements about numbers as designata of numerals". His nominalistic opponent replies: "You are wrong; there are no numbers. The numerals may still be used as meaningful expressions. But they are not names, there are no entities designated by them. Therefore the word "number" and numerical variables must not be used (unless a way were found to introduce them as merely abbreviating devices, a way of translating them into the nominalistic thing language)." I cannot think of any possible evidence that would be regarded as relevant by both philosophers, and therefore, if actually found, would decide the controversy or at least make one of the opposite theses more probable than the other. (To construe the numbers as classes or properties of the second level, according to the Frege-Russell method does, of course, not solve the controversy, because the first philosopher would affirm and the second deny the existence of classes or properties of the second level.) Therefore I feel compelled to regard the external question as a pseudo-question, until both parties to the controversy offer a common interpretation of the question as a cognitive question; this would involve an indication of possible evidence regarded as relevant by both sides.

There is a particular kind of misinterpretation of the acceptance of abstract entities in various fields of science and in semantics, that needs to be cleared up. Certain early British empiricists (e. g., Berkeley and Hume) denied the existence of abstract entities on the ground that immediate experience presents us only with particulars, not with universals, e. g., with this red patch, but not with Redness or Color-in-General; with this scalene triangle, but not with Scalene Triangularity or Triangularity-in-General. Only entities belonging to a type of which examples were to be found within immediate experience could be accepted as ultimate constituents of reality. Thus, according to this way of thinking, the existence of abstract entities could be asserted only if one could show either that some abstract entities fall within the given, or that abstract entities can be defined in terms of the types of entity which are given. Since these empiricists found no abstract entities within the realm of sense-data, they either denied their existence, or else made a futile attempt to define universals in terms of particulars. Some contemporary philosophers, especially English philosophers following Bertrand Russell, think in basically similar terms. They emphasize a distinction between the data (that which is immediately given in consciousness, e. g. sense-data, immediately past experiences, etc.) and the constructs based on the data. Existence or reality is ascribed only to the data; the constructs are not real entities; the corresponding linguistic expressions are merely ways of speech not actually designating anything (reminiscent of the nominalists' *flatus vocis*). We shall not criticize here this general conception. (As far as it is a principle of accepting certain entities and not accepting others, leaving aside any ontological, phenomenalistic and nominalistic pseudo-statements, there cannot be any theoretical objection to it.) But if this conception leads to the view that other philosophers or scientists who accept abstract entities thereby assert or imply their occurrence as immediate data, then such a view must be rejected as a misinterpretation. References to space-time points, the electromagnetic field, or electrons in physics, to real or complex numbers and their functions in mathematics, to the excitatory potential or unconscious complexes in psychology, to an inflationary trend in economics, and the like, do not imply the assertion that entities of these kinds occur as immediate data. And the same holds for references to abstract entities as designata in semantics. Some of the criticisms by English philosophers against such references give the impression that, probably due to the misinterpretation just indicated, they accuse the semanticist not so much of bad metaphysics (as some nominalists would do) but of bad psychology. The fact that they regard a semantical method involving abstract entities not merely as doubtful and perhaps wrong, but as manifestly absurd, preposterous and grotesque, and that they show a deep horror and indignation against this method, is perhaps to be explained by a misinterpretation of the kind described. In fact, of course, the semanticist does not in the least assert or imply that the abstract entities to which he refers can be experienced as immediately given either by sensation or by a kind of rational intuition. An assertion of this kind would indeed be very dubious psychology. The psychological question as to which kinds of entities do and which do not occur as immediate data is entirely irrelevant for semantics, just as it is for physics, mathematics, economics, etc., with respect to the examples mentioned above. [1]

5. Conclusion

For those who want to develop or use semantical methods, the decisive question is not the alleged ontological question of the existence of abstract entities but rather the question whether the use of abstract linguistic forms or, in technical terms, the use of variables beyond those for things (or phenomenal data), is expedient and fruitful for the purposes for which semantical analyses are made, viz. the analysis, interpretation, clarification, or construction of languages of communication, especially languages of science. This question is here neither decided nor even discussed. It is not a question simply of yes or no, but a matter of degree. Among those philosophers who have carried out semantical analyses and thought about suitable tools for this work, beginning with Plato and Aristotle and, in a more technical way on the basis of modern logic, with C. S. Pierce and Frege, a great majority accepted abstract entities. This does, of course, not prove the

---

[1] Wilfrid Sellars (*Acquaintance and Description Again*, in *Journal of Philos.* 46 (1949), pp. 496-504, see pp. 502 f.) analyzes clearly the roots of the mistake "of taking the designation relation of semantic theory to be a reconstruction of *being present to an experience*".

case. After all, semantics in the technical sense is still in the initial phases of its development, and we must be prepared for possible fundamental changes in methods. Let us therefore admit that the nominalistic critics may possibly be right. But if so, they will have to offer better arguments than they did so far. Appeal to ontological insight will not carry much weight. The critics will have to show that it is possible to construct a semantical method which avoids all references to abstract entities and achieves by simpler means essentially the same results as the other methods.

The acceptance or rejection of abstract linguistic forms, just as the acceptance or rejection of any other linguistic forms in any branch of science, will finally be decided by their efficiency as instruments, the ratio of the results achieved to the amount and complexity of the efforts required. To decree dogmatic prohibitions of certain linguistic forms instead of testing them by their success or failure in practical use, is worse than futile; it is positively harmful because it may obstruct scientific progress. The history of science shows examples of such prohibitions based on prejudices deriving from religious, mythological, metaphysical, or other irrational sources, which slowed up the developments for shorter or longer periods of time. Let us learn from the lessons of history. Let us grant to those who work in any special field of investigation the freedom to use any form of expression which seems useful to them; the work in the field will sooner or later lead to the elimination of those forms which have no useful function. *Let us be cautious in making assertions and critical in examining them, but tolerant in permitting linguistic forms.*

University of Chicago.

12

The Problem
of Counterfactual
Conditionals

by **NELSON GOODMAN**

Reprinted from *The Journal of Philosophy,* 44 (1947).

THE PROBLEM OF COUNTERFACTUAL CONDITIONALS[1]

I. THE PROBLEM IN GENERAL

THE analysis of counterfactual conditionals is no fussy little grammatical exercise. Indeed, if we lack the means for interpreting counterfactual conditionals, we can hardly claim to have any adequate philosophy of science. A satisfactory definition of scientific law, a satisfactory theory of confirmation or of disposition terms (and this includes not only predicates ending in "ible" and "able" but almost every objective predicate, such as "is red"), would solve a large part of the problem of counterfactuals. Accordingly, the lack of a solution to this problem implies that we have no adequate treatment of any of these other topics. Conversely, a solution to the problem of counterfactuals would give us the answer to critical questions about law, confirmation, and the meaning of potentiality.

I am not at all contending that the problem of counterfactuals is logically or psychologically the first of these related problems. It makes little difference where we start if we can go ahead. If the study of counterfactuals has up to now failed this pragmatic test, the alternative approaches are little better off.

What, then, is the *problem* about counterfactual conditionals? Let us confine ourselves to those in which antecedent and consequent are inalterably false—as, for example, when I say of a piece of butter that was eaten yesterday, and that had never been heated,

If that piece of butter had been heated to 150° F., it would have melted.

Considered as truth-functional compounds, all counterfactuals are of course true, since their antecedents are false. Hence

If that piece of butter had been heated to 150° F., it would not have melted

would also hold. Obviously something different is intended, and the problem is to define the circumstances under which a given

[1] Slightly revised version of a paper read before the New York Philosophical Circle, May 11, 1946. My indebtedness in several matters to the work of C. I. Lewis and of C. H. Langford has seemed too obvious to call for detailed mention.

counterfactual holds while the opposing conditional with the contradictory consequent fails to hold. And this criterion of truth must be set up in the face of the fact that a counterfactual by its nature can never be subjected to any direct empirical test by realizing its antecedent.

In one sense the name "problem of counterfactuals" is misleading, because the problem is independent of the form in which a given statement happens to be expressed. The problem of counterfactuals is equally a problem of factual conditionals, for any counterfactual can be transposed into a conditional with a true antecedent and consequent; e.g.,

Since that butter did not melt, it wasn't heated to 150° F.

The possibility of such transformation is of no great importance except to clarify the nature of our problem. That "since" occurs in the contrapositive shows that what is in question is a certain kind of connection between the two component sentences; and the truth of this kind of statement—whether it is in the form of a counterfactual or factual conditional or some other form—depends not upon the truth or falsity of the components but upon whether the intended connection obtains. Recognizing the possibility of transformation serves mainly to focus attention on the central problem and to discourage speculation as to the nature of counterfacts. Although I shall begin my study by considering counterfactuals as such, it must be borne in mind that a general solution would explain the kind of connection involved irrespective of any assumption as to the truth or falsity of the components.

The effect of transposition upon another kind of conditional, which I call "semifactual," is worth noticing briefly. Should we assert

Even if the match had been scratched, it still would not have lighted,

we would uncompromisingly reject as an equally good expression of our meaning the contrapositive,

Even if the match lighted, it still wasn't scratched.

Our original intention was to affirm not that the non-lighting could be inferred from the scratching, but simply that the lighting could not be inferred from the scratching. Ordinarily a semifactual conditional has the force of denying what is affirmed by the opposite, fully counterfactual conditional. The sentence

Even had that match been scratched, it still wouldn't have lighted

is normally meant as the direct negation of

Had the match been scratched, it would have lighted.

That is to say, in practice full counterfactuals affirm, while semifactuals deny, that a certain connection obtains between antecedent and consequent.[2] Thus it is clear why a semifactual generally has not the same meaning as its contrapositive.

There are various special kinds of counterfactuals that present special problems. An example is the case of "counteridenticals," illustrated by the statements

If I were Julius Caesar, I wouldn't be alive in the twentieth century,

and

If Julius Caesar were I, he would be alive in the twentieth century.

Here, although the antecedent in the two cases is a statement of the same identity, we attach two different consequents which, on the very assumption of that identity, are incompatible. Another special class of counterfactuals is that of the "countercomparatives," with antecedents such as

If I had more money, . . .

The trouble with these is that when we try to translate the counterfactual into a statement about a relation between two tenseless, nonmodal sentences, we get as an antecedent something like

If "I have more money than I have" were true, . . .

although use of a self-contradictory antecedent was plainly not the original intent. Again there are the "counterlegals," conditionals with antecedents that either deny general laws directly, as in

If triangles were squares, . . .

or else make a supposition of particular fact that is not merely false but impossible, as in

If this cube of sugar were also spherical, . . .

All these kinds of counterfactuals offer interesting but not insurmountable special difficulties.[3] In order to concentrate upon the

[2] The practical import of a semifactual is thus different from its literal meaning. Literally a semifactual and the corresponding counterfactual are not contradictories but contraries, and both may be false (cf. footnote 8). The presence of the auxiliary terms "even" and "still," or either of them, is perhaps the idiomatic indication that a not quite literal meaning is intended.

[3] Of the special kinds of counterfactuals mentioned, I shall have something to say later about counteridenticals and counterlegals. As for countercomparatives, the following procedure is appropriate:—Given "If I had arrived one minute later, I would have missed the train," first expand this to "($\exists t$). t is a time. I arrived(d) at t. If I had arrived one minute later than t, I would

major problems concerning counterfactuals in general, I shall usually choose my examples in such a way as to avoid these more special complications.

As I see it, there are two major problems, though they are not independent and may even be regarded as aspects of a single problem. A counterfactual is true if a certain connection obtains between the antecedent and the consequent. But as is obvious from examples already given, the consequent seldom follows from the antecedent by logic alone. (1) In the first place, the assertion that a connection holds is made on the presumption that certain circumstances not stated in the antecedent obtain. When we say

If that match had been scratched, it would have lighted,

we mean that conditions are such—i.e., the match is well made, is dry enough, oxygen enough is present, etc.—that "That match lights" can be inferred from "That match is scratched." Thus the connection we affirm may be regarded as joining the consequent with the conjunction of the antecedent and other statements that truly describe relevant conditions. Notice especially that our assertion of the counterfactual is *not* conditioned upon these circumstances obtaining. We do not assert that the counterfactual is true *if* the circumstances obtain; rather, in asserting the counterfactual we commit ourselves to the actual truth of the statements describing the requisite relevant conditions. The first major problem is to define relevant conditions; to specify what sentences are meant to be taken in conjunction with an antecedent as a basis for inferring the consequent. (2) But even after the particular relevant conditions are specified, the connection obtaining will not ordinarily be a logical one. The principle that permits inference of

That match lights

from

That match is scratched. That match is dry enough. Enough oxygen is present. Etc.

is not a law of logic but what we call a natural or physical or causal law. The second major problem concerns the definition of such laws.

have missed the train." The counterfactual conditional constituting the final clause of this conjunction can then be treated, within the quantified whole, in the usual way. Translation into "If 'I arrive one minute later than t' were true, then 'I miss the train' would have been true" does not give us a self-contradictory component.

II. The Problem of Relevant Conditions

It might seem natural to propose that the consequent follows by law from the antecedent and a description of the actual state-of-affairs of the world, that we need hardly define relevant conditions because it will do no harm to include irrelevant ones. But if we say that the consequent follows by law from the antecedent and *all* true statements, we encounter an immediate difficulty:—among true sentences is the negate of the antecedent, so that from the antecedent and all true sentences everything follows. Certainly this gives us no way of distinguishing true from false counterfactuals.

We are plainly no better off if we say that the consequent must follow from *some* set of true statements conjoined with the antecedent; for given any counterfactual antecedent A, there will always be a set S—namely, the set consisting of $-A$—such that from $A \cdot S$ any consequent follows. (Hereafter I shall regularly use "A" for the antecedent, "C" for the consequent, and "S" for the set of statements of the relevant conditions.)

Perhaps then we must exclude statements logically incompatible with the antecedent. But this is insufficient; for a parallel difficulty arises with respect to true statements which are not logically but are otherwise incompatible with the antecedent. For example, take

If that radiator had frozen, it would have broken.

Among true sentences may well be (S)

That radiator never reached a temperature below 33° F.

Now it is certainly generally true that

All radiators that freeze but never reach below 33° F. break,

and also that

All radiators that freeze but never reach below 33° F. fail to break;

for there are no such radiators. Thus from the antecedent of the counterfactual and the given S, we can infer any consequent.

The natural proposal to remedy this difficulty is to rule that counterfactuals can not depend upon empty laws; that the connection can be established only by a principle of the form "All x's are y's" when there are some x's. But this is ineffectual. For if empty principles are excluded, the following non-empty principles may be used in the case given with the same result:

Everything that is either a radiator that freezes but does not reach below 33° F., or that is a soap bubble, breaks;

Everything that is either a radiator that freezes but does not reach below 33° F., or is powder, does not break.

By these principles we can infer any consequent from the A and S in question.

The only course left open to us seems to be to define relevant conditions as the set of all true statements each of which is both logically and non-logically compatible with A where non-logical incompatibility means violation of a non-logical law.[4] But another difficulty immediately appears. In a counterfactual beginning

If Jones were in Carolina, . . .

the antecedent is entirely compatible with

Jones is not in South Carolina

and with

Jones is not in North Carolina

and with

North Carolina plus South Carolina is identical with Carolina;

but all these taken together with the antecedent make a set that is self-incompatible, so that again any consequent would be forthcoming.

Clearly it will not help to require only that for *some* set S of true sentences, $A \cdot S$ be self-compatible and lead by law to the consequent; for this would make a true counterfactual of

If Jones were in Carolina, he would be in South Carolina,

and also of

If Jones were in Carolina, he would be in North Carolina,

which can not both be true.

It seems that we must elaborate our criterion still further, to characterize a counterfactual as true if and only if there is some set S of true statements such that $A \cdot S$ is self-compatible and leads by law to the consequent, while there is no such set S' such that $A \cdot S'$ is self-compatible and leads by law to the negate of the consequent.[5] Unfortunately even this is not enough. For among true sentences will be the negate of the consequent: $-C$. Is $-C$ compatible with A or not? If not, then A alone without any additional condi-

---

[4] This of course raises very serious questions, which I shall come to presently, about the nature of non-logical law.

[5] Note that the requirement that $A \cdot S$ be self-compatible can be fulfilled only if the antecedent is self-compatible; hence the conditionals I have called "counterlegals" will all be false. This is convenient for our present purpose of investigating counterfactuals that are not counterlegals. If it later appears desirable to regard all or some counterlegals as true, special provisions may be introduced.

tions must lead by law to C. But if $- C$ is compatible with A (as in most cases), then if we take $- C$ as our S, the conjunction $A \cdot S$ will give us $- C$. Thus the criterion we have set up will seldom be satisfied; for since $- C$ will normally be compatible with A—as the need for introducing the relevant conditions testifies—there will normally be an A (namely, $- C$) such that $A \cdot S$ is self-compatible and leads by law to $- C$.

Part of our trouble lies in taking too narrow a view of our problem. We have been trying to lay down conditions under which an A that is known to be false leads to a C that is known to be false; but it is equally important to make sure that our criterion does not establish a similar connection between our A and the (true) negate of C. Because our S together with A was to be so chosen as to give us C, it seemed gratuitous to specify that S must be compatible with C; and because $- C$ is true by supposition, S would necessarily be compatible with it. But we are testing whether our criterion not only admits the true counterfactual we are concerned with but also excludes the opposing conditional. Accordingly, our criterion must be modified by specifying that S be compatible with both C and $- C$.[6] In other words, S by itself must not decide between C and $- C$, but S together with A must lead to C but not to $- C$. We need not know whether C is true or false.

Our rule thus reads that a counterfactual is true if and only if there is some set S of true sentences such that S is compatible with C and with $- C$, and such that $A \cdot S$ is self-compatible and leads by law to C; while there is no set S' compatible with C and with $- C$, and such that $A \cdot S'$ is self-compatible and leads by law to $- C$. As thus stated, the rule involves a certain redundancy; but simplification is not in point here, for the criterion is still inadequate.

The requirement that $A \cdot S$ be self-compatible is not strong enough; for S might comprise true sentences that although *compatible with A*, were such that *they would not be true if A were true*. For this reason, many statements that we would regard as definitely false would be true according to the stated criterion. As an example, consider the familiar case where for a given match M, we would affirm

(I) If match M had been scratched, it would have lighted,

[6] It is natural to inquire whether for similar reasons we should stipulate that S must be compatible with both A and $- A$, but this is unnecessary. For if S is incompatible with $- A$, then A follows from S; therefore if S is compatible with both C and $- C$, then $A \cdot S$ can not lead by law to one but not the other. Hence no sentence incompatible with $- A$ can satisfy the other requirements for a suitable S.

but deny

(II) If match M had been scratched, it would not have been dry.[7]

According to our tentative criterion, statement II would be quite as true as statement I. For in the case of II, we may take as an element in our S the true sentence

Match M did not light,

which is presumably compatible with A (otherwise nothing would be required along with A to reach the opposite as the consequent of the true counterfactual statement, I). As our total $A \cdot S$ we may have

Match M is scratched. It does not light. It is well made. Oxygen enough is present . . . etc.;

and from this, by means of a legitimate general law, we can infer

It was not dry

and there would seem to be no suitable set of sentences S' such that $A \cdot S'$ leads by law to the negate of this consequent. Hence the unwanted counterfactual is established in accord with our rule. The trouble is caused by including in our S a true statement which though compatible with A would not be true if A were. Accordingly we must exclude such statements from the set of relevant conditions; S, in addition to satisfying the other requirements already laid down, must be not merely compatible with A but "jointly tenable" or "cotenable" with A. A is cotenable with S, and the conjunction $A \cdot S$ self-cotenable, if it is not the case that S would not be true if A were.[8]

Parenthetically it may be noted that the relative fixity of conditions is often unclear, so that the speaker or writer has to make explicit additional provisos or give subtle verbal clues as to his meaning. For example, each of the following two counterfactuals would normally be accepted:

[7] Of course, some sentences similar to II, referring to other matches under special conditions, may be true; but the objection to the proposed criterion is that it would commit us to many such statements that are patently false. I am indebted to Morton G. White for a suggestion concerning the exposition of this point.

[8] The double negative can not be eliminated here; for ". . . if S would be true if A were" actually constitutes a stronger requirement. As we noted earlier (footnote 2), if two conditionals having the same counterfactual antecedent are such that the consequent of one is the negate of the consequent of the other, the conditionals are contraries and both may be false. This will be the case, for example, if every otherwise suitable set of relevant conditions that in conjunction with the antecedent leads by law either to a given consequent or its negate leads also to the other.

If New York City were in Georgia, then New York City would be in the South. If Georgia included New York City, then Georgia would not be entirely in the South.

Yet the antecedents are logically indistinguishable. What happens is that the direction of expression becomes important, because in the former case the meaning is

If New York City were in Georgia, and the boundaries of Georgia remained unchanged, then . . .

while in the latter case the meaning is

If Georgia included New York City, and the boundaries of New York City remained unchanged, then . . .

Without some such cue to the meaning as is covertly given by the word-order, we should be quite uncertain which of the two consequents in question could be truly attached. The same kind of explanation accounts for the paradoxical pairs of counteridenticals mentioned earlier.

Returning now to the proposed rule, I shall neither offer further corrections of detail nor discuss whether the requirement that S be cotenable with A makes superfluous some other provisions of the criterion; for such matters become rather unimportant beside the really serious difficulty that now confronts us. In order to determine the truth of a given counterfactual it seems that we have to determine, among other things, whether there is a suitable S that is cotenable with A and meets certain further requirements. But in order to determine whether or not a given S is cotenable with A, we have to determine whether or not the counterfactual "If A were true, then S would not be true" is itself true. But this means determining whether or not there is a suitable S_1, cotenable with A, that leads to $- S$ and so on. Thus we find ourselves involved in an infinite regressus or a circle; for cotenability is defined in terms of counterfactuals, yet the meaning of counterfactuals is defined in terms of cotenability. In other words to establish any counterfactual, it seems that we first have to determine the truth of another. If so, we can never explain a counterfactual except in terms of others, so that the problem of counterfactuals must remain unsolved.

Though unwilling to accept this conclusion, I do not at present see any way of meeting the difficulty. One naturally thinks of revising the whole treatment of counterfactuals in such a way as to admit first those that depend on no conditions other than the antecedent, and then use these counterfactuals as the criteria for the cotenability of relevant conditions with antecedents of other counterfactuals, and so on. But this idea seems initially rather unpromising in view of the formidable difficulties of accounting by such a step-by-step method for even so simple a counterfactual as:

If the match had been scratched, it would have lighted.

III. The Problem of Law

Even more serious is the second of the problems mentioned earlier: the nature of the general statements that enable us to infer the consequent upon the basis of the antecedent and the statement of relevant conditions. The distinction between these connecting principles and relevant conditions is imprecise and arbitrary; the "connecting principles" might be conjoined to the condition-statements, and the relation of the antecedent-conjunction $(A \cdot S)$ to the consequent thus made a matter of logic. But the same problems would arise as to the kind of principle that is capable of supporting a counterfactual; and it is convenient to consider the connecting principles separately.

In order to infer the consequent of a counterfactual from the antecedent A and a suitable statement of relevant conditions S, we make use of a general statement, namely, the generalization [9] of the conditional having $A \cdot S$ for antecedent and C for consequent. For example, in the case of

If the match had been scratched, it would have lighted

the connecting principle is

Every match that is scratched, well made, dry enough, in enough oxygen, etc., lights.

But notice that *not* every counterfactual is actually supported by the principle thus arrived at, *even* if that principle is *true*. Suppose, for example, that all I had in my right pocket on V–E day was a group of silver coins. Now we would not under normal circumstances affirm of a given penny P

If P had been in my pocket on V–E day, P would have been silver,[10]

[9] The sense of "generalization" intended here is that explained by C. G. Hempel in "A Purely Syntactical Definition of Confirmation," *Journal of Symbolic Logic*, Vol. 8 (1943), pp. 122–143.

[10] The antecedent in this example is intended to mean "If P, while remaining distinct from the things that were in fact in my pocket on V–E day, had also been in my pocket then," and *not* the quite different, counteridentical "If P had been identical with one of the things that were in my pocket on V–E day." While the antecedents of most counterfactuals (as, again, our familiar one about the match) are—literally speaking—open to both sorts of interpretation, ordinary usage normally calls for some explicit indication when the counteridentical meaning is intended.

even though from

P was in my pocket on V–E day

we can infer the consequent by means of the general statement

Everything in my pocket on V–E day was silver.

On the contrary, we would assert that if P had been in my pocket, then this general statement would not be true. The general statement will *not* permit us to infer the given consequent from the counterfactual assumption that P was in my pocket, because the general statement will not itself withstand that counterfactual assumption. Though the supposed connecting principle is indeed general, true, and perhaps even fully confirmed by observation of all cases, it is incapable of supporting a counterfactual because it remains a description of accidental fact, not a law. The truth of a counterfactual conditional thus seems to depend on whether the general sentence required for the inference is a law or not. If so, our problem is to distinguish accurately between causal laws and casual facts.[11]

The problem illustrated by the example of the coins is closely related to that which led us earlier to require the cotenability of the antecedent and the relevant conditions, in order to avoid resting a counterfactual on any statement that would not be true if the antecedent were true. But decision as to the cotenability of two sentences must depend upon decisions as to whether or not certain general statements are laws, and we are now concerned directly with the latter problem. Is there some way of distinguishing laws from non-laws among true universal statements of the kind in question, such that a law will be the sort of principle that will support a counterfactual conditional while a non-law will not?

Any attempt to draw the distinction by reference to a notion of causative force can be dismissed at once as unscientific. And it is clear that no purely syntactical criterion can be adequate, for even the most special descriptions of particular facts can be cast in a form having any desired degree of syntactical universality. "Book *B* is small" becomes "Everything that is *Q* is small" if "*Q*" stands for some predicate that applies uniquely to *B*. What then does distinguish a law like

All butter melts at 150° F.

[11] The importance of distinguishing laws from non-laws is too often overlooked. If a clear distinction can be defined, it may serve not only the purposes explained in the present paper but also many of those for which the increasingly dubious distinction between analytic and synthetic statements is ordinarily supposed to be needed.

from a true and general non-law like

All the coins in my pocket are silver?

Primarily, I would like to suggest, the fact that the first is accepted as true while many cases of it remain to be determined, the further, unexamined cases being predicted to conform with it. The second sentence, on the contrary, is accepted as a description of contingent fact *after* the determination of all cases, no prediction of any of its instances being based upon it. This proposal raises innumerable problems, some of which I shall consider presently; but the idea behind it is just that the principle we use to decide counterfactual cases is a principle we are willing to commit ourselves to in deciding unrealized cases that are still subject to direct observation.

As a first approximation then, we might say that a law is a true sentence used for making predictions. That laws are used predictively is of course a simple truism, and I am not proposing it as a novelty. I want only to emphasize the idea that rather than a sentence being used for prediction because it is a law, it is called a law because it is used for prediction; and that rather than the law being used for prediction because it describes a causal connection, the meaning of the causal connection is to be interpreted in terms of predictively used laws.

By the determination of all instances, I mean simply the examination or testing by other means of all things that satisfy the antecedent, to decide whether all satisfy the consequent also. There are difficult questions about the meaning of "instance," many of which Professor Hempel has investigated. Most of these are avoided in our present study by the fact that we are concerned with a very narrow class of sentences: those arrived at by generalizing conditionals of a certain kind. Remaining problems about the meaning of "instance" I shall have to ignore here. As for "determination," I do not mean final discovery of truth, but only enough examination to reach a decision as to whether a given statement or its negate is to be admitted as evidence for the hypothesis in question.

The limited scope of our present problem makes it unimportant that our criterion, if applied generally to all statements, would classify as laws many statements—e.g., true singular predictions—that we would not normally call laws.

A more pertinent point is the application of the proposed criterion to vacuous generalities. As the criterion stands, no conditional with an empty antecedent-class will be a law, for all its instances will have been determined prior to its acceptance. Now since the antecedents of the statements we are concerned with will be generalizations from self-cotenable and therefore self-compatible conjunctions, none will be known to be vacuous.[12]   For example, since

M is scratched. M is dry . . . (etc.)

is a self-compatible set, the antecedent of

For every x, if x is scratched and x is dry (etc.), then x lights

will not be known to be false.   But now we would still want the generalized principle just given to be a law if it should just *happen* to be the case that nothing satisfies the antecedent.   This discloses a defect in our criterion, which should be amended to read as follows: A true statement of the kind in question is a law if we accept it before we *know* that the instances we have determined are *all* the instances.

For convenience, I shall use the term "lawlike" for sentences which, whether they are true or not, satisfy the other requirements in the definition of law.   A law is thus a sentence that is both law-like and true, but a sentence may be true without being lawlike, as I have illustrated, or lawlike without being true, as we are always learning to our dismay.

Now the property of lawlikeness as so far defined is not only rather an accidental and subjective one but an ephemeral one that sentences may acquire and lose.   As an example of the undesirable consequences of this impermanence, a true sentence that had been used predictively would cease to be a law when it became fully tested—i.e., when none of its instances remained undetermined. The definition, then, must be restated in some such way as this: A general statement is lawlike if and only if it is acceptable prior to the determination of all its instances.   This is immediately objectionable because "acceptable" itself is plainly a dispositional term; but I propose to use it only tentatively, with the idea of eliminating it eventually by means of a non-dispositional definition.   Before trying to accomplish that, however, we must face another difficulty in our tentative criterion of lawlikeness.

Suppose that the appropriate generalization fails to support a given counterfactual because that generalization, while true, is un-lawlike, as is

Everything in my pocket is silver.

[12] Had it been sufficient in the preceding section to require only that $A \cdot S$ be self-*compatible*, this requirement might now be eliminated in favor of the stipulation that the generalization of the conditional having $A \cdot S$ as antecedent and C as consequent should be non-vacuous; but this stipulation would not guarantee the self-*cotenability* of $A \cdot S$.

All we would need do to get a law would be to broaden the antecedent strategically. Consider, for example, the sentence

Everything that is in my pocket or is a dime is silver.

Since we have not examined all dimes, this is a predictive statement and—since presumably true—would be a law. Now if we consider our original counterfactual and choose our S so that $A \cdot S$ is

P is in my pocket. P is in my pocket or is a dime,

then the pseudo-law just constructed can be used to infer from this the sentence "P is silver." Thus the untrue counterfactual is established, if one prefers to avoid an alternation as a condition-statement; the same result can be obtained by using a new predicate such as "dimo" to mean "is in my pocket or is a dime." [13]

The change called for, I think, will make the definition of lawlikeness read as follows: A sentence is lawlike if its acceptance does not depend upon the determination of any given instance.[14] Naturally this does not mean that acceptance is to be independent of all determination of instances, but only that there is no particular instance on the determination of which acceptance depends. This criterion excludes from the class of laws a statement like

That book is black and oranges are spherical

on the ground that acceptance requires knowing whether the book is black; it excludes

Everything that is in my pocket or is a dime is silver

on the ground that acceptance demands examination of all things in my pocket. Moreover, it excludes a statement like

All the marbles in this bag except Number 19 are red, and Number 19 is black

on the ground that acceptance would depend on examination of or knowledge gained otherwise concerning marble Number 19. In fact the principle involved in the proposed criterion is a rather powerful one and seems to exclude most of the troublesome cases.

We must still, however, replace the notion of the acceptability

13 Apart from the special class of connecting principles we are concerned with, note that under the stated criterion of lawlikeness, any statement could be expanded into a lawlike one; for example: given "This book is black" we could use the predictive sentence "This book is black and all oranges are spherical" to argue that the blackness of the book is the consequence of a law.

14 So stated, the definition counts vacuous principles as laws. If we read instead "given class of instances," vacuous principles will be non-laws since their acceptance depends upon examination of the null class of instances. For my present purposes the one formulation is as good as the other.

of a sentence, or of its acceptance *depending* or *not depending* on some given knowledge, by a positive definition of such dependence. It is clear that to say that the acceptance of a given statement depends upon a certain kind and amount of evidence is to say that given such evidence, acceptance of the statement is in accord with certain general standards for the acceptance of statements that are not fully tested. So one turns naturally to theories of induction and confirmation to learn the distinguishing factors or circumstances that determine whether or not a sentence is acceptable without complete evidence. But publications on confirmation not only have failed to make clear the distinction between confirmable and non-confirmable statements, but show little recognition that such a problem exists.[15] Yet obviously in the case of some sentences like

Everything in my pocket is silver

or

No twentieth-century president of the United States will be between 6 feet 1 inch and 6 feet 1½ inches tall,

not even the testing with positive results of all but a single instance is likely to lead us to accept the sentence and predict that the one remaining instance will conform to it; while for other sentences such as

All dimes are silver

or

All butter melts at 150° F.

or

All flowers of plants descended from this seed will be yellow

positive determination of even a few instances may lead us to accept the sentence with confidence and make predictions in accordance with it.

There is some hope that cases like these can be dealt with by a sufficiently careful and intricate elaboration of current confirmation theories; but inattention to the problem of distinguishing between confirmable and non-confirmable sentences has left most confirmation theories open to more damaging counterexamples of an elementary kind.

Suppose we designate the 26 marbles in a sack by the letters of

---

[15] The points discussed in this and the following paragraph have been dealt with a little more fully in my ''Query on Confirmation,'' this JOURNAL, Vol. XLIII (1946), pp. 383–385.

the alphabet, using these merely as proper names having no ordinal significance. Suppose further that we are told that all the marbles except d are red, but we are not told what color d is. By the usual kind of confirmation theory this gives strong confirmation for the statement

Ra. Rb. Rc. Rd. . . . . *Rz*

because 25 of the 26 cases are known to be favorable while none is known to be unfavorable. But unfortunately the same argument would show that the very same evidence would equally confirm

Ra. Rb. Rc. Re. . . . . *Rz.—Rd,*

for again we have 25 favorable and no unfavorable cases. Thus "*Rd*" and "*— Rd*" are equally and strongly confirmed by the same evidence. If I am required to use a single predicate instead of both "*R*" and "*— R*" in the second case, I will use "*P*" to mean:

is in the sack and either is not d and is red, or is d and is not red.

Then the evidence will be 25 positive cases for

All the marbles are *P*

from which it follows that d is P, which implies that d is not red. The problem of what statements are confirmable merely becomes the equivalent problem of what predicates are projectible from known to unknown cases.

So far, I have discovered no way of meeting these difficulties. Yet as we have seen, some solution is urgently wanted for our present purpose; for only where willingness to accept a statement involves predictions of instances that may be tested does acceptance endow that statement with the authority to govern counterfactual cases, which can not be directly tested.

In conclusion, then, some problems about counterfactuals depend upon the definition of cotenability, which in turn seems to depend upon the prior solution of those problems. Other problems require an adequate definition of law. The tentative criterion of law here proposed is reasonably satisfactory in excluding unwanted kinds of statements, and in effect, reduces one aspect of our problem to the question how to define the circumstances under which a statement is acceptable independently of the determination of any given instance. But this question I do not know how to answer.

NELSON GOODMAN

UNIVERSITY OF PENNSYLVANIA

13

Toward a Theory of Interpretation and Preciseness

by ARNE NAESS

Reprinted from *Theoria*, 15 (1949).

Toward a theory
of interpretation and preciseness

by

ARNE NÆSS

Introduction.

The present article intends to give a survey of the attempts
which the author and his collaborators have made to work out a
system of basic concepts suitable for a theory of interpretation
and preciseness that is confirmable by means of systematic observation under standardized conditions. In spite of much valuable
work, there is so far little done to arrive at sufficiently precise
delimitations of such observations. Thus, there is little done to
construct tools by which to decide whether two persons misinter-
pret each other or not. There are no standardized procedures or
observations by means of which different interpretations can be
distinguished. The theories are therefore apt to degenerate into
vague vocabularies, or reduced to furnish classifications without
solid observational basis, but often filled up with methodological
magic words of the time, as »behavioral» or »operational». The
author believes that he has at least been aware of the dangers
inherent in this situation.[1]

The work was originally motivated by a feeling that so-called

---

[1] The work has as yet not been printed, but parts of it has been published in
mimeographed form under the title *Interpretation and Preciseness*, I—II Survey
of Basic Concepts, III. »To Define» and To Make Precise, IV. Misinterpretation
and Pseudodisagreement. Oslo. Universitetets Studentkontor 1947—1948.

analytical trends in contemporary philosophy, with which the author has much sympathy, will either give birth to scientific disciplines covering their activities, or will have to give up the basic aspirations which distinguish them from other trends in philosophy. So far, the analytical trends have given birth to new scientific disciplines in the borderline zone between logic and methodology. As regards what has been called semantics, or more generally, semiotics, only investigations of artificial, very simple languages have reached scientific status. The more empirically laden questions have mainly been dealt with by attempts at working out more or less vague research programs, not by research proceding from testable working hypotheses to systematic observation and using such observation as the basis of new hypotheses.

The work has also been motivated by the conviction that many fields of psychology, sociology, political science, public opinion research, law and literary criticism, may directly profit by investigations within the broad limits of a theory of interpretation and preciseness as conceived here.

Writers within the semantics and significs movements and analytical philosophers have contributed to theories of interpretation. But there is at present a discord between the broad claims and aspirations and the narrow scientific basis of their claims.

Underlying our methodological approach is a belief in hypothetic-deductive methods as they are used in the theory of heredity, in econometrics, in some theories of learning (Hull *et al.*) and, with the greatest success, in physics and chemistry. We are interested in empirical research guided by fairly precise hypotheses which are constructed on the basis of a small number of operationally defined concepts.

The basic concepts are introduced by making more precise — especially from an operational viewpoint — some old and rather vague concepts. As the designations for these old concepts may be used as a starting point for interpretations in various directions, several of which give fruitful concepts, it is convenient to introduce some schemes which by proper specification can be turned into specific operationally defined concepts.

Synonymity.

One such scheme is the following:

The sentence (or designation) »a» is for the person p_i in the kind of situation s_j *synonymous* with the sentence (or designation) »b» for the person p_m in the kind of situation s_n.

The word »synonymous» is used for sentences as well as designations instead of the more common use of »equipollent» for sentences and »synonymous» for designations.[2]

For short representation, the scheme is written in symbols thus:

$$S(ap_is_j, bp_ms_n).$$

Roughly the basic kind of relation indicated by this scheme is that of a part of a speech or a text »a» being observed and related to a person p_i who tentatively is supposed to be the assertor of »a». The verbal or non-verbal context of »a» is symbolized by s_j. It may be described more or less completely, the selection of described characteristics being picked out for particular purposes. In case no definite p_i is found, or it is deemed irrelevant to find such a person, or the interpretation is referred to indirectly by use of a system of sentences, e. g. a system said to express the rules for »correct» use, in all such cases it is convenient to use a more simple scheme where person and situation are symbolized by one letter.

S is only defined for the case that a and b are both formulations or both designations.

In case of p_i and p_m being the same person, we shall speak of »intrapersonal» synonymity. Its definition, discovery and description are, when a moderate level of accuracy and preciseness

---

[2] It is not possible to go into further terminological clarifications, as our present purpose is to give an introductory outline, not a condensed technical description.

is aimed at, somewhat less problematical than the »interpersonal» synonymity. By that expression we refer to cases where p_i and p_j are different persons. If the level of aspiration is more exacting, much the same problems are encountered in both cases.

In case of s_j and s_n being the same, we shall occasionally speak of »intrasituational», otherwise of »intersituational» synonymity. The difference is of little importance because, unlike in the case of persons, the delimitation of individual situations is rather arbitrary. As a limiting case, we shall by a »situation» refer to a single historical event, an historical instance of »a»'s occurrence. Normally, however, it will be synonymous with »type of situation».

»a» (or »b») is not except in very special cases to be identified with any single occurrence (specimen) of sentence »a», but with the class of occurrences of »a». Thus, if »a» is said to be »Theorists of interpretation are pedantic», this does not limit the symbol »a» to just this occurrence on this page, but to the class of occurrences of that sentence, f. inst. including those in previous drafts of this manuscript. Due to the possibility of repetition of situations s_n, or to the occurrence of »a» 100 times within s_n, we cannot assert that »any sentence is synonymous with itself». This would amount to a denial of homonymity (ambiguity).

We have so far only introduced a conceptual scheme, no individual operationally defined concept. To make sentences (hypotheses) about synonymity testable and to be able to delimit which are the kinds of observations that are relevant to the hypotheses, fairly precise concepts must be worked out. Some kinds, (1), may be constituted by introducing standardized questionnaires on synonymity. Certain kinds of positive answers are by definition said to be a confirmation of an hypothesis of synonymity. Others, (2), may be introduced by methods of text analysis, certain regularities of occurrences being considered by definition to confirm synonymity hypotheses. Others, (3), may be introduced by a set of decisions that certain regularities of behavior, verbal *or non-verbal*, are definitorial criteria of certain sentences or designations being synonymous (for certain persons in certain situations). Lastly, (4), definitional criteria may be introduced which are combinations of the previous ones.

By being connected with definite kinds of procedure the sentences on synonymity and such concepts reducible to synonymity get a chance of being tested in a way acceptable to scientific methodology. Otherwise we shall continue to have a literature involving endless disputes on »the meaning» of this or that.

There is no space here for full description of procedures, only the most superficial ones can be referred to. Qs1 and Qs5 are two questionnaires which can be described as follows:

Qs1

A person — the tester or »analyst» — invites an other person to read carefully a text containing the formulation T. An other formulation, U, is held in reserve.[3]

Having read the text, the analyst says: This text was offered you as an example of a text containing the formulation — — (here, T is mentioned). What I should like to know is the following:

Suppose the formulation U (here, U is mentioned) had occurred in the text instead of T, and in T's place. Would U have expressed the same proposition to you as T did when you read T?»

The wording is sometimes modified, (creating subclasses of questionnaires), thus other words are introduced instead of the vague and controversial word »proposition».

Qs5

The analyst presents a formulation T within a context C. He then presents the same context, but now with a formulation U in the place of T, and asks:

»Are you able to imagine circumstances (conditions, situations) in or by which you would accept T and reject U or vice versa?

---

[3] In non-symbolic texts we write T for »a» and U for »b».

Or, would you either accept both or reject both under any conceivable circumstances?»

— If the subject answers positively on the first question, this is taken (1) either by definition to mean that, or (2) taken as confirmation that T and U are not always, perhaps never, synonymous for him. If the subject answers negatively this is related to a corresponding non-synonymity (heteronymity).

— The two questionnaires are only adapted to cases of intrapersonal synonymity. One may confront 100 persons with the same formulations T and U in different contexts, but one cannot decide with reasonable certainty whether T for p_1 in s_1 means the same as U for p_2 in s_1. If 100 persons answer Qs1 with the same answer, this indicates that there is a high degree of constancy as regards the relation of T to U within the system of speech habits of different persons. It cannot, however, without further assumptions be taken as a confirmation that T (or U) means the same to all 100, or that T means for any one the same as U means to some other. Questionnaires on interpersonal synonymity are much more complex.

Attempts to use behavioral approaches to questions of cognitive meaning have not been very encouraging so far. It sounds so easy, reading e. g. Malinowski's enthusiastic account of how the meaning of words is »seen» from the activities of people engaged in work requiring cooperation. But he should try to delimit the meaning of »The distance to the sun is 92.000.000 miles» by that method! Even the analysis of Bridgman of sentences about length does not give any description of the operations corresponding to measurements of length, by means of which such measurements can be distinguished from any other. Bridgman *speaks* about such operations, he *says* he observes what the physicists »do» with the concepts, but he does not go into the details of descriptions of the units or clusters of behavior patterns corresponding to any concept or proposition. The whole molar behavioral avenue of attack is so far a *planned* avenue, not one that is opened up anywhere. The theories are mostly disguised programs.

This does not mean that we have given up the molar behavioral point of view, but that we have cooled down after enjoying the first beautiful vistas of future sciences that some time will be opened up by molar behavioristic research. What is now needed is the establishment of methods of observation, rather than elaboration of behavioristic terminology. And even if we shall succeed in describing identities of molar behavioral units, there will still be demand for short cut methods which can lead to fairly reliable hypotheses of synonymity as regards a pair of formulations T and U, by some weeks or even days of work. The investigation of non-verbal habits within a population, e. g., of physicists, necessarily involves extensive observation, if we are not going to rely on their own descriptions of usage, i. e. go back to verbal level methods, especially questionnaires distributed among highly qualified physicists.

Ambiguity.

A conceptual scheme of ambiguity concepts is introduced by the negation of a synonymity relation involving one sentence (or designation). In symbols: $S(ap_i s_j, ap_m s_n)$. In words: »a for p_i in s_j is not synonymous with a for p_m in s_n». One of the standard questionnaires on intrapersonal synonymity reads as follows:

Qb1

A person — the analyst — invites another person P to read carefully two texts both containing the formulation T.

Having read the texts, the analyst says: »You were confronted with these texts because they both contain the sentence T. What we should like to know is whether T in the two cases expressed the same proposition to you, or T to you expressed in the first text a proposition different from the one it expressed to you in the second text».

By means of special questionnaires, the »meta questionnaires», we try to find out how our questions are interpreted. As regards the term »same», e. g., there are important differences of interpretation, some taking it in more absolutistic and rigoristic connotations, others in more »latidudinarian» senses.

More precise than.

If two sentences T and U are synonymous (equipollent) for at least some persons in some situations, T will be said to be a possible interpretation of U and U a possible interpretation of T. If all interpretations of T are also interpretations of U, whereas some interpretations of U are not interpretations of T for some persons in some situations, we say that T is more precise than U for those persons in those situations.

In the vernacular we sometimes say that mathematical sentences are more precise than psychological ones. If T is a formulation in mathematics and U one in psychology, they may be interpretations of each other, or have some interpretations in common, but the normal would be that they have none. Even if they have none, we may in the vernacular say that T is more precise than U. Not so according to the terminology here introduced. According to the definition they must have at least one interpretation in common.

The definition is constructed in this way to facilitate inferences from formulations of the type »T is more precise than U» to those of the kinds »T may with profit be substituted for U» and »T is apt to provoke less misunderstanding and deeper understanding than U». We cannot substitute mathematical for psychological theorems. If »2 + 2 = 4» is found to be more precise than »When habit strength is zero, reaction-evocation potential is zero» (Hull), we cannot infer that »2 + 2 = 4» may with profit be placed in Hull's text to replace the psychological sentences. Thus the vernacular term »precise» is too broad for our purposes.

One of the reasons why »less ambiguous than» is not used instead of »more precise than» is that the differences of interpretation we are usually interested in here, are very much smaller than those said to cause ambiguity (in the vernacular or in linguistic books on »words and their meaning»). There is a negative valence attached to »ambiguous» which is misleading in our discussions.

If »a is more precise than b» is symbolized by P(ab), »x and y are synonymous for z in t» by S(xyzt), and »e» stands for definitional identity, the definition of 'more precise than' may be formulated in terms of synonymity relations as follows:

$$P(a\ b)e(Ey).(Ez)(Et)S(b\ y\ z\ t)\ \&\ -\ (Ez)(Et)S(a\ y\ z\ t)$$
$$:\&:\ -\ (Ey).(Ez)(Et)S(a\ y\ z\ t)\ \&\ -\ (Ez)(Et)S(b\ y\ z\ t)$$

From the definition of 'more precise than' it follows that if »a» is more precise than »b» within a context, »a» will be more precise than »b» within the same limit of application. When the schemas of synonymity are given empirical sense by operational definition, some of the theorems on relations of preciseness are turned into empirical hypotheses testable by questionnaires, procedures of textual analysis or behavioral observation and inference. Some of the theorems have been tested, but only in the case of the questionnaire methods. As subjects we used students taking part in courses in interpretation and logical analysis. Numerous purely practical and didactical difficulties are involved. But on the whole the students have answered as predicted when testing theorems on, e. g., symmetry of concepts of interpretation and transitivity of concepts of preciseness.

Definiteness of intention.

If one tries to measure preciseness of certain terms or sentences within groups of readers or listeners, what seems most striking is not so much the lack of preciseness, as the lack of having considered even the possibility of distinctions. This has made us put more and more stress on the possibility of measuring what we call »definiteness (or vagueness) of intention (or delimitation)». Concepts with this designation are introduced by procedures roughly as follows.

In some text or speech the analyst makes use of a certain

sentence, e. g. ». . . The ship was of 5.000 tons . . .», or ». . . This would mean a step towards democracy . . .». Suddenly the context is broken and the audience is invited to answer detailed questionnaires as regards their interpretation of the sentence as it occurred in the text. It is stressed that their hypotheses on how they interpreted the sentence should not be conceived as confirmable only (or mainly) by retrospective introspection, but by inferences from past verbal and non-verbal behavior.

If the sentence is that involving measure of ships, each individual of the audience is confronted by lists of interpretations (precizations) where the niceties of ship measurements are introduced. Thus the distinction between »ton» as measure of weight and as measure of volume.

If volume of displacement of water was meant, it is asked whether saltwater or freshwater was intended — there being a difference in volume because of difference in weight. Sooner or later a situation arises where the subject must admit, if honest, that (1) if he made a definite interpretation of the sentence at all, he either must have intended a or non-a (a certain distinction). Further, (2) that he neither intended a nor non-a, being unaware of the possibility of making the distinction at issue (e. g. between ton as measure of volume and ton a measure of weight). In such cases the subject is given a minus in definiteness of intention.

Scores are constructed in relation to definite sets of discrimination possibilities. So far, the practical difficulties of formulating such sets of discrimination possibilities have hindered the quantification of results.

Much critique of present discussions in politics, in art, in the various fields of contemporary problems of society, should be directed against indefiniteness of intention rather than against ambiguity of formulations.

Interpersonal preciseness.

The problems involved in constructing precise and fruitful concepts of interpersonal synonymity are grave and manysided.

The discussions about intersubjectivity of knowledge and other questions of philosophy are involved, and pseudo-questions of solipsism are lurking in the background.

There is no reason to believe that we have other kinds of methods to find out our own usage than those used when investigating that of others. The introspectional »feeling» of understanding has never proved an adequate clue to find out just what is »understood». We have, however, a much more extended and reliable knowledge of our own speech habits.

Roughly speaking, the concepts of interpersonal synonymity to be introduced will be closely adapted to one of the usual ways in which we in scientific debate try to make others understand what we mean by a sentence in a certain text. Suppose the text is the introductory treatise on theoretical mechanics by A. E. H. Love, published 1897, and that the formulation, »a», to be discussed is the following: »Every body, and every individual part of a body, has a constant mass, and the mass of the body is the sum of the masses of its parts». Let us suppose the two readers p and q are post-graduate students of physics, and that they upon reading the formulation »a» within the time-interval t, agree to make an attempt to find out whether, or to what degree, they understood »a» in the same way within the time interval t. We suppose that they during t established a hypothesis of interpretation, explicitly or implicitly, we suppose that they understood what Love intended by the formulation »a».

One of the ways by which p and q would try to explore each other's interpretations of »a», consists in expressing what they understood by it in other words, after having observed each other apply the sentence to concrete cases. (However closely they study applications, instances, subsumptions, procedures of confirmations, the reports of such studies cannot, however, replace general formulation of the sentence »a» within the text under consideration.) Suppose they reformulate »a» and say: »I understood »b» by »a», did you do that, or did you interpret »a» otherwise?» In »b», they have, for inst., replaced the word »mass» by some definition of mass. (More correctly formulated: »by a definiens in some definition of »mass»). Then they might replace the definiens of the definition of mass by an expression in which some terms of the definiens are replaced by some definienses of definitions of those terms. Thus, they might discuss how they interpret Love's introduction of 'mass': If we associate the number 1 with any particular material figure A, then we can associate a definite positive number m with any other material figure B, this number is the mass-ratio of the two figures A and B. We call it »the mass of B» (p. 87). Using this text to construct a definiens formulation of 'mass', the interpretation of the formulation will depend very much on the interpretation of the expressions »mass-ratio» and »material figure». Both are explicitly defined by Love, and the investigation of interpretations of »a» naturally leads to the definiens formulations of those expressions, and so forth.

Maybe p would have understood the same as q understood by »a», within t, if the text had contained a strong popularization of »a». If p says to q that he by »a» understands the same as by »b», and q answers that he does not, this difference may more naturally be attributed to ambiguities of the popularization, than to a difference of interpretation of »a». Thus, in replacing »a» by other formulations, p and q ought not to replace it by any synonymous formulations, arbitrarily selected. But just which synonymities should be selected is the great question.

Briefly, p ought to select precizations of »a» which are apt to disclose possible differences in interpretation of »a», thereby that they themselves only permit some of the interpretations which »a» permits. Asking q whether he thinks »a» synonymous with these formulations, p may hope that in case q answers positively in relation to a formulation »b» and negatively to a formulation »c», *the difference in meaning between these two formulations will be approximately the same for q as for p.* He cannot be sure of this approximate identity, but he may from general considerations of the similarity of education and training, etc., have reasons to suppose that »b» and »c» are able to disclose the difference intended by p, or one closely similar.

This procedure of reformulation does not lead to anything else than to establish two maps of synonymity and heteronymity relations, one map showing relations within the usage of p, the other showing relations within the usage of q.

If there is a one to one correspondence of points of the two intrapersonal synonymity maps, and the points are selected with due consideration of relations of preciseness and ambiguity *within each map*, we shall say that there is *maximum confirmation of interpersonal synonymity* of »a» in relation to p and q in s, and in relation to the reference class of formulations defined by the maps, i. e. by the reformulations used.

Comparing two maximum confirmations, the one in relation to a reference class which is part of the other class, that confirmation will by definition be called strongest which is maximal in relation to the most comprehensive reference class most comprehensively tested.

The introduced concept of interpersonal synonymity may be said to be equivalent to a concept of identical structure of intrapersonal synonymity and heteronymity relations within a system of formulations making up highly qualified reference classes of the formulation investigated. This is, vaguely speaking, in agreement with tendencies to define intersubjective characteristics of scientific knowledge by means of identity of structure of systems.

Suppose the persons p and q try to find out their interpretations of »a» by means of a list r_1, of reformulations of »a». The members of the list are reformulations which p and q tentatively suppose to be more precise than »a». The formulations make up a preliminary class of precizations of »a», a »first order reference class».

Applying tests of preciseness to the members of r_1, we shall usually find out that the working hypotheses that they are more precise than »a» is not completely confirmed, and by reformulating each member of r_1, we construct a »second order reference class», r_2. The members of this class may in turn be tested, and so on.

Let us call the number of members of a reference class r, $/r/$, and /v/ the ordinal number of the order of the highest order r. Let $S(a\ p\ s, a\ q\ s)$ stand for »a for p in s is interpersonally synonymous with a for q in s». Further, let N be agreements and M disagreements in replies on questions about synonymity answered by the persons p and q in relation to reformulations of »a», adopted in a reference class. We may introduce a concept »degree of interpersonal synonymity», DS, in the following way:

$$DS\ eD\ \text{Degree of}\ S(a\ p\ s, a\ q\ s)$$
$$eD\ \lim\ \frac{N}{N+M}\ {}_{/v/\ \to\ \infty}^{/r/\ \to\ \infty}$$

It is not our purpose to maintain that just this quantitative concept is fruitful, and we shall therefore leave undiscussed the many practical and theoretical difficulties we should meet if we try to apply it. We mention the concept because fruitful quantitative concepts can be worked out with it as a crude starting point.

At the present stage of preliminary research, we have found it more fruitful to give *condensed descriptions* of the outcome of questionnaires on first and second order reference classes. It seems premature to try to work out fruitful quantification as long as methods of systematic observation are still rather undeveloped.

Synonymity and preciseness of imperatives.

Suppose »T!» is a sentence which does not for p in s express any assertion, but a command or request (an »imperative»), made by the person pronouncing T! or imagined to be the command or request by some other person or personalized institution.

Two sentences $T_1!$ and $T_2!$ are in this work said to express the same imperative for a person p in a situation s, if and only if every designation »d» which to p in s designates a satisfaction of $T_1!$ also designates a satisfaction of $T_2!$, and vice versa; and every designation »d'» which to p in s designates a non-satisfaction of $T_1!$ also designates a non-satisfaction of $T_2!$, and vice versa.

Two sentences satisfying these demands we call synonymous sentences for p in s.

By the expression »a designation »d» expresses for p in s a state of satisfaction of the imperative T!» we mean the same as »if p considers the state characterized by »d» to be realized, he considers T! to have been followed».

To illustrate the definitional formulation we may select the following »constants»:

T_1! — In this paper the word »formulation» shall be used as indicated in »Interpretation and Preciseness» I.

T_2! — In the article in which this sentence occurs, the word »formulation» shall be used as indicated in part I of »Interpretation and Preciseness».

p — Arne Naess.

s — This page.

I guess there is no designation which weakens the requirements stated above. As an example of a pair of confirmatory formulas we select the following:

d_1 — In this work the word »formulation» is used as indicated in part I of »Interpretation and Preciseness».

d_2 — In the work in which this sentence occurs, the word »formulation» is used as indicated in part I of »Interpretation and Preciseness».

On the basis of this concept scheme of normative synonymity, concepts of preciseness may be introduced as follows:

The formulation »U!» is more precise than »T!» means in this work the same as »there is an interpretation of an expression of complete conditions of realization of »T!», which is not an interpretation of any expression of complete conditions of realization of »U!», whereas there is no expression of complete conditions of realization of »U!» which is not also an expression of complete conditions of realization of »T!».

The above introduction of workable concepts does of course not pretend to treat or solve any of the foundation problems regarding validity of norms.

Pseudoagreement and pseudodisagreement.

It is a common observation that people at one moment may believe they disagree on something they suppose they both express by a sentence S, then they may drop their initial hypothesis and believe they agree on the proposition expressed by S, and explain their »disagreement» as only terminological. Still later they may find out that after all they disagreed on the proposition, but that some disagreement was due to terminological differences. If the sentence is an imperative more complicated possibilities arise.

Which are the criteria of confirmation and disconfirmation of hypotheses stating that there at a certain stage of a discussion, say among philosophers, politicians, mathematicians or what else, is a misinterpretation or a terminological disagreement covering a »real» agreement? So far, no criteria are worked out which are testable by systematic observation.

As in the case of synonymity and of preciseness, we favor a triple approach to the problem of developing a science of mis-interpretation and disagreement:

(1) An approach on the verbal level involving direct participation of the communicating persons and with concepts operationally defined by questionnaires.

(2) An approach on the verbal level but centring around analysis of texts. (In many cases the direct participation is impossible, e. g. in case we are discussing the following question: »Which are the criteria and symptoms justifying statements that Kant misinterpreted Hume on the question of causality — as judged from the texts available?»)

(3) An approach on a mixed verbal and non-verbal, molar behavioral level, connecting criteria of misinterpretation with certain situations of frustration, disruption of means-end sequences of behavioral patterns, etc.

At a future highly developed stage of research, the third approach may be most fruitful even in studies of research-behavior itself (involving, e. g., misinterpretation among mathematicians, theoreticians of æsthetics and of other complicated fields of controversy).

The approach involving questionnaires is the simplest and will probably continue to be of importance even in the remote future — especially with experts as respondents to the questions posed. In this paper only the questionnaire approach will be mentioned.

By »acts of assenting» we refer to verbal and non-verbal actions such as saying »yes», »sure», »agreed», »that is so», and to noddings and socially accepted gestures of assenting. If a person A asserts a sentence »a» with B as the audience, and B assents, we shall say there is verbal agreement between A and B in relation to »a» and to the situation at hand. If it can by means of procedures outlined above be confirmed that »a» for A means the same as »a» for B, that is, that there is an interpersonal synonymity S(aAs, aBs) we shall say there is a communicated proposition agreement between A and B as regards »a» in the situation s. Any conclusion of this kind is apt to be highly tentative because of the tentativity of hypotheses on interpersonal synonymity.

If interpersonal non-synonymity is confirmed, at least two cases should be distinguished: (1) What A unsuccessfully tried to convey to B, is a proposition agreed to by B. In this case, we talk of »pseudoexpressed propositional agreement». (2) What A did not succeed in conveying to B is a proposition not agreed to by B. In this case, we talk of pseudoagreement.

We shall give a schematical example of pseudodisagreement:

1) A: Nothing exists (T_0)   Step (1)
   B: No. Your foolish assertion exists.   (2)
   A: I meant: Nothing exists in the sense in which
         Parmenides used »to exist»   (3)
   B: I agree, but why did you not say that at once
         instead of saying something quasi-profound?   (4)

At step (2) we have a case of verbal disagreement. At stage (3) A introduces a »T_1» presumably chosen among precizations of T_0 for A, and with the hope that T_1 means the same for B as it does for A.

At step (4) we may say that in relation to the succession ((1)—(4)) there was at step (2) a misinterpretation on the part of B. There was at that stage of the discussion a pseudo-disagreement. If the aim of A to make more precise what he at step (1) intended to express is presumed to be successful at step (4), there is at that stage propositional agreement. We may, however, say that there are symptoms of propositional agreement at (4) and pseudodisagreement at (2).

One of the main purposes of introducing concepts of pseudo-agreement on the previously introduced concepts of synonymity is to link together vast fields of observation by a small group of basic concepts operationally introduced. One of these fields of observation is made up of the acts of assent followed by various kinds of discussional confusion, e. g., the acts of assenting to sentences on·»democracy» in Yalta or Potsdam declarations and subsequent discussion on misinterpretation, pseudoagreement, misuse of the word »democracy», etc. What are the observational basis and exact meaning, if there are any, of hypotheses on mis-interpretation? Which are the assumptions (e. g. about certain interpersonal synonymities) made when people say they agree or disagree?

By means of the already mentioned concepts of synonymity of imperatives, corresponding concepts of pseudoagreements involving imperatives can be introduced, mutatis mutandis.

»To define» and to make precise.

The use of the word »definition» among experts offers a con-fused picture. There are still groups competing with each other to monopolize this vague and ambiguous word as a concept designation. What we contend is only that some of the sentences called »definitions» are equipollent with hypotheses about past or present use of certain words or sentences or sentence schemes. If sufficiently precise, such so-called definitions can be reformulated into synonymity hypotheses. We therefore introduce the following (roughly indicated) concept of »descriptive definition of usage»:

»A formulation shall in the MS of A.N. be called a formulation expressing a descriptive definition of usage, if and only if it states that a certain expression, the so-called definiendum expression, is used strictly synonymous with a certain other expression, the so-called definiens expression, within a certain class of situations, the so-called intended field of application of the descriptive definition of usage.»

With this and related concepts as tools of clarifying discussions on definitions, it is of importance to stress the complex character of the hypotheses involved.

Using previous symbols a descriptive definition may be symbolized by

$$S(a\ p_i\ s_j, b\ p_m\ s_n)$$

where

a   — definiendum expression

b   — definiens expression

$p_i\ s_j$ — intended field of application

p_m — person whose interpretation of »b» shall determine the interpretation of »a»

s_n — »standard» situation in which the person p_m shall be when making the »standard» interpretation of »b».

Judging the extensive and violent discussion on the »correct», »proper», »true», »main», »traditional», »old», etc., etc., definition of, e. g. »democracy» on the basis of the requirements of a description of past or present usage, heavy shortcomings are revealed and easily formulated.

Thus, looking up statements on »democracy» which seem to be intended to be descriptions of usage, the factors symbolized in $S(a\ p_i\ s_j, b\ p_m\ s_n)$ are very seldom expressed, and if they are, then only rather vaguely, making it difficult or impossible to test the hypotheses. Thus, for p_i »we» may be found, for s_j »when used correctly» or »hitherto», for »b», the definiens expression, some expressions the preciseness of which seems very questionable. Explicit indications about p_m and s_n are seldom found. More often, only »a» and »b» are indicated, e. g. as in formulas »a means b». The widely held contempt for »definitions» seems well motivated if it were turned against formulations intended to give descriptive definitions which have the defects indicated above and are not based on empirical research.

Analysis of hypotheses involved in subsuming instances under ways of use.

In the writings of authors belonging to analytical movements in present day philosophy, we find a great number of hypotheses stating that such and such philosopher or scientist is using such and such a word in such and such a sense. Sometimes instances of use (occurrences of the word) are quoted in support of the hypothesis at issue. »Subsumption analysis» aims to find out what kind of assumptions are implicitly made when an author subsumes an instance in this way. Not only presumptions of synonymity and preciseness are often involved, but also hypotheses within the field of science to which the analyzed text refers. Thus, an analytic philosopher may be found to reason as follows: if the scientist A by his sentence »a» means »a_1», then he says something stupid, which is improbable; if he means »a_2» he says something which is intelligent and suits the context, therefore A means »a_2» by »a». A great number and variety of assumptions are here made, for instance, that A means either »a_1» or »a_2». If »a_1» and »a_2» seem very imprecise it is of interest to find out how the analytical philosopher can subsume anything at all under »a_1» or »a_2».

Of the empirical findings in subsumption analysis the finding of H. Tønnessen ought to be mentioned: subjects interrogated as to how they managed to perform a certain subsumption revealed a tendency to interpret a descriptive definition on the basis of instances given of subsumption under the definition, and then to judge subsumptions on the basis of the interpretation

»found». This involves a kind of vicious circle which may be in part responsible for the low level of reliability and stability of hypotheses on the usage or usages exemplified by certain occurrences of certain words, e. g. hypotheses on inconsistency or contradiction.

Slogan analysis and slogan character.

Many designations considered to express concepts of central importance in philosophy (including political philosophy) are what has been called slogans in the social sciences (in content-analysis, propaganda-analysis, public opinion analysis, ideology analysis, etc.). Thus, »liberty», »justice», »democracy», »truth», »scientific attitude», »spiritual», »material».

There are vast theories of great political importance which depict the function of slogans in ideological conflicts to be that of confusing and hiding »real», non-ideological issues (Marx, Nordau, Nietzsche, Pareto, Sorel, Veblen, Beard *et al*). If an author belongs to an ideological camp, it is normal that he at least uses such theories to explain the verbal behavior of those of the opposite camps.

Theories about the slogan function of basic terms in political and philosophical discussion have never been worked out sufficiently clearly to permit of systematic testing. There are, however, a large number of approaches developing. (Cf. e. g., the bibliography of Smith, Lasswell and Casey, »Propaganda, Communication and Public Opinion). One of the approaches is that of linking the slogan analysis to the previous kinds of investigation. A study on »private enterprise»[4] has been a pilot study in the field.

Concluding word.

From time to time critical and empirical movements in philosophy and the border-line of the sciences have developed out of questioning the foundations of some older movements. There

---

[4] H. Tønnessen, *Det private initiativ*, Universitetets studentkontor, Oslo 1948.

seems to be no bottom to be reached, rather some kinds of circularity of chains of arguments.

The enormous speculative edifices of Kant are considered critical and sceptical in relation to metaphysicians such as Wolff. Logical empiricism and related analytic trends have undermined the belief in such speculative edifices by questioning their meaning. It is time to study the assumptions inherent in the analytical approaches. But such studies cannot bring positive results without linking them up with contemporary methods of psychology and social science and especially with the requirements of testability roughly indicated by the slogan »operational». The approach surveyed in this article is an attempt to work out some tools of wide applicability within the problem situation indicated.

14

The Analytic and the Synthetic: An Untenable Dualism

by MORTON G. WHITE

Reprinted from *John Dewey: Philosopher of Science and Freedom*, New York: The Dial Press, 1950.

The Analytic and the Synthetic:
an Untenable Dualism[1]

by Morton G. White

DEWEY HAS spent a good part of his life hunting and shooting at dualisms: body-mind, theory-practice, percept-concept, value-science, learning-doing, sensation-thought, external-internal. They are always fair game and Dewey's prose rattles with fire whenever they come into view. At times the philosophical forest seems more like a gallery at a penny arcade and the dualistic dragons move along obligingly and monotonously while Dewey picks them off with deadly accuracy. At other times we may wonder just who these monsters are. But vague as the language sometimes is, on other occasions it is suggestive, and the writer must confess to a deep sympathy with Dewey on this point. Not that distinctions ought not to be made when they are called for, but we ought to avoid making those that are unnecessary or unfounded. It is in this spirit that I wish to examine a distinction which has come to dominate so much of contemporary philosophy—the distinction between analytic and synthetic statements in one of its many forms. It must be emphasized that the views which will be put forth are not strict corollaries of Dewey's views; indeed, he sometimes deals with the question so as to suggest disagreement with what I am about to argue. But I trace the source of my own general attitudes

---

[1] The present paper is a revised version of one read at the annual meeting of the Fullerton Club at Bryn Mawr College on May 14, 1949. It owes its existence to the stimulus and help of Professors Nelson Goodman and W. V. Quine. My debt to them is so great that I find it hard to single out special points. My general attitude has also been influenced by discussion with Professor Alfred Tarski, although I would hesitate to attribute to him the beliefs I defend.

on this point to Dewey, even though my manner and method in this paper are quite foreign to his.

Recent discussion has given evidence of dissatisfaction with the distinction between analytic and synthetic statements. A revolt seems to have developed among some philosophers who accepted this distinction as one of their basic tenets a few short years ago. So far as I know, this attitude has not been given full expression in publications, except for a few footnotes, reviews, and undeveloped asides. In this paper I want to present some of the reasons for this decline of faith in such a pivotal distinction of recent philosophy, or at least some of the reasons which have led to the decline of my own assurance. On such a matter I hesitate to name too many names, but I venture to say, under the protection of the academic freedom which still prevails on such matters, that some of my fellow revolutionaries are Professor W. V. Quine of Harvard and Professor Nelson Goodman of the University of Pennsylvania. As yet the revolution is in a fluid stage. No dictatorship has been set up, and so there is still a great deal of freedom and healthy dispute possible within the revolutionary ranks. I, for one, am drawn in this direction by a feeling that we are here faced with another one of the dualisms that Dewey has warned against.

There is some irony in the fact that some of our most severely formal logicians have played a role in creating doubt over the adequacy of this great dualism—the sharp distinction between analytic and synthetic. It is ironical because Dewey has never looked in this direction for support; indeed he has shunned it. But such a phenomenon is not rare in the history of philosophy. Dewey has told of his attachment to Hegel's language at a time when he was no longer a Hegelian, and in like manner the contemporary revolt against the distinction between analytic and synthetic may be related to Dewey's anti-dualism. Perhaps this is the pattern of philosophical progress—new wine in old bottles.

There are at least two kinds of statements which have been called analytic in recent philosophy. The first kind is illustrated by true statements of formal logic in which only logical constants and variables appear essentially, *i.e.* logical truths in the narrowest sense. For example:

$$(p \text{ or } q) \text{ if and only if } (q \text{ or } p)$$
$$p \text{ or not-}p$$
$$\text{If } p, \text{ then not-not-}p$$

and similar truths from more advanced chapters of modern logic. With the attempts to define "analytic" as applied to these I shall not be concerned. Nor am I interested here in the ascription of analyticity to those which are derived from them by substitution of constants for variables. This does not mean that I do not have related opinions of certain philosophical characterizations of this type of statement, but rather that my main concern here is with another kind of statement usually classified as analytic.

My main worry is over what is traditionally known as essential predication, best illustrated by "All men are animals," "Every brother is a male," "All men are rational animals," "Every brother is a male sibling," "Every vixen is a fox"—Locke's *trifling propositions*. I am concerned to understand those philosophers who call such statements analytic, as opposed to true but merely synthetic statements like "All men are bipeds," "Every brother exhibits sibling rivalry," "Every vixen is cunning." The most critical kind of test occurs when we have a given predicate like "man," which is said to be analytically linked with "rational animal" but only synthetically linked with "featherless biped," although it is fully admitted that all men are in fact featherless bipeds and that all featherless bipeds are in fact men. The most critical case occurs when it is said that whereas the statement "All and only men are rational animals" is analytic, "All and only men are featherless bipeds" is true but synthetic. And what I want to understand more clearly is the ascription of analyticity in this context. What I will argue is that a number of views which have been adopted as papal on these matters are, like so many papal announcements, obscure. And what I suggest is that the pronouncements of the modern, empiricist popes are unsuccessful attempts to bolster the dualisms of medieval, scholastic popes. From the point of view of an anti-dualist, their distinctions are equally sharp, even though the moderns make the issue more linguistic in character. But the similarities between the medievals and the moderns are great; both want to preserve the distinction between essential and accidental predication and both have drawn it obscurely.

Quine[2] has formulated the problem in a convenient way. He has pointed out (with a different illustration) that the statement "Every man is a rational animal" is analytic just in case it is the result of putting synonyms for synonyms in a logical truth of the first type mentioned. Thus we have the logical truth:

(1) Every P is P

From which we may deduce by substitution:

(2) Every man is a man.

Now we put for the second occurrence of the word "man" the expression "rational animal" which is allegedly synonymous with it, and we have as our result:

(3) Every man is a rational animal.

We may now say that (3) is analytic in accordance with the proposed criterion. Quine has queried the phrase "logical truth" as applied to (1) and the phrase "is synonymous with" as applied to "man" and "rational animal," but I am confining myself to the latter.

Quine has said that he does not understand the term "is synonymous with" and has suggested that he won't understand it until a behavioristic criterion is presented for it. I want to begin by saying that I have difficulties with this term too, and that this is the negative plank on which our united front rests. I should say, of course, that the complaint when put this way is deceptively modest. We begin by saying we do not understand. But our opponents may counter with Dr. Johnson that they can give us arguments but not an understanding. And so it ought to be said that the objection is a little less meek; the implication is that many who *think* they understand really don't either.

---

[2] "Notes on Existence and Necessity," *Journal of Philosophy*, Vol. XL (1943), pp. 113-127.

Now that the problem is introduced, a few preliminary observations must be made.

First: it might be pointed out that we are searching for a synonym for the word "synonym" and we must, therefore, understand the word "synonym" to begin with. Now it *would* be peculiar to frame the thesis by saying that a synonym for "synonym" has not been found, for then it would appear as if I did not understand the word "synonym." Obviously, if I did not understand the word "synonym" and I formulated my complaint in this way, I could hardly be said to understand my own complaint. But such criticism is avoided by saying, not that there is no synonym available for the word "synonym," but rather that no one has presented even an extensional equivalent of it which is clearer than it. In short, rather weak demands are made on those who hold that the word "synonym" may be used in clearing up "analytic"; they are merely asked to present a criterion, another term which is extensionally equivalent to "synonym." In other words, a term which bears the relation to "synonym" that "featherless biped" bears to "man" on their view.

Second: whereas Quine appears to require that the criterion for being synonymous be behavioristic or at least predicts that he won't understand it if it's not, I make less stringent demands. The term formulating the criterion of being synonymous will satisfy me if I understand it more clearly than I understand the term "synonymous" now. And I don't venture conditions any more stringent than that. It should be said in passing that Quine's behaviorism would appear quite consonant with Dewey's general views.

Third: it is obvious that if the problem is set in the manner outlined, then the statement " 'All men are rational animals' is analytic" is itself empirical. For to decide that the statement is analytic we will have to find out whether "man" is in fact synonymous with "rational animal" and this will require the empirical examination of linguistic usage. This raises a very important problem which helps us get to the root of the difficulty and to ward off one very serious misunderstanding.

The demonstration that "All men are rational animals" is analytic depends on showing that it is the result of putting a synonym for its synonym in a logical truth. In this situation we find ourselves asking whether a statement in a natural language or what Moore calls ordinary language—a language which has not been formalized by a logician—is analytic. We find ourselves asking whether two expressions in a natural language are synonymous. But this must be distinguished from a closely related situation. It must be distinguished from the case where we artificially construct a language and propose so-called definitional rules. In this case we are not faced with the same problem. Obviously we may *decide* to permit users of our language to put "rational animal" for "man" in a language L_1. (For the moment I will not enter the question of how this decision is to be formulated precisely.) In that same language, L_1, which also contains the phrase "featherless biped" in its vocabulary, there may be no rule permitting us to put "featherless biped" for "man." Thus we may say that in artificial language L_1 "All men are rational animals" is analytic on the basis of a convention, a rule explicitly stated. In L_1, moreover, "All men are featherless bipeds" is not analytic. But it is easy to see that we can construct a language L_2 in which the reverse situation prevails and in which a linguistic shape which was analytic in L_1 becomes synthetic in L_2, etc.

Now no one denies that two such languages can be constructed having the features outlined. But these languages are the creatures of formal fancy; they are dreamed up by a logician. If I ask: "Is 'All men are rational animals' analytic in L_1?" I am rightly told to look up the rule-book of language L_1.[3] But natural languages have no rule-books and the question of whether a given statement is analytic in them is much more difficult. We know that dictionaries are not very helpful on this matter. What some philosophers do is to pretend that natural languages are really quite like these artificial languages; and that even though there is no rule-book for them, people do behave *as if* there were such a book. What some philoso-

---

[3] Even here, Quine asks, how do you know a rule when you see one? Only by the fact that the book has the word 'Rule-Book' on it, he answers.

phers usually assume is that the artificial rule-book which they construct in making an artificial language is the rule-book which ordinary people or scientists *would* construct, if they were asked to construct one, or that it is the rule-book which, in that vague phrase, presents *the* rational reconstruction of the usage in question. But suppose a logician constructs L_1 and L_2 as defined above, and now suppose he approaches L_3, a natural language, with them. Can he say in any clear way that L_1 is *the* rational reconstruction of L_3 and that L_2 is not? My whole point is that no one has been able to present the criterion for such claims. And the reason for this is that no one has succeeded in finding a criterion for synonymy.

The moral of this is important for understanding the new revolt against dualism. I hope it makes clear that whereas I understand fairly well the expressions "analytic in L_1" and "analytic in L_2," where L_1 and L_2 are the artificial languages mentioned, I do not understand as well the phrase "analytic in the natural language L_3."[4] More important to realize is that my understanding of the first two expressions in no way solves the serious problem of analyticity as I conceive it, and I want to repeat that my major difficulties will disappear only when a term is presented which is coextensive with "synonymous" and on the basis of which I can (operationally, if you like) distinguish analytic sheep from synthetic goats. I want to repeat that I am not doing anything as quixotic as seeking a synonym for "synonym."

Those who refuse to admit the distinction between "analytic in L_1" and "analytic in the natural language L_3" will, of course, disagree completely. But then, it seems to me, they will have to refrain from attributing analyticity to any statement which has not been codified in a formalized language. In which case they will find it hard to do analysis in connection with terms in *ordinary language*. They may say, as I have suggested, that people using natural languages behave *as if* they had made rules for their language just like those of L_1 and L_2, but then how do we establish when people behave *as if* they had done something which they haven't

[4] For many years Quine has also pointed to the unclarity of the phrase "analytic in L," where "L" is a variable even over formal languages.

done? As we shall see later, clearing this problem up is just as difficult as the one we start with, for it involves the equally vexatious
problem of contrary-to-fact conditional statements. I suppose it
would be granted that those who use natural language do not make
conventions and rules of definition by making a linguistic contract
at the dawn of history. What defenders of the view I am criticizing
want to hold, however, is that there are other'ways of finding out
whether a group of people has a convention. And what I am saying is that philosophers should tell us what these ways are before
they dub statements in natural languages "analytic" and "synthetic."

The point at issue is closely related to one discussed at length by
Professor C. I. Lewis in *An Analysis of Knowledge and Valuation*
(1946). We agree in seeing a problem here which is overlooked by
what I shall call crude conventionalism, but differ in our conception of where the solution must be sought. Lewis is led to say that
whether "All men are rational animals" is analytic in a natural
language depends on whether all men are necessarily rational animals, and this in turn depends on whether the *criterion in mind*
of *man* includes the *criterion in mind* of *rational animal*. Lewis has
dealt with this matter more extensively than any recent philosopher
who advocates a sharp distinction between analytic and synthetic,
and his arguments are too complex to be treated here. In any case,
his views are quite different from those upon which I am concen-
trating in this paper. He holds that I need only make what he calls
an "experiment in imagination" to find out whether all men are
necessarily rational animals. And when I try this experiment I am
supposed to conclude that I *cannot* consistently think of, that I cannot conceive of, a man who is not a rational animal. But how shall
we interpret this "cannot"? How shall we understand "thinkable"?
I suspect that this view leads us to a private, intuitive insight for
determining what each of us individually *can* conceive. How, then,
can we get to the analyticity of the *commonly* understood statement?
Lewis' most helpful explanation turns about the word 'include' in
the following passage: "The question, 'Does your schematism for
determining application of the term *"square"* include your schema-

tism for applying *"rectangle"*? is one determined in the same general fashion as is the answer to the question, 'Does your plan of a trip to Chicago to see the Field Museum include the plan of visiting Niagara to see the Falls?' " The inclusion of plans, furthermore, is a sense-apprehensible relationship for Lewis. One either sees or doesn't see the relationship and that is the end of the matter. It is very difficult to argue one's difficulties with such a position and I shall only say dogmatically that I do not find this early retreat to intuition satisfactory. I will add, however, that in its recognition of the problem Lewis' view is closer to the one advanced in this paper than those which do not see the need for clarification of "analytic in natural language." My difficulties with Professor Lewis are associated with the difficulties of intensionalism but that is a large matter.

I want to consider now two views which are avowedly anti-intensional and more commonly held by philosophers against whom my critical comments are primarily directed.

1—*"Analytic statements are those whose denials are self-contradictory."* Consider this criterion as applied to the contention that "All men are rational animals" is analytic in a natural language. We are invited to take the denial of this allegedly analytic statement, namely "It is not the case that all men are rational animals." But is this a self-contradiction? Certainly looking at it syntactically shows nothing like "*A* and not-*A*." And even if we transform it into "Some men are not rational animals" we still do not get a self-contradiction in the syntactical form. It might be said that the last statement is self-contradictory *in the sense* in which "man" is being used. But surely the phrase "in the sense" is a dodge. Because if he is asked to specify that sense, what can the philosopher who has referred to it say? Surely not "the sense in which 'man' is synonymous with 'rational animal' " because that would beg the question. The point is that the criterion under consideration is not helpful if construed literally and if not construed literally (as in the attempt to use the phrase "in the sense") turns out to beg the question.

Let us then suppose that the criterion is not used in this question-begging manner. A self-contradiction need not literally resemble in shape "*A* and not -*A*" or "Something is *P* and not -*P*." All it has to do is to produce a certain feeling of horror or queerness on the part of people who use the language. They behave as if they had seen someone eat peas with a knife. Such an approach is very plausible and I would be satisfied with an account of the kind of horror or queer feelings which people are supposed to have in the presence of the denials of analytic statements. But on this I have a few questions and observations.

(a) Who is supposed to feel the horror in the presence of the opposites of analytic statements? Surely not all people in the community that uses the language. There are many who feel no horror at seeing people eat peas with a knife just as there are many who are not perturbed at statements that philosophers might think self-contradictory. Who, then?

(b) Let us remember that on this view we will have to be careful to distinguish the horror associated with denying firmly believed synthetic statements from that surrounding the denials of analytic statements. The distinction must not only be a distinction that carves out two mutually exclusive classes of sentences but it must carve them out in a certain way. It would be quite disconcerting to these philosophers to have the whole of physics or sociology turn out as analytic on their criterion and only a few parts of mathematics.

(c) If analytic statements are going to be distinguished from synthetic true statements on the basis of the degree of discomfort that is produced by denying them, the distinction will not be a sharp one[5] and the current rigid separation of analytic and synthetic will have been surrendered. The dualism will have been surrendered, and the kind of *gradualism* one finds in Dewey's writings will have been vindicated. The most recent justification of the distinction between essential and accidental predication will have been refuted. It may be said that sharp differences are compatible with matters of

[5] On this point see Nelson Goodman's "On Likeness of Meaning," in *Analysis* October 1949, pp. 1-7. Also W. V. Quine's forthcoming *Methods of Logic*, section 33 (Henry Holt, N.Y., probably 1950).

degree. Differences of temperature are differences of degree and yet we may mark fixed points like 0^0 centigrade on our thermometers. But it should be pointed out that a conception according to which "analytic" is simply the higher region of a scale on which "synthetic" is the lower region, breaks down the radical separation of the analytic and the synthetic as expressive of different kinds of knowledge. And this is a great concession from the view that K. R. Popper[6] calls "essentialism." It is reminiscent of the kind of concession that Mill wanted to wrest from the nineteenth century in connection with the status of arithmetical statements. Once it is admitted that analytic statements are just like synthetic statements, only that they produce a little more of a certain quality—in this case the quality of discomfort in the presence of their denials—the bars are down, and a radical, gradualistic pragmatism is enthroned. This is the kind of enthronement which the present writer would welcome.

2—"*If we were presented with something which wasn't a rational animal, we would not call it a man.*" Such language is often used by philosophers who are anxious to clarify the notion of analytic in the natural languages. In order to test its effectiveness in distinguishing analytic statements let us try it on "All men are featherless bipeds" which by hypothesis is *not* analytic. Those who use this criterion would have to deny that if we were presented with an entity which was not a biped or not featherless we would not call it a man. But we *do* withhold the term "man" from those things which we know to be either non-bipeds or non-featherless. Obviously everything turns about the phrase "we would not call it a man" or the phrase "we would withhold the term 'man.' " Again, who are we? And more important, what is the pattern of term-withholding? Suppose I come to a tribe which has the following words in its vocabulary plus a little logic: "man," "rational," "animal," "featherless," and "biped." I am told in advance by previous visiting anthropologists that "man" is synonymous with "ra-

* See *The Open Society and its Enemies*, especially chapter 11 and its notes (Routledge, London, 1945).

tional animal" in that tribe's language, whereas "featherless biped" is merely coextensive with it. I wish to check the report of the anthropologists. How do I go about it?

In the spirit of the proposed criterion I must show that if anything lacked rationality it would not be reputed a man by the people in question. So I show them cocoanuts, trees, horses, pigs, and I ask after each "man?" and get "no" for an answer. They will not repute these things to be men. I must now show that there is a difference in their attitudes toward "rational animal" and "featherless biped" *vis-a-vis* "man." I originally produced things which lacked rational animality. But these very things also lack feathers and are not bipeds, and so the negative responses of the natives might just as well be offered as an argument for the synonymy of "man" and "featherless biped" as for the theory that "man" is synonymous with "rational animal." It would appear that such crude behaviorism will not avail. They don't call non-featherless-bipeds men just as they don't call non-rational-animals men. The criterion, therefore, is one that will not help us make the distinction.

We might pursue the natives in another way. We might ask them: Would you call something a man if it were not a featherless biped? To which they answer in the negative. Would you call something a man if it weren't a rational animal? To which they answer "no" again. But now we might ask them: Aren't your reasons different in each of these cases?—hoping to lead them into saying something that will allow us to differentiate their responses. Aren't you surer in concluding that something is not a man from the fact that it is not a rational animal, than you are in concluding it from the fact that it is not a featherless biped? If the savage is obliging and says "yes," we have the making of a criterion. But notice that it is a criterion which makes of the distinction a matter of degree. Not being a rational animal is simply a better sign of the absence of manhood than is the property of not being a featherless biped, just as the latter is a better sign than the property of not wearing a derby hat. It should be noticed in this connection that we are precluded from saying that the inference from "*a* is not a rational animal" to "*a* is not a man" is logical or analytic for them, since we are trying to explain "analytic." To use it in the explanation would hardly be helpful.

Probably the most helpful interpretation of this mode of distinguishing analytic and synthetic is that according to which we observe the following: when the natives have applied the word "man" to certain objects and are then persuaded that these objects are not rational animals, they immediately, without hesitation, withdraw the predicate "man." They contemplate no other means of solving their problem. But when they have applied the word "man" and are then persuaded that the things to which they have applied it are not featherless bipeds, they do not withdraw the predicate "man" immediately but rather contemplate another course, that of surrendering the hypothesis that all men are featherless bipeds. Now I suspect that this criterion will be workable but it will not allow us to distinguish what we think in advance are the analytic equivalences. It will result in our finding that many firmly believed "synthetic" equivalences are analytic on this criterion.

I am sure that there are a number of other ways of constructing the criterion that are similar to the ones I have just considered. No doubt students of language who have thought of this problem can develop them. But I want to call attention to one general problem that criteria of this sort face. They usually depend on the use of the contrary-to-fact conditional: if . . . were . . . then . . . would be . . . But in appealing to this (or any variety of causal conditional) we are appealing to a notion which is just as much in need of explanation as the notion of *analytic* itself. To appeal to it, therefore, does not constitute a philosophical advance. Goodman[7] has reported on the lugubrious state of this notion, if there are some who are not fazed by this circumstance. It would be small consolation to reduce "analytic" to the contrary-to-fact conditional, for that is a very sandy foundation right now.

After presenting views like these I frequently find philosophers

---

[7] "The Problem of Counterfactual Conditionals," *Journal of Philosophy*, Vol. XLIV (1947), pp. 113-128.

agreeing with me. Too often they are the very philosophers whose views I had supposed I was criticizing. Too often, I find, the criticisms I have leveled are treated as arguments *for* what I had supposed I was opposing. For example, there are some philosophers who construe the argument merely as an argument to show that words in natural language and scientific language are ambiguous—that "man" is synonymous with "rational animal" in one situation and with "featherless biped" in another—and who immediately embrace the views here set forth. But this is not what is being emphasized. Many philosophers who defend the view I have criticized admit that a word may have many meanings, depending on context. For example, John Stuart Mill, who admits that a biologist might regard as the synonym of "man," "mammiferous animal having two hands," and not "rational animal." But Mill also holds that in common usage "rational animal" is the synonym. Because of this admission of a varying connotation Mill regards himself (justifiably) as superior to the benighted philosopher who holds what has been called "The one and only one true meaning" view of analysis. If the benighted philosopher is asked "What is the synonym of 'man'?" he immediately replies "rational animal." If he is a Millian, he says it depends on the situation in which it is used, etc.

I am not concerned to advocate this view here, because it is quite beside the point so far as the thesis of this paper is concerned. The difference between the Millian (if I may call him that without intending thereby to credit Mill with having originated the view) and his opponent (I would call him an Aristotelian if such matters were relevant), is comparatively slight. The Millian takes as his fundamental metalinguistic statement-form: "X is synonymous with Y in situation S," whereas his opponent apparently refuses to relativize synonymy. The opponent merely says: "X is synonymous with Y." What I want to emphasize, however, is that by so relativizing the notion of synonymy he is still far from meeting the difficulty I have raised. For now it may be asked how we establish synonymy *even in a given situation*. The problem is analogous to the following one in mechanics. Suppose one holds that the question:

"Is *x* moving?" is unanswerable before a frame of reference is given. Suppose, then, that motion is relativized and we now ask such questions in the form: "Is *x* moving with respect to *y*?" But now suppose we are not supplied with a clear statement of how to go about finding out whether *x* is in motion with respect to *y*. I venture to say that the latter predicament resembles that of philosophers who are enlightened enough to grant that synonymy is relative to a linguistic context, but who are unable to see that even when relativized it still needs more clarification than anyone has given it.

I think that the problem is clear, and that all considerations point to the need for dropping the myth of a sharp distinction between essential and accidental predication (to use the language of the *older* Aristotelians) as well as its contemporary formulation—the sharp distinction between analytic and synthetic. I am not arguing that a criterion of analyticity and synonymy can never be given. I argue that none has been given and, more positively, that a suitable criterion is likely to make the distinction between analytic and synthetic a matter of degree. If this is tenable, then a dualism which has been shared by both scholastics and empiricists will have been challenged successfully. Analytic philosophy will no longer be sharply separated from science, and an unbridgeable chasm will no longer divide those who see meanings or essences and those who collect facts. Another revolt against dualism will have succeeded.

Bibliography

Ajdukiewicz, K. "Sprache und Sinn," *Erkenntnis,* 4 (1934), pp. 100-38.

Bergmann, G. "Pure Semantics, Sentences, and Propositions," *Mind,* 53 (1944), pp. 238-57.

Black, M. *Language and Philosophy.* Ithaca: Cornell University Press, 1949.

Carnap, R. *The Logical Syntax of Language.* New York: Harcourt, Brace and Co., 1937.

————. *Introduction to Semantics.* Cambridge: Harvard University Press, 1942.

————. *Meaning and Necessity.* Chicago: University of Chicago Press, 1947.

————. *The Foundations of Logic and Mathematics.* International Encyclopedia of Unified Science, I, 3. Chicago: University of Chicago Press, 1939.

————. *Logical Foundations of Probability.* Chicago: University of Chicago Press, 1950.

————. "Testability and Meaning," *Philosophy of Science,* 3 (1936), pp. 419-71; 4 (1937), pp. 1-40.

————. "On Inductive Logic," *Philosophy of Science,* 12 (1945), pp. 72-97.

————. "Remarks on the Paradox of Analysis: A Reply to Leonard Linsky," *Philosophy of Science,* 16 (1949), pp. 347-50.

Chisholm, R. "The Contrary-to-Fact Conditional," *Mind,* 55 (1946), pp. 289-307. (Reprinted in Feigl and Sellars, *Readings.*)

Church, A. Articles in *The Dictionary of Philosophy,* edited by D. D. Runes. New York: The Philosophical Library, 1942.

————. "Carnap's Introduction to Semantics," *Philosophical Review,* 52 (1943), pp. 298-304.

————. Review of Quine's "Notes on Existence and Necessity," *Journal of Symbolic Logic,* 8 (1943), pp. 45-47.

————. "On Carnap's Analysis of Statements of Assertion and Belief," *Analysis,* 10 (1950), pp. 97-99.

————. "The Need for Abstract Entities in Semantic Analysis," *Proceedings of the American Academy of Arts and Sciences,* 80 (1951), pp. 100-12.

————. Review of Lewis' "Modes of Meaning," *Journal of Symbolic Logic,* 9 (1944), pp. 28-29.

Feigl, H., and Sellars, W. (editors). *Readings in Philosophical Analysis.* New York: Appleton-Century-Crofts, 1949.

Frege, G. "Ueber Sinn und Bedeutung," *Zeitschrift fuer Philosophie und philosophische Kritik,* 100 n.s. (1892), pp. 25-50. (Reprinted in English, in Feigl and Sellars, *Readings.*)

———. "Ueber Begriff und Gegenstand," *Vierteljahrsschrift fuer Wissenschaftliche Philosophie,* 16 (1892), pp. 192-205. (Translation by P. T. Geach in *Mind,* 60 (1951), pp. 168-80.)

———. *The Foundations of Arithmetic.* New York: Philosophical Library, 1950.

Geach, P. T. "Subject and Predicate," *Mind,* 59 (1950), pp. 461-82.

Goodman, N. *The Structure of Appearance.* Cambridge: Harvard University Press, 1951.

Hallden, S. *The Logic of Nonsense.* Uppsala: Uppsala Universitets Arsskrift, 1949:9.

Hempel, C. "Vagueness and Logic," *Philosophy of Science,* 6 (1939), pp. 163-80.

———. "Studies in the Logic of Confirmation," *Mind,* 54 (1945), pp. 1-26, 97-121.

———. Review of Lewis' *An Analysis of Knowledge and Valuation,* in *Journal of Symbolic Logic,* 13 (1948), pp. 40-45.

———. "The Concept of Cognitive Significance," *Proc. Am. Acad. Arts and Sciences,* 80 (1951), pp. 61-71.

Johnson, A. *Treatise on Language,* edited by David Rynin. Berkeley: University of California Press, 1947.

Kalish, D. "Meaning and Truth," *University of Calif. Publications in Philosophy,* 25 (1950), pp. 99-117.

———. "Logical Form," *Mind,* 61 (1952), pp. 57-71.

Kaplan, A. "Definition and Specification of Meaning," *Journal of Philosophy,* 43 (1946), pp. 281-88.

Kokoszynska, M. "Ueber den absoluten Wahrheitsbegriff und einige andere semantische Begriffe," *Erkenntnis,* 6 (1936), pp. 143-65.

Lewis, C. *An Analysis of Knowledge and Valuation.* La Salle, Ill.: Open Court, 1946.

Linsky, L. "Some Notes on Carnap's Concept of Intensional Isomorphism and the Paradox of Analysis," *Philosophy of Science,* 16 (1949), pp. 343-47.

———. "On Using Inverted Commas," *Methodos,* 2 (1950), pp. 232-36.

———. "Description and the Antinomy of the Name-Relation," *Mind,* 61 (1952), pp. 273-75.

Marhenke, P. "Propositions and Sentences," *University of Calif. Publications in Philosophy,* 25 (1950), pp. 273-98.

Mates, B. "Analytic Sentences," *Philosophical Review,* 60 (1951), pp. 525-34.

Morris, C. *Foundations of the Theory of Signs.* International Encyclopedia of Unified Science, I, 2. Chicago: University of Chicago Press, 1938.

———. *Signs, Language, and Behavior.* New York: Prentice-Hall, 1946.

Nagel, E. "Logic Without Ontology," in *Naturalism and the Human Spirit.* New York: Columbia University Press, 1944. (Reprinted in Feigl and Sellars, *Readings.*)

Ogden, C., and Richards, I. *The Meaning of Meaning,* 5th ed. New York: Harcourt, Brace and Co., 1938.

Quine, W. *Mathematical Logic,* revised ed. Cambridge: Harvard University Press, 1952.

———. "Designation and Existence," *The Journal of Philosophy,* 36 (1939), pp. 701-09. (Reprinted in Feigl and Sellars, *Readings.*)

———. "On Universals," *Journal of Symbolic Logic,* 12 (1947), pp. 74-84.

———. "The Problem of Interpreting Modal Logic," *Journal of Symbolic Logic,* 14 (1947), pp. 43-48.

———. "Two Dogmas of Empiricism," *Philosophical Review,* 60 (1951), pp. 20-43.

———. "Truth by Convention," in *Philosophical Essays for A. N. Whitehead,* edited by O. H. Lee. New York: Longmans, Green and Co., 1936. (Reprinted in Feigl and Sellars, *Readings.*)

Russell, B. *An Inquiry into Meaning and Truth.* New York: W. W. Norton, 1940.

———. "On Denoting," *Mind,* 14 (1905), pp. 479-93. (Reprinted in Feigl and Sellars, *Readings.*)

Smullyan, A. "Modality and Description," *Journal of Symbolic Logic,* 13 (1948), pp. 31-37.

Tarski, A. *Introduction to Logic.* New York: Oxford University Press, 1941.

———. "Der Wahrheitsbegriff in den formalisierten Sprachen," *Studia Philosophica,* 1 (1935), pp. 261-405.

Will, F. "The Contrary-to-Fact Conditional," *Mind,* 56 (1948), pp. 236-49.

Wittgenstein, L. *Tractatus Logico-Philosophicus.* New York: Harcourt, Brace and Co., 1922.